IKE'S FINAL BATTLE

IKE'S FINAL BATTLE

THE ROAD TO LITTLE ROCK AND
THE CHALLENGE OF EQUALITY

KASEY S. PIPES

World Ahead Publishing, Inc.

IKE'S FINAL BATTLE: The Road to Little Rock and the Challenge of Equality
A World Ahead Book
Published by World Ahead Media
Los Angeles, CA

Cover Design by Brandi Laughey

World Ahead Books are distributed to the trade by:

Midpoint Trade Books
27 West 20th Street, Suite 1102
New York, NY 10011

World Ahead Books are available at special discounts for bulk purchases. World Ahead Publishing also publishes books in electronic formats. For more information call (310) 961-4170 or visit www.worldahead.com.

First Edition

ISBN 10-Digit 0977898458
ISBN 13-Digit 9780977898459
Library of Congress Control Number: 2006933775

Printed in the United States of America

For Lacie

In memory of Robert Woodson, Jr.

"...the young man or woman writing today has forgotten the problems of the human heart in conflict with itself which alone can make good writing because only that is worth writing about, worth the agony and the sweat."

William Faulkner

CONTENTS

PREFACE

HISTORIANS, like archaeologists, often search for the Rosetta Stone. Something new, different, earth-shattering; a code that will unlock history's hidden treasures. Failing this, they return to their laboratories to conduct experiments on the past, hoping to determine a defining moment, a turning point or a seminal day when an immortal man shaped the steel of life with his own fire.

But history isn't archaeology. And politics is not a science, despite its frequent misnomer in the academy. The writing of history and the practice of politics are both arts. They require the broad strokes of empathy and a myriad of colors to fill the canvas with an array of people, emotions, ideas, and actions.

Having spent ten years in politics, including stints in a congressional office and at the White House, I know that politics does not neatly fit into theories or categories. Simply put, politics is about people. And people can make mistakes and make a difference. Usually, they do both. A writer must take both into account. Only in Hollywood do heroes always wear a white hat.

To borrow another metaphor, history more often resembles geometry: Different angles and various pieces fit together to form a whole. Anything else is merely the diameter, not the circumference.

Ike's Final Battle attempts to tell the whole story. The book offers the reader no exact turning points, no simple explanations for the events that transpired. It does offer a compelling, comprehensive human drama of a great man struggling to do the right thing in a difficult situation.

Like an engine, a penetrating question drives any great narrative. In this story, Dwight Eisenhower—war hero and president—must decide how to grapple with the dawn of the modern civil rights movement. He must reconcile the related, but sometimes competing, interests of freedom and equality. Like all great narratives, this one seeks to bring the reader into the story with detailed descriptions of the action, the scenes, the players, and the stakes. And it strives to provide some context to the times and the issues that engulfed Ike throughout his career.

"There is some Myth for every man," William Butler Yeats wrote, "which, if we but knew it, would make us understand all that he did and thought." Undoubtedly, this book falls short of determining Eisenhower's Myth. It could not be otherwise. Only the man himself could answer that.

Rather than presume to view events from Ike's mind, this book attempts the reverse: to use the events in a way that at least partly reveals his mindset. It presents him as he was, in his own words, fighting his own battles. The facts and the events speak for themselves. The conclusions will be drawn by the reader.

An unconventional biography, this book focuses on one issue—race—as a window into the soul of the main character. Great narratives offer great personal drama. Less concerned with policy-making than with soul-searching, this book seeks to determine not just what decisions Ike made on civil rights, but how he arrived at the decisions. What was he concerned about? Why did he struggle with the issue? Where was he headed? How did he talk about race with his friends and staff?

This fundamental tension—a struggle essentially within himself about what he ought to do—makes the story so human, so compelling, so interesting. The story is unique, but the application is universal. Every person struggles with a moral issue at some point.

The first book on Eisenhower and civil rights in twenty-five years, *Ike's Final Battle* breaks new ground. Until now, most scholars, including the estimable Stephen Ambrose, have judged Eisenhower as a man who simply did what he had to do on civil rights. In a way, that's all true...but that's not all the truth. Mainly drawing upon primary source material, including newly released documents, this book shows a man who struggled mightily with the issue but generally was headed in the right direction throughout his life. As his attorney general later wrote, "His heart was in the right place." And a man's actions eventually will reflect his heart. So it was with Ike.

The theme of redemption flows through the book's pages. Human beings are seldom static. They are dynamic. They change, grow, evolve, and move forward over time. Ike himself sensed this, once explaining a blemish on his civil rights record to a young, black aide by speaking of "forgiveness." This book is a compassionately critical look at the man, his struggles, his redemption, and, yes, his triumph.

"Books," Barbara Tuchman wrote, "are humanity in print." And here is Eisenhower in all his humanity—strong and vacillating, pro-active and reactive, certain and unsure, often right and sometimes wrong, searching, struggling, seeking, and, in the end, getting it right.

"I say don't worry about plot," the writer Anne Lamont advised. "Worry about characters." *Ike's Final Battle* centers on the man himself: as a young officer, as supreme commander and chief of staff, at Columbia and NATO, on the campaign trail and in the White House, and finally, in Gettysburg as an elder statesman. At each step in this journey, Ike found himself confronted by race. Only when all these pieces are fitted together does the whole story finally materialize and make sense.

This project, like its subject, evolved and grew over time. What started as an account of the showdown at Little Rock Central High in 1957 soon expanded into an exploration of its causes leading back to the Battle of the Bulge. What began as a project about civil rights transformed into a character study of Eisenhower. He is the character. He drives the story. He makes the book.

As a child, young Ike's temper often got the best of him, once leading him to violently smash his fists into a tree. His mother, Ida, consoled the bleeding boy with the words: "He who conquers his own soul is greater than he who taketh a city."

Ike's Final Battle is the story of Eisenhower overcoming the greatest challenge any human ever faces—himself.

A word about language: Any author writing about race enters a linguistic minefield. As a general rule, I tried to navigate this by using the vernacular of the times of which I wrote. As the book progresses, the term "Negro" gives way to "black," which then gives way to "African-American." I hope the reader can tell that I tried to exercise great care and caution on these matters.

G.K. Chesterton observed there are three kinds of stories: a battle, a journey, and a riddle. All three elements appear in this book. Finding a way to balance minority rights with majority rule served as a riddle. Ike's growth on civil rights showed quite a journey. But above all, this book describes a battle; a battle that Dwight David Eisenhower waged to overcome his own doubts and his own concerns. The lessons of this life and the legacy of this battle speak to us even today.

That he wrestled with himself intrigues. That he searched his soul instructs. That he triumphed in the end inspires.

Kasey S. Pipes
August 8, 2006
Sacramento, California

ACKNOWLEDGMENTS

"HISTORY TEACHES," David McCullough says, "that there is no such thing as a self-made man." In writing a book, as in living a life, we all need help. I know I did on this project.

Writing this book would have been inconceivable without my family. First among them is my wife, Lacie. How I ever managed without her love, support, and grace remains a mystery to me.

I'm also grateful to my parents, Jerry and Sue Pipes, for their lifelong support; Bruce and Chanda Harville; Kerry, Beth, Ella and Nina Pipes; Guinn and Elsie Arrington; Christine Pipes; Joe, Karen, David and Jeffrey Arrington; Tommy and Judy Pipes; Nick and Trisha Troutz; Chris, Karen, Allee, Logan and Riley Pipes; and Dennis Pipes.

A number of people helped me during the researching, thinking and writing processes. Many listened to me as I tested material. Some helped chisel and refine the story. But all encouraged me.

Congresswoman Kay Granger gave me my first start in politics and has been a dear friend for more than ten years. I couldn't have done this without her.

Eric Schmutz, Chris Gavras, Jeff Harris and Robert Camacho all read the manuscript as I wrote it and provided detailed edits.

Daun van Ee of the Library of Congress, Mack Teasley of the Eisenhower Foundation and Dr. Jack McCallum of Texas Christian University all reviewed the book once it was completed and provided insightful critiques.

Matt Dowling, Chandler Harris, and Courtney Russell helped organize my research, fact-check my work, and find information.

During my research in Kansas, the entire Eisenhower Center team was helpful. I especially want to thank Linda Smith, Jim Leyerzapf, David Haight, Chalsea Millner, Michelle Kopfer, and Barbara Joyce Splichal.

ACKNOWLEDGMENTS

And during my frequent trips to Kansas, Bob and Karyl Ford opened their lovely Abilene home to me. They became family to me.

Other people listened and helped along the way, including: Ken Mehlman, Matthew Dowd, Michael P. Shannon (especially for his help in creating the title), Blaine Bull, Mark McKinnon, Secretary Don Evans, Senator Robert J. Dole, George F. Will, Maria Shriver, Mary Matalin, Governor William Scranton, Robert Head, Lawrence E. Walsh, Max Everett, Joel Scanlon, Barry S. Jackson, Chad Kolton, Steve Schmidt, Katie Levinson, Scott and Corrie Corley, Chris Cox, Scott Dunaway, Dylan Hogarty, Adrian Gray, Darren Grubb, John McConnell, Julie Camacho, Rudy and Micaela Camacho, David and Harriet Watson, Andrew Hall, Corey and Lisa Stone, Greg and Stacey Losher, Bryan Eppstein, John Shultz, Ron Lewis, Jonathan Rice, Chris Keffer, Linda Walter, Sally Gavras, Talisa Harris, Justin and Lauren Stone, Pat and Sue Six, Larry Stone, Danny Sims, Dr. Travis Thompson, and Robert and Brenna Head.

I thank my Navy colleagues, including: CDR Tom Gresback, CDR Randy Britton, CDR Robert Durand, CDR Jon Lundberg, LCDR Pam Warnken, CDR John Wallach, LCDR John Bernard, LCDR Dave Hodge, LCDR John Mills, LT Bill Clinton, LT Bill Davis, LT Ed Sisk, LT James Stockton, ENS William Knight, PS1 Lorna Mae Devera, LT Ron Carpinella, ENS Dilshad Kasmani, MC1 Leslie Shively, LT Reggie Jackson, LTJG Damita Woolridge, MC2 Lucinda Thierry, LT Mike Randazzo, MC1 Erin Perez, Carol Moore, CDR Vincent Quidachay, CDR Warden Heft, MC2 Chaz Isom, LT Kris Hooper, CDR Abe McGull, and Charlotte Malone.

I also thank Alison Edwards, Kim Eppstein, Fred Gray, Betsy Holahan, David Langdon, Matt Boyer, Brian McLaren, Greg Taylor, General Carl Reddel, Catherine Grimes, Brad and Angela Cheves, Dave Clevenger, Jody Dean, Greg and Kristen Campbell, Doug Price, Brian Lamb, Eric Fox, Darin Gardner, George P. and Mandi Bush, Albon Head, Jay Druley, Jeff Echols, Jennifer Johnson, Jeff Barker, Jim Bognet, Jim Morrell, Craig Stevens, W. Joe O'Rourke, Clif Weigand, Jon Berrier, Sarah Starcevich, Alicia McGee, Julie Soderlund, Karen Van Wagner, Cliff and Jill Angelo, Travis Thomas, Adam Goldman, Danner Bethel, Jeremy Katz, Kevin McLaughlin,

ACKNOWLEDGMENTS

Allison and Jeff Swope, Peter Davidson, Maurice Kurland, Bret Saxon, Mayor Robert Cluck, and Glen Whitley.

Also, I am grateful to Dan and Alise Daggett, Norma Ellis, La Marilys Doering, Lisa Page, Matt David, J.D. and Martha Granger, Chelsea and Joe Hughes, Brandon and Rosy Granger, Bonnie O'Leary, Danielle Gonzalez, Larry and Barbara Ragland, Kelsey de la Torre, Caitlin Carroll, Terry Edwards, Sally Burt, Marcie Etie, Michael Gonzales, Barrett Benge Karr, Johnnie Kaberle, Violet Love, Bill and Dodie Souder, Rachel Carter, Jeff Stockdale, Tom Wood, Amy Tenhouse, Stacey Kounelias, Melody Parlett, Pat Svacina, Reed Galen, Ron Hadfield, Sara Taylor, Neil Zimmerman, Bill Clark and Alicia Peterson Clark, Kris Purcell, Rebekah McDonald, Israel Hernandez, Scott Stanzel, Stacy Nipper, Greg Sedberry, Taylor Griffin, Tracey Schmitt, Dr. Tevi Troy, Pete Wehner, Sarah Simmons, Yvette Hanshaw, Dr. Mel Hailey, Dr. Gary McCaleb, Andy Davis, Ed Renehan, Celia Sandys, David Eisenhower, Susan Eisenhower, Irwin Gellman, Dr. Amos Ross, Danny and Kerry Troutz, Brian and Vicki Tinsley, John Grammer, Jack and Laura Goleman, Lana Goleman, Christine Harville, Bill and Anita Bell, Conrad and Arlene Peterson, Vince and Janie Harville, Barrett and Jennifer Fischer, Jordan Breal, Jacque Steinmetz, Katy Johnson, Samantha Suttle, Matt and Karen Meeks, Bill and Mary Tate, Don and Susie Haggard, Cindy Meyers, Dustin and Aubrey Meyers, Brandon and Charleton Meyers, and Casey and Virginie Meyers, Nat and Lynn O'Day, Tim and Elaine Petrus, Bill Smith, and Paula Bledsoe for first sparking my interest in writing many years ago.

I thank Elliot and Heather Goldman, Joseph P. and Sali Regan, Jerry Keys, and Justin A. Hoover for their work in helping make the dream of this book a reality.

The entire World Ahead team was magnificent: Eric Jackson, Ami Naramor, Judy Abarbanel, and Norman Book. I thank them all.

Of course, this book would never have been written without the advice and support of Richard Norton Smith. As a former director of the Eisenhower Center, his knowledge is indisputable. As a friend for more than ten years, his support is indispensable.

ACKNOWLEDGMENTS

Finally and most importantly, I thank God for His daily blessings and His eternal love.

THE FIRST DAY

"A blessing in disguise."

—Martin Luther King, Jr.

THE FIRST LIGHT dawned bright and broad, peeling back the curtain of dusk to unveil a crystal sky unbroken by clouds.

Below the azure canopy, a little city could be seen snuggled between the rolling, dark river and the gentle, green hills. And there, in the heart of the town, it could be seen: standing tall, proud, beautiful, even majestic. A certain noble presence graced its being.

At once Gothic and Art Deco, the architecture seemed almost out of place. Rising like a colossus, it was canvassed by the ordinary, wooden-framed homes and brick buildings that populated so many Southern towns of the era. Finding its home at the corner of 14th and South Park Streets, it lorded over its neighbors. Everyone noticed its beauty; everyone loved its grandeur. Built in 1927, the building featured a brief colonnade a little like Rome, and a red-brick texture a lot like Princeton.

It cost one-and-a-half million dollars to build. But the folks in town said it was worth every penny. Plenty of locals could recite the building's résumé. It was huge, covering two city blocks. And at its zenith, it reached seven stories to touch the face of the sky.[1]

But the real power lay not in the brick and mortar of the building but in the hearts and minds of the people in town. They loved it, revered it, talked about it. It occupied the heart of the city in more than just a geographic sense. For a small city to host such a beautiful structure was a source of great pride to many people.

On that particular late summer morning, as the sunlight above continued to spread like a wave and give life to the day, so too the town itself began to breathe. That morning, the streets filled with cars; cafes served coffee; stores opened for business. And the edifice on the corner of 14th and South Park unlocked its doors and prepared to share its glories with the chosen few who would grace its halls.

The procession began in front: Cars pulled up and unloaded people. Not just any people: Young people adorned in the poodle skirts and blue jeans so common in those days. Yellow buses trimmed in black did the same; only they unloaded dozens of these youngsters at once. Others made the pilgrimage by pouring out of the neighborhoods and streaming toward the proud edifice: some on bikes, some on foot. As they came, their voices, like the birds humming above, filled the air with a harmony of joyous sounds: laughing, talking, joking, singing.

As the golden sun continued its ascent, those in the town could be forgiven for hoping for a glorious day, filled with hope and promise.

And then...it happened.

Seldom does danger announce itself. It comes silently, secretly, suddenly. And so it was on that day. A darkness began to manifest itself; a darkness not of weather, but of man.

It was first seen in front of the grand building. There, amid the children, a group of men appeared. Ominously, they appeared dressed for war, not for school. Uniformly clothed in olive drab, they adorned the building with their presence: standing at the front door, guarding its entrance with their martial order. Most surprising of all, they were carrying guns. And they were carrying out orders. Their actions that day would challenge the nation and change history.

For this was no ordinary place...and these were no ordinary times. This was Little Rock Central High School; September, 1957.

◇

Across town, Melba Pattillo made her preparations for the day. A bright, talented girl not yet sixteen years old, she was striking in her jet-black hair and soft, gleaming face. She was ready for Central High.[2] But she wasn't sure Central High was ready for her. Melba was many things, but one thing she was not: white.

She did live close to Central High though, which made her eligible to enroll there. When a teacher at her previous school asked whether she wanted to go to Central, Melba said she did. Youth often brings its own courage. From that day forward, she had been both excited and nervous about what lay ahead. In the summer of 1957, the Little Rock School District announced that seventeen African-American students had been chosen to integrate the city's crown jewel—Central High School. The showplace school would open its doors, if not its arms, to black children.

Before school started, eight of the kids, at last succumbing to fears about their safety, thought better of it. But not Melba. She wanted to go to Central. In a few moments, she would step out of her house and step into history.

It was Wednesday morning, September 4th, 1957.

As Melba left her wood-framed, pale-colored home on Cross Street that morning, her grandmother grabbed her with both arms. "God is always with you," she told Melba, her voice thick with emotion, her eyes damp with tears.[3] Melba climbed into the car with her mother. The vehicle started. They began to drive. As the steel belts hummed their way along the concrete, Melba could sense her anxiety growing. At 7:55 a.m. they parked their car a short distance away from the school. They got out and began to walk. As they made their way toward the school, they could see it towering over the neighborhood.

Something else they noticed as they walked: They were not alone. A stream of people was heading in the same direction. Only they weren't students. They were adults. And they were angry. As Melba and her mother approached the school, an ominous rumbling could be heard in the distance. Like a thunderstorm over the horizon, the din was growing and terrifying. As the sound and fury grew, Melba and her mother marched closer to the roar and the danger.

Finally, at around 8:00 a.m., Melba arrived at the corner of 14th and South Park. She may have wished she hadn't.

Spread out before her eyes was a canvas filled with dark colors of chaos, rage, and evil. The picture could only be seen to be believed.[4] Immediately across the street from the school, masses of people were shouting, threatening, taunting. Racism is democratic—it can affect anyone. And so it was that September morning. It was not only the men who were angry: Middle-aged white mothers shook their fists; little white children hurled insults. Everyone was spewing venom at the black children.

As Melba approached the building, the storm of anger unleashed its thunder on her. "Niggers, go home!" she heard. "Niggers, go back where you belong!" The volume of the noise was matched only by its brutality. Enraged and enormous, the crowd posed an immediate threat to Melba. Sensing the danger, Melba's mother grabbed her by the hand and led her away. "We have to find the others," she said. They would seek shelter from the storm.

The original plan had been for all nine black students to gather together before entering the school. Faced with 1,500 white students, having the nine black kids together seemed to make more sense then sending them into the school one at a time. At least that was the plan.

But not everyone got the message.

◇

So often, great events turn on minor details. The night before the Little Rock Nine (as they would soon be known) were to enter school, Daisy Bates called to give instructions. Bates was the president of the Arkansas NAACP. Her incandescent smile masked a steely resolve. She was intimately involved in the planning and preparation for the integration of Central High. And so it fell to her to call each of the nine children and tell them where to meet in the morning so that they would enter the building together.

She called eight of the kids. Then she realized: Elizabeth Eckford's family had no phone.[5] There was no way to get a hold of her.

On September 4th, as Melba Pattillo and her mother made their way through the fierce crowd besieging the school, they were looking for the other African-American kids. Suddenly, in front of the school they saw a scene both harrowing and inspiring.

"Oh, my Lord," Melba's mother uttered in horror when she first saw what was happening at the front doors of the school.

Since little Elizabeth Eckford had never gotten the message to meet up before school with the other kids, she did the natural thing. She walked to the front of the building and tried to enter. All around her was a ferocious sea of hatred and cursing. Immediately in front of her was the military beachhead set up by the troops of the Arkansas National Guard. Officially, they were to keep the peace. In reality, they were to keep African-Americans out.

Each of the soldiers wore a steel helmet and carried an automatic rifle. Hoisted above the muzzle of each gun was an unsheathed bayonet glistening in the morning light. The soldiers' focus was now turned on five-foot-tall Elizabeth, in her white dress, trimmed with a checkered pattern at the bottom. Her feet were hidden inside ballet shoes, and she was armed only with a notebook.

Amazingly, Elizabeth moved forward. She approached one soldier. When he turned her away, she would confront another. The roar of the mob across the street would grow more piercing. Years later, Melba would remember watching her friend and would marvel at how "erect and proud she stood."[6]

Having failed to breach the military ring, Eckford now slowly retreated. She would fight another day. She made her way back, alone, to the bus stop. A torrent of epithets followed her. Later, she was rescued by a school bus, which whisked her away to the safety of her home. Meanwhile, Melba and the other black students escaped the wrath of the crowd and returned home.

It was a searing experience. Elizabeth Eckford would recall looking in vain for a friendly face that morning. At one point, she thought she had found one. "When I looked at her again, she spat on me."

◇

Across town, the governor of Arkansas was keeping a close eye on events. Unlike several other Southern governors, Orval Faubus was not an obstructionist; he was an opportunist.[7] He may not have been a racist; but he was certainly a realist. He had the politician's gift for seeing opportunity in any problem. And in September of 1957, he saw the opportunity of a lifetime.

Faubus had a real political problem: He was not trusted by many in his party on the race issue. And for good reason. Elected just months after the Supreme Court had outlawed segregation in public schools, Governor Faubus began encouraging school districts in the state to look at ways to desegregate. He even helped to desegregate state buses and public transportation.

But Faubus was also a populist. And populists, by definition, want to be with the people. In 1957, it was not at all clear that the people of Arkansas were with Faubus. They were not ready for blacks on their buses. And they certainly weren't ready for blacks in their schools. If he needed any evidence of this, Faubus could have looked to his own internal polling that showed eighty-five percent of Arkansans opposed to integration.

But Faubus didn't need to look at any research poll. He had just experienced something much more accurate: the polling booth. In the 1956 Democratic Primary, segregationist Jim Johnson had challenged the incumbent governor. It was an experience that would not only change Faubus, but also change history.

Johnson had accused Faubus of supporting integration so that he could get a "mess of nigger votes." His campaign had been putting points on the board until Faubus decided to use one of the oldest tricks in the political playbook: He would co-opt the issue. Unburdened by ideology, there was no reason why Faubus couldn't now join the segregationists. And so, Faubus reversed himself during the 1956 campaign and began proposing plans to stall desegregation.

It worked. When the votes came in, Governor Faubus had survived the test of strength with Johnson. Still, the challenger carried one out of every three votes in the primary. And anti-integration measures on the ballot were approved as well. The voters had spoken. And Faubus was now listening.

But Arkansas politics did not change the Supreme Court's ruling. The Court had struck down the "separate but equal" segregation policy in 1954. A year later, it had ordered local school districts to develop plans for bringing black children into white schools. Now, in 1957, Little Rock was ready to make good on its pledge.

But the governor was ready to make good on his pledge, too. Like Marlowe's Faustus, he had exchanged his political soul for the power of an electoral Helena. He had vowed during the campaign to stall integration. And that's what he set out to do, beginning with a television address on September 2nd, 1957. To viewers in living rooms throughout the state, the governor's face was ashen with sadness; his words dripped with concern. His coal-colored hair was slicked back, tinged with a slight dose of gray.[8]

He told the people of Arkansas that he worried about "caravans" rumored to be en route to Little Rock Central. He feared "the harm that may occur on the morrow." He dreaded the thought that there might be violence. He simply had no other choice, he told the people as he peered out from the screen. He would mobilize the state militia to keep law and order at the school. And all the public schools in Little Rock must be "operated on the same basis" as they had before. The schools would remain segregated.

The day after the speech, September 3rd, the school board ordered the black students to stay home. But a federal judge soon ordered that they be allowed to integrate the school as planned. And so it was that the chaos began on the morning of September 4th.

As he watched the events of that September morning, Faubus must have been pleased. The black children had been turned away. The white voters had been reassured. He had crossed his political Rubicon. No more fears of a Jim Johnson-led uprising. No more insurrections in his own party. From now on, Orval Faubus would be the voice of segregation in Arkansas. He would take up the fight, and he would take on Washington. The lines had been drawn. The battle had been joined.

Like Faustus, Faubus made a fateful decision.

<>

Not everyone watching the events at Central High that day lived in Little Rock. In another part of the South, a young minister was going about his business when he learned of the mob at the school. Almost immediately and almost alone among observers, he realized what was at stake.

These were heady days for young Martin Luther King, Jr. A man with a song of a voice, King's melodies could inspire and inform, energize, and educate. But he was beginning to see that his pulpit was not confined to Dexter Avenue Baptist Church and that his sermons were needed beyond the pews of Montgomery.

The previous year, he had achieved the unthinkable: He had taken on a Southern city and won. After Rosa Parks had refused to move to the back of a Montgomery bus, King was chosen to lead the Montgomery Bus Boycott. For the first time, a successful organized campaign was undertaken to make local officials rethink their segregation policies.

In the 1950s, most civil rights victories were in the courtroom. Lawsuits were filed in the hope that a judge would rule in favor of integration. This was the approach taken by the NAACP and its top lawyer, Thurgood Marshall. Their most spectacular success was the Supreme Court ruling in *Brown v. Board of Education of Topeka, Kansas,* which effectively outlawed segregation in schools.

But if Thurgood Marshall had led the legal campaign, Martin Luther King was now leading the political one. King was beginning to envision a series of protests in Southern cities that would lead political and business leaders to capitulate as they had done in Montgomery. Here was a whole new front in the civil rights battle. While Marshall was in courtrooms, King would be in the streets rallying black citizens and urging city fathers to change their ways. At long last, the civil rights movement was coming into its own. It was a powerful, new team effort. And it would have to be reckoned with.

Most people probably would have laughed at this strategy...except that it worked. King's leadership of the bus boycott in Montgomery was astonishing. During the day, he had organized a complicated series of alternative transportation for blacks, including carpools and groups of walkers. At night, he would reenergize the tired protestors with his emotional oratory. His fiery words warmed the hearts chilled by white hostility. The boycott endured. And the boycott prevailed.

After nearly a year, the buses were desegregated. On the first day of the new bus policy, King himself was the first to ride a desegregated bus.

King was a great preacher. But he was an even better prophet. His knowledge of history gave him the foresight to see where events were leading and how things would play out. He had studied Ghandi as well as the Founding Fathers. And he felt certain that history was on his side. More important, as he watched his television screen in Alabama, he knew that Little Rock was a part of the larger struggle to bring racial justice to all Americans. And he foresaw that Faubus was unwittingly setting the stage for a showdown of historic proportions.

King was horrified by what he saw in Little Rock: the rage, the venom, the chaos.[9] To him, the scenes from Central High added up to a "tragic revelation of what prejudice can do to blind the visions of men and darken their understanding."

Yet he also glimpsed in Little Rock a "blessing in disguise." After Montgomery, King was not afraid of battle. He believed that too many blacks had waited too long to get justice. It was time to get it out in the open, to settle the issues. And it might just as well be at Little Rock.

<>

Half a continent away, the nation's capital looked on from its marbled monuments and fabled edifices. Over on First Street, the Supreme Court was preparing for the opening of its new session once September receded into October.

Few at the Supreme Court could have been surprised by the chaos unfolding in Little Rock. After all, only three years before, in May of 1954, this same tribunal had overturned history when it had pronounced a death sentence on segregation in public schools. In a unanimous ruling, the Court had overruled the infamous *Plessy v. Ferguson* decision and had established that separate facilities were inherently unequal. A year later, in a subsequent ruling, the court ordered local school districts to develop plans for integration with "all deliberate speed."

The man least surprised by the reaction in Little Rock on September 4th was the judge most responsible for outlawing segregation. In September of 1957, Earl Warren was a bitter man. The chief justice was angry that more had not been done to encourage the South to change. He was horrified at the displays of resistance that had developed in the region. Wasn't this a nation of laws? Why were people resisting?

But resist they did in the three years since the original *Brown* ruling. During that time, the eleven states of the old Confederacy passed 141 laws in opposition to desegregation. Even the American Bar Association had said little to support the ruling. "They're always worried about their Southern members," Warren lamented.[10]

Still, in August, he was unaware that a squall would soon disrupt the quiet and peaceful days of Little Rock. The chief justice and his wife journeyed to London, where the ABA was having its annual conference. Warren then left for Dublin. He was joined by the United States attorney general, Herbert Brownell. Both men received honorary degrees from the local university.

A few more days of vacation in the British Isles and the Warrens returned home just in time for the building drama to unfold in Little Rock.

Warren had long foreseen this day. He was saddened, but not surprised, by what he later called the governor's "obstructive conduct."[11] Warren's preferred course of action probably shocked those who heard it. Even before Little Rock, Warren had voiced what he believed must be done to enforce desegregation in the event that a local community resisted. "If I were president," he said, "I would send the U.S. Marshals in there."[12]

◇

As the first day of school ended, a shadow fell softly on Little Rock. Soon, the people in town realized they were not alone: They had an audience. Millions of Americans were eye-witnesses to the drama. A few years before, the scenes of that September day might well have faded into memory. But not now; not in 1957. Television brought the horror into homes all over the country.

And because Elizabeth Eckford hadn't gotten a phone call, she became a living symbol of the oppression at Little Rock and throughout the South. Television made sure of that.

On September 4th, 1957, the Battle of Little Rock—indeed, the struggle of the modern civil rights movement—had only just begun. As Melba, Elizabeth, and the rest of the Little Rock Nine repaired to their homes, they must have wondered what had just happened to them, and what would happen next. Would they ever go to school at Central? Would they be safe if they did? After all, hadn't the governor promised that "blood would run in the streets" if black children entered a white school?

The crisis of September of 1957 did not begin in Little Rock. Nor would its impact end there. It was part of a larger story, a longer journey that had begun years before…and would continue long after. For Melba, Elizabeth, and the others, their journey had its origin in Topeka, Kansas, where segregation in the classroom had been the issue that had engaged the Supreme Court in 1954.

But on the evening of September 4th, as the sun quietly exited the sky, night had fallen on the Little Rock Nine. They had been turned away from the school by soldiers and the power of the state government. How would they ever find a way in?

And why did the white people inside the school building fear them so much? A few teachers had been heard to complain about the troops keeping blacks out.[13] Not because these teachers supported integration. Far from it: They worried that without black janitors they themselves would have to clean their own rooms, and perhaps even prepare food in the cafeteria.

On September 5th, the Little Rock School Board confirmed the Little Rock Nine's worst fears when it recommended that integration be halted until law and order could be restored. The next day, all nine stayed home. In the most important test yet for the civil rights movement, segregation was winning.

◇

For the man who would ultimately decide the fate of the Little Rock Nine, and the challenge of racial equality, it was a long, hard journey, indeed.

Raised in a small Kansas town only a few miles down the road from Topeka, he would grapple with the challenge of civil rights as he did with almost no other issue throughout his storied life and career. His was a very human story of struggling to find the right thing and trying to do it in the right way.

In coming to terms with the dawn of the civil rights era, he would come to symbolize the American people as they, too, came to terms with it. His doubts were their doubts. His values were their values. He was a living metaphor for America; a man who claimed he spoke *for*, not *to*, the American people.

Creating a society based on equal rights was a challenge that had confounded American leaders from Washington to Truman. By the 1950s, America was a nation that had accomplished profound and historic milestones. It had given birth to modern democracy, won world wars, and become a global superpower. But it had yet to find a way to simply treat all its citizens equally.

In the South, Americans may have quoted the words of Thomas Jefferson. But they lived by the laws of Jim Crow: separate restrooms, separate seats, separate water fountains, and separate schools. At mid-century, segregation showed no signs of fading gently into the night.

Ironically, the party of Lincoln bore much responsibility for the racial caste system of the 1950s. To keep a Republican in the White House after a presidential election that was too close to call, the party in 1877 made a deal to end Reconstruction and remove the troops from the South. The "Compromise of 1877" made Rutherford B. Hayes president. But it also helped make segregation a possibility. And a segregated society is exactly what came to pass.

Now, eighty years later, segregation was still a reality. The man Americans had chosen to lead them in the 1950s had entered the world stage just as the civil rights movement was coming into its own. For years, they traveled in the same direction. Many times at a distance. Sometimes together. For him, there were steps forward and steps backward. And the journey was uneasy.

He was the greatest hero in one of the greatest wars America ever fought. As a commander, he vanquished one of the most lethal regimes in history. His ability was unquestioned; his leadership was undeniable. But in September of 1957, what he would do in Little Rock was unknown.

PROLOGUE

This was a battle he did not want, but could not avoid. It was a cause about which he had concerns, but also one where he knew he had responsibilities. How he would balance these, and how he would temper his own beliefs and doubts, would alter history forever.

For a great warrior, this was his last, great battle; a Shakespearean drama about a man struggling to find his way.

For a great movement, this was the turning point; a seminal struggle that would define the future of race relations in America.

And for a great nation, this was the last, great unfinished business of the American Revolution.

The convergence of this man and this movement at the same intersection of history would have profound consequences on the nation and the world. And at Little Rock, it became the most serious constitutional crisis America had faced since the Civil War and Reconstruction. The stakes could not have been higher. The results could not have been more profound. The drama could not have been more compelling.

The greatest American leader of his time was forced to confront the greatest American dilemma of all time.

For years, he had navigated through the rugged terrain and explosive minefields of war and politics. Throughout his crowded life, his was a devotion to duty above all else. Amid the blood and brutality of war, he could always see the colors flying; out of the din and death of combat, he never once failed to hear the trumpet call. Now he must face a very different war, a very different enemy. This was the greatest personal challenge of his lifetime.

And in the end, this final battle was a battle within himself; a battle that first commenced in bitter wars years ago and on bloody fields far away...

PART ONE

REVEILLE

*"It's not so much where we stand today,
but in what direction we're heading."*

—Oliver Wendell Holmes, Sr.

CHAPTER ONE

THE IRON HEWER

"Calamity acted on Eisenhower like a restorative and brought out all the greatness in his character."

—Alan Brooke[1]

A T LAST, the gods of war were smiling. In the fall of 1944, a brutal, vicious war of attrition was entering its sixth year. As the battle lines continued to realize eastward, and the storm of fire and steel seemed to grow, so too did the prospects for an end. Allied troops were moving across Europe. Victory appeared to be in sight, if not in hand. And no one was more eager to have the war over than Dwight David Eisenhower.

The Second World War was hard on millions, but it was hell on Eisenhower. For the supreme commander of the Allied Expeditionary Force, the stakes were impossibly enormous. The pressure almost unbearable. The days never-ending. Eisenhower wrote a friend that he sometimes felt like he was "1,000 years old."[2]

But if he was aging, he was also winning. The Allies, as the remarkable multi-national coalition was simply known, were moving the tip of their spear ever closer to the heart of Hitler's Germany. In the fall of 1944, the success of Eisenhower's command could be traced by following the progression of headquarters. The Supreme Headquarters, Allied Expeditionary Force (SHAEF) had leapfrogged dramatically—from Algiers in 1943, to England in 1944, and now, as the year came to a close, to Versailles. Eisenhower took up residence in a villa previously used by German field marshall Karl Rudolf Gerd von Rundstedt: another sign of the war's changing fortunes. He set up shop at the Hotel Trianon, crafted of cut stone and enclosed by a pastoral array of trees and gardens.

Inside, the man chosen to lead America's sons into the mouth of war went about his business. Eisenhower's office was, like the man, simple, unpretentious, and effective.[3] A log in the fireplace warmed the room. American, British, and SHAEF flags adorned the wall behind the desk. Eisenhower himself occupied only one-half of the long, narrow space. He was sheltered by a partition dividing the room, and guarded by a secretary who worked the desk outside the divide. She kept away those who didn't belong and ushered in those who did.

On any given day, Eisenhower usually rose after five hours or less of rest.[4] Typically, he was already smoking when he met with his staff for a working breakfast at 7:00 a.m. The cigarettes were a bad habit, but he didn't know it. Doctors of the era found nothing too dangerous about them. Besides, they offered a good way to relieve some of the stress. Sometime around 8:00 a.m., he entered his office and sat behind his simple, wooden desk. A black telephone resided on top of the desk, as did an ashtray that always seemed to be curiously empty. "He believes cigarette ashes are good for carpets," one of his aides joked. A pair of reading glasses was usually perched on the desk, ready to be called into action. Mamie Eisenhower kept a close watch on her husband from her picture that sat on the desk. So, too, the president of the United States looked on approvingly from his framed image. A cigar box was there as well, adorned with the words "Help yourself" on the outside. For Eisenhower, this was his battle station. And these were his weapons.

From dawn to dusk, he would smoke cigarettes, drink coffee, and fight the Nazis. Before the day was over, he would smoke up to four packs, consume several pots of coffee, and push the Third Reich closer to the abyss.

Many days, he went to the front to see the battle lines and visit the troops. It was a tonic to his soul. But when he was at Versailles, his typical schedule was a whirlwind of meetings, conferences, and strategy sessions. Though it was hard on him, he thrived on the work. Serious, stressful labor was what fueled his fire. When the stress was at its worst, he was at his best. "Calamity acted on Eisenhower like a restorative," British general Alan Brooke wrote, "and brought out all the greatness in his character."[5]

Around 1:00 p.m. he might have a quick lunch. But it was still business. "If he does have lunch, it's always with somebody," Sgt. Mickey McKeough, Eisenhower's driver, told a reporter. "Usually brasshats, British or American generals, and big shots." There was almost never a moment alone for the general. "He can't waste time eating by himself," McKeough observed.

In the afternoon, Eisenhower would once more face the challenge of paperwork and the burden of decision-making. A general is forever writing: orders, letters, memos, speeches. Ike did it all, and he did it well. Years of writing orders had sharpened and tightened his use of words. He would often dictate; pacing the floor, arms crossed, eyes wandering beyond the walls of his office and into the battlefields of Europe, where his boys fought and died.

Once, his boss in Washington, General George C. Marshall, sent the text of a speech he wanted the supreme commander to give. Eisenhower read it and hated it. When told by his staff that Marshall expected him to deliver the speech as it was, Eisenhower snarled: "Like hell, I am!" His words, like everything else around him, were to be his and his alone.

Later that night, around 8:00 p.m., he would leave the office "with a briefcase full of papers to work on at home." He would often be up until the early morning hours. The routine was repeated each day, seven days a week. "Holidays, Sundays, didn't mean a thing," one of the WAAC secretaries observed years later. In the run-up to the war, Winston Churchill famously accused the British of taking their weekends in the country while Hitler took his countries on the weekend. Eisenhower, like Churchill, understood that World War II was no time for time off.

The hours were so long, and the work so hard, because the stakes were so high. And no one realized this more than the man known since childhood as "Ike." Confronting him was a ferocious military power that was wed to, and motivated by, a vicious racial ideology. This unholy union had produced an offspring of evil: an empire desirous of ruling Europe, and perhaps the whole world. Already, there were stories of concentration camps, death chambers, and torture for anyone who dared disagree with the Nazis.

But if Ike's obstacles were many, so were his advantages. He now commanded one of history's greatest, largest, and most powerful military operations. His troops were well-trained, well-equipped, and well-aware of what they were fighting for. For his part, Ike's war was personal. He had the simple values whence he came—the Great Plains of America. He believed that America was a place where ordinary people could do extraordinary things. He knew this because he had done so himself.

And if America was a beacon of light, then in Ike's view, Nazi Germany was an abyss of darkness. As he labored each day to win the war, he was motivated by a "deep-seated hatred I felt for Hitler and all that he stood for."[6] And so he pushed on. Hour after hour. Day after day. Making decisions. Charting strategy. Cheering up the troops. Lobbying Washington for more men and more equipment. Writing condolence letters to parents of dead soldiers. Cajoling the various Allied leaders to get along.

Still, he needed help. He believed in teamwork and counted on his team enormously. General Walter Bedell (pronounced "Beetle") Smith was an effective, if abrasive, chief of staff. All day long, he would lead people in and out of Eisenhower's office: intelligence briefings, reports from the field, advice from officers. The meetings, like the war itself, took a toll. But Eisenhower was tough. And so was his chief of staff. "Remember, Bedell is a Prussian," Eisenhower would laugh, "and one must make allowances for it."[7]

◇

But the staff also made allowances for Eisenhower's own German temperament. To those who worked closely with him, he was a marvelous enigma of a man. His nature was a curious union of fire and ice. An unseen switch resided somewhere inside the man himself, allowing his temper, or his goodwill, to turn on or off.

In front of his personal staff, his rage could thunder like a bolt from Zeus. Yet, more often, his goodwill radiated like a warm spring morning. He could both intimidate and inspire, sharply correct or calmly comfort.

At five-foot-eleven he cut an impressive physical figure. He was only slightly taller than most of his colleagues. But he seemed bigger in person. He stood erect and was blessed with presence, grace, and charisma. At age fifty-four, he had put on some weight, as most middle-aged men do. But he still looked remarkably like the college football player he had been. He was vibrant, energetic, and, for the most part, quite healthy. Yes, the brown hair was turning gray and growing less. But a handsome man he remained. When *Time* Magazine named Eisenhower Person of the Year for 1944, it noted that he gave "a subtle impression of having grown bigger as a man and as a commander."[8]

Nowhere was this more evident than in his face. His was an agile countenance that telegraphed his emotions. When hearing something he didn't agree with, his eyebrows raised, and his forehead pinched into disapproving wrinkles. Anger caused a vein in his temple to bulge in displeasure.[9] But when seeing an old friend, his broad smile curled upward until it covered almost the entire width of his face. "Eisenhower had the most expressive face I ever painted," the artist Norman Rockwell once said. "When he smiled, it was just like the sun came out."

Even in conversation, his vibrant personality was on full display. He would often use his hands to demonstrate the point he was making. And though he carried himself like the general he was, he cussed like the enlisted men he commanded. God had a way of entering his sentences, usually as a means to condemn somebody or something.

In his casual speech, he sometimes sounded like a football coach.[10] There was a reason why: He was. For years, he had coached football teams at various Army bases. This enabled him to effortlessly use simple metaphors that made sense to his young troops. "Get that ball across the goal line," he often would say to soldiers who were thrilled to hear a man talk like them. Sports has its own language. And Ike, like his men, spoke it very well.

His voice was an arresting, resonant baritone. Thanks to having grown up in the heartland of the country, Ike had no discernable dialect or accent. By this point in his career, he had been a leader long enough to know that being in command of an army meant being in control of himself. Even when angry, he seldom lost control. His voice usually didn't get louder, but it did get more intense. He could, and did, use his cadence to make his point. Like a car engine, his voice would roll along smoothly until suddenly it revved up to emphasize a key word or concept: "This…is…*vital!*" he would say to his commanders.

His probing, sky-blue eyes were soft with emotion, befitting a man whose lot it was to send young soldiers into harm's way. He once told a staffer, "It's hard to look a soldier in the eye when you fear you are sending him to his death." He cared enormously about the men he commanded. He loved visiting with his boys. Concerned about their appearance and comfort, he even helped design a new uniform for them. The "Ike Jacket," as it came to be known, was an olive-colored, woolen jacket that cut off at the waist and fit snugly around the torso. If worn in the field, it wouldn't show any mud or dirt. In the office, it made for a fine work uniform. Ike wore it almost every day. Only the stars on his shoulder boards distinguished him from his soldiers.

His connection with people was real. Just as electric power can light or heat a room, the currents of Ike's personality could brighten the darkest realities of war or warm the coldest foxhole. He had a way with his men; a magician's gift for using surprise and suspense to make them smile and draw them to him. Before the war, Sgt. McKeough had served on Ike's staff in Texas. Once the shooting started, McKeough was startled to learn that Eisenhower had sent for him. When McKeough arrived in Washington, he presented himself to the general, snapped to attention, and crisply saluted. "But he didn't salute me," McKeough remembered. "He stuck out his hand and said, 'Hello, Mickey, sure am glad to see you again.'"[11] To Ike, friendship often trumped protocol.

Sue Sarafian was one of his secretaries.[12] She was scared of him. But she also loved him. In the mornings, on the way to his office, he would often walk right past her desk. As Ike sauntered into the office, he gave the impression of a man rolling on wheels: so graceful was his gait, so confident was his demeanor.[13] "Good morning, Sue," he would say, again discarding her formal military title in favor of the more personal first name. Without exception, she would stand at attention and respond: "Good morning, Sir." After years of laboring in his office, Sarafian would later say, "I think there wasn't anyone else who could have been the Supreme Commander." Ike's personality could warm the cold of life in war. His troops saw this, were drawn to it, and gained strength from it. They would follow him anywhere. And why not?

Here was a man: a hardened leader with a soft heart, raised in the heartland, forged by war, refined by decades of service throughout the Army and throughout the world. To his boys, he was one with them...and he was one of them. He believed in fighting and winning the war. But he feared the terrible human cost. This fusion of hope and fear made him perfectly suited to lead the Allies.

This was obvious to anyone entering his office. Like the omnipresent cigarette smoke, an air of controlled chaos and confidence filled the room, emanating from the man himself. He was friendly but firm, patient but persistent, profane but spiritual, strong-willed but kind-hearted; he was a warrior who hated war, a policymaker who claimed he hated politics. At times, it seemed that Ike was at war not only with the Nazis but also with himself.

◇

How fitting that his name was Eisenhower: an American commander with a German surname. And a name that roughly translated into "iron hewer." That was Ike—he was made of steel, but the fire of life was constantly shaping him, refining him, strengthening him through adversity.

The first time he met the British commander, General Bernard Law Montgomery, Ike got a glimpse of a difficult relationship he would endure for the next few years. For his part, Montgomery was a little like Greenland—almost completely covered in ice. His face adorned with a mustache, his head adorned with a beret, he exuded not even a trace of warmth. As his first meeting with Ike opened, Montgomery asked Ike to put out his cigarette. It was the first time Monty forgot who was in charge. But it wouldn't be the last. Still, Ike winked at a colleague and then politely disposed of the cigarette. No reason to argue with an ally over nicotine. Afterward, to his staff in the car, he roared about the gall of that "son of a bitch."[14]

More often, Ike's temper came in milder rebukes to staffers and friends who lost sight of the big picture. When his son John, recently graduated from West Point, arrived after D-Day to visit his father, he was eager to demonstrate the lessons gleaned from his military education. Upon seeing too many vehicles located too closely together in the battle zone, John told his father, "You'd never get away with this if you didn't have air supremacy." Rather than acknowledge the correct military doctrine from which John spoke, Ike snapped back, "If I didn't have air supremacy, I wouldn't be here."[15]

Wars have a way of stripping away a man's airs; as fire refines gold, battle can sear and shape a man. The flames remove the excess particles and chisel the innate fibers within.

So it was with Ike. Fighting the Nazis accentuated his two dominant character traits—his goodwill and his toughness.

His goodwill and optimism were the first to be singed by the combat. Earlier in the fighting, as he sat inside the cold, wet caves of Gibraltar waiting on reports from the North African invasion, Ike realized that optimism was the most important tool he could bring to bear on the construction of the Allied war effort. There and then, he decided that "my mannerisms and speech in public would always reflect the cheerful side of victory—that any pessimism and discouragement that I might ever feel would be reserved for my pillow."[16]

His sunny persona was thus, at least in part, born in the dark caves of Gibraltar. Surrounded by doubt, he embraced hope as the natural cure. He knew that positive thinking flowed from the top down. Eisenhower hadn't chosen World War II; but he did choose to respond to it with an optimistic spirit. He would continue to display this trait throughout his life—he couldn't always control the environment, but he could control how he responded. Despite his naturally fiery disposition, he sought to control himself so that he could lead others. He chose to exude goodwill and confidence to his troops. And his investment in optimism was already paying dividends.

But his toughness was also enhanced by the war. An aide in Algiers once overheard a conversation Ike was having with General George S. Patton. The troops deserved nothing less than the best leadership, the two men agreed. And that included, indeed required, absolute ruthlessness. Ike had already shown his acceptance of this grim reality. When American troops were routed at Kasserine Pass in 1943, Ike promptly removed General Lloyd Fredendall from command.[17]

And so the twin pieces of Ike's character—the tender and the tough—were, if not created, seasoned by the demands of war. This remodeling of Ike's basic structure would hold up well in the coming years, just as it had served him well so far in the war. His leadership had already secured one of the greatest military victories in history.

<>

On June 6th, 1944, Eisenhower had presided over the largest amphibious assault in military history. A convoy of 125,000 soldiers, escorted by six battleships, two monitors, twenty-two cruisers, and sixty-three destroyers, and supported by 2,219 warplanes, crossed the English Channel and established a beachhead in Normandy. These real forces were only half of the attack. Eisenhower coordinated an elaborate deception that included decoys to fool the German radar and convince the Nazis that the landing would take place at Pas-de-Calais. The ghost armada worked. Having avoided the straight and short path to Pas-de-Calais, Eisenhower eschewed the frontal assault and surprised the Germans at Normandy.[18]

Just hours before the assault, Ike showed up at the departure point for the 101st Airborne. His advisors told him the 101st could expect a seventy percent casualty rate once they landed behind the German lines in Normandy. If the paratroopers were afraid, they didn't show it. Their commander found them busy covering their faces with burnt cork and cocoa.

They were thrilled to meet the man they, too, called "Ike." Eisenhower reassured the men; "If you see planes overhead," he vowed, "they will be ours." One sergeant told the general not to be concerned. "Hell, we ain't worried," he said. "It's the Krauts that ought to be worrying now." Eisenhower marveled at their courage. Before he left, a private spoke for the whole unit: "Look out, Hitler, here we come." As he watched them load into their planes, Ike's eyes filled with tears. "Well," he said to an aide, "it's on."[19]

Officially, he wrote to Washington with optimism, telling Marshall that his boys had "the light of battle in their eyes."[20] Privately, he was less certain. "I hope to God I know what I'm doing," one staffer heard him say.[21] Early the next morning, the 101st, along with all the other Allied troops, answered his prayers and vanquished his doubts. D-Day was a success.

Eisenhower became the first commander to successfully cross the English Channel in a military invasion since William the Conqueror in 1066. Not Napoleon, not Wellington, not Rommel—no one in 1,000 years had pulled it off. It was a stunning military achievement, virtually unmatched in design and daring. No less a source than Churchill—a self-styled military historian himself—called it the "most difficult and complicated operation that has ever taken place."[22]

But if D-Day permanently etched Ike's place in history, it had not ended the war.

As the Allies pushed across Europe, the Nazis fought bitterly for every inch of terrain. It was more than a clash of two giant armies. It was a clash of two vastly different ideologies. There would be no armistice this time around. No negotiated settlement to paper over differences. One side—either the Allies or the Axis—was going to be extinguished. No peace accord could make these two ideologies co-exist.

Perhaps nothing more effectively demonstrated the two competing philosophies of World War II than the men chosen to fight it. To lead their war machine, the Nazis picked characters right out of Nietzsche: über-commanders thought to be smarter, tougher, and better than anyone else. To confront them, the Allies had chosen a man right out of the American heartland: an über-American who talked, thought, and acted like the men he commanded. He didn't just lead the American war effort…he personified it.

◇

Saturday, December 16th, 1944, started out as a happy one for Ike. It was nine days from Christmas. Though it was cold and raining outside, there was good reason for good cheer.

The night before, Eisenhower had learned that a fifth star would soon adorn his uniform.[23] General of the Army and five stars! Even for a man as inherently modest as Eisenhower, it was a thrill to know that the nation thought enough of him to award him this unprecedented decoration. Earlier in his career, he seemed to be an officer destined to march in place. For sixteen years he was a major. Now, in the middle of the greatest war in history, Ike found himself rapidly scaling heights few had ever crested. From a temporary brigadier general at the beginning of the war, he would now be a five-star general.

The real happiness of December 16th, however, was not in his star but in his staff. Sgt. Mickey McKeough was getting married. And Ike was pleased as a doting father. He warmly approved of Mickey's decision to marry Pearlie Hargreaves, a staff secretary. And he looked forward to the wedding.

After tending to some business in the morning, he made his way to the Chapel of Louis XIV, not far from his headquarters.[24] There, he joined the other guests as they watched the wedding ceremony and froze in the cold. Afterward, the supreme commander hosted a reception for the happy couple back at his headquarters. His wedding gift was, appropriately enough, a one-hundred-dollar war bond. He kissed the bride, then left the wedding to return to business.

It was 4:00 p.m. when Eisenhower met at his villa with General Omar Bradley. They were classmates and friends from West Point. Brad's rumpled face and calm demeanor were a contrast to General George S. Patton and General Bernard Law Montgomery, who both seemed to be as tightly strung as a violin.

Now, Ike and Bradley were fighting side by side in the greatest of wars. Chet Hansen, one of Bradley's aides, congratulated Eisenhower on his new star. "God," Ike beamed, "I just want to see the first time I sign my name as General of the Army."

The meeting began as most did in those days—with a discussion of manpower. Eisenhower had many problems. None loomed larger than the dwindling number of troops at his disposal.

The issue demanded attention because Ike's strategy demanded troops. In the Pacific, Eisenhower's old boss, Douglas MacArthur, was using a "leapfrogging" method to skip over islands and avoid Japanese troops where possible. The Eisenhower approach was very different. Ike's plan in many ways resembled Ulysses S. Grant's approach to fighting Robert E. Lee in the Civil War. Previous Union generals had sought to capture Richmond, the Confederate capital.

But not Grant. Starting at the Wilderness in 1864, he targeted Lee's famous Army of Northern Virginia as the real goal. Grant fought Lee with a broad-front, covering as much territory and killing as many Confederates as possible.[25] Unlike his predecessors who chose to fight set-piece battles, Grant believed in applying constant pressure. It was a long, brutal process that was painful and bloody. The theory was that by taking on the enemy directly and accepting casualties now, the war would end sooner and thus reduce casualties.

As a child, Eisenhower sometimes showed less interest in his schoolwork so that he could spend time reading biographies of great generals of the past. He loved Hannibal and Lee, perhaps most of all. He knew the commanders, strategies, and outcomes of virtually every great battle. And to listen to him talk about the battles of yore was to feel the might of the ancient cannon and hear the roll of the vanished drum. Like the poet T.S. Eliot, he appreciated the mystical power and presence of the past. He drew inspiration *from* it; and often inspired others *with* it.

The broad-front strategy had worked for Grant. Ike believed it would work for him.

To liberate Europe, Eisenhower knew his armies would have to roll like a high tide, washing over Europe and dissolving the Nazi war machine.

Unlike MacArthur, he couldn't afford to skip isolated areas. This was not the large waters and small islands of the Pacific, but the huge land mass of Europe. Even a small town held by the

Germans could become a sword in the side of the Allies. Ike knew that he had to brush away every vestige of Nazi control.

Not everyone saw it that way. Montgomery urged him to make a beeline for Berlin. If the German capital were captured, wouldn't the end of the war be at hand? Churchill, too, was not so sure.

Still, Eisenhower wouldn't budge. As a young military officer assigned to Panama, he had gotten an unofficial graduate school education in military strategy and tactics. His tutor had been General Fox Connor, a renaissance man who insisted that young Eisenhower read the works of the martial masters. He did. Three times Eisenhower read the strategist Carl von Clausewitz.

Clausewitz, a veteran of the Napoleonic Wars, wrote that the key to fighting a war is to determine the center of gravity. Rather than blindly attacking a capital city, a good commander should pick and choose his battles carefully. And in picking a battle, he must decide where the enemy's center of gravity is.

Perhaps it's a city. Maybe it's a garrison. Possibly it's an army of troops. Whatever it is, a commander must determine the center of gravity and hit it relentlessly.

For Ike, the German center of gravity was the German army. Wherever they were, he would go, too. Attacking. Harassing. Destroying. This was the way of Clausewitz. And Grant. And now, Eisenhower.

As the winter snows fell on the frozen terrain of central Europe, victory seemed within grasp for the Allies. On December 16th, Eisenhower had reason to believe his broad-front strategy was working. France was largely liberated. And his troops were poised to reach into Germany. Earlier in the war, he had bet General Montgomery that the end would come by Christmas 1944. Now, Montgomery reminded him of their wager. "I still have nine days," Ike had written to Monty as he left the office that morning to head to the McKeough-Hargreaves wedding.

All kidding aside, Eisenhower was worried. The last time he had received a promotion, it was immediately followed by a battlefield setback. On February 14th, 1943, he earned his fourth star. The next day, he suffered his first defeat in the Battle of Kasserine

Pass in North Africa. Could a similar fate await him now that a fifth star was his?

He was already a bit superstitious. Earlier in the war, a little girl from Detroit had sent him some lucky coins and told him that she prayed for him every day. Ike, calling the girl his "little god-mother" began a correspondence with her. He also began carrying the seven lucky coins with him, which he rubbed when praying for God's blessings.

He didn't have to be superstitious to know the Germans would fight to protect their endangered homeland. Like a bear viciously defending her den, Ike knew the Germans would fiercely defend Germany. Taking France away from them was one thing. But their own country? That would take time, effort, and blood.

Not long after Eisenhower arrived for the meeting with Bradley after the wedding, he did indeed get some bad news. His premonitions had been right. His chief intelligence officer, Major General Kenneth Strong, reported that there was new information that the Germans were launching a counter assault.

Bradley seemed unconcerned. "A spoiling attack," he opined, referring to the standard maneuver that defensive armies use to thwart an advancing army.[26] By attacking, the defenders hope to disrupt the offensive army. It made sense that the Germans would try it.

Ike disagreed. All his life he had played poker. He knew the difference between a strong hand and a bluff. Plus, he could read a map. And he knew that there weren't enough American troops in the Ardennes to justify such a maneuver.

"That's no spoiling attack," the supreme commander told Bradley. He knew by instinct the Germans were trying to smash the Allied line precisely where it was the most vulnerable. The weakness of the Eisenhower broad-front strategy was that he couldn't be strong everywhere. Some pieces of the line were very thin, indeed. In the Ardennes, four American divisions held a seventy-five-mile front. It was precisely there that the Nazis gambled and attacked.

Eisenhower's sunny demeanor soon darkened. He realized he was in for a fight. This was probably the last, best chance the

Germans had. They would fight to the death to keep the Third Reich alive.

To hold the line in the Ardennes, Eisenhower knew he needed more troops. Desperate, he ordered two of General George S. Patton's divisions to be sent to the Ardennes. It was a necessary, but temporary, solution. When Bradley said that Patton would object, Ike snapped: "Tell him Ike is running this goddamn war!"[27]

The Battle of the Bulge—the longest, largest, and deadliest single battle in American history—had just begun.

◇

One day into the battle, Eisenhower wrote to the War Department in optimistic terms. He predicted that the Allies would blunt the attack and "be able to profit from it." Privately, he wasn't so sure.

At Verdun on the 19th, Ike met with his high command. They assembled in a barracks' squad room. Sitting around a large table and facing maps on the wall, the Allied leaders discussed their options.

Typically, Eisenhower began the meeting with a word of encouragement: "The present situation is to be regarded as one of opportunity for us and not of disaster."[28] He went on to say that there would be "only cheerful faces at this conference table."

Patton was in rare form. Known as "Blood and Guts" for his ferocious approach to war and life, he and Eisenhower had been friends for years. At six-foot-one, he was an impressive combustion of a man. Theirs was a complicated, often difficult relationship. Ike appreciated Patton's sharp mind but fretted over his sharp elbows. Patton's military genius was matched only by his egomania. The same fire that torched the Nazis could also singe his colleagues.

Ike had scarcely opened the meeting when Patton's bravado was on full display. "Hell, let's have the guts to let the Krauts run all the way to Paris," he said, a smile clinging on his handsome, patrician face. "Then we can really chew 'em up." Patton seemed genuinely pleased that the Germans were on the move. He was ready to make them pay for it.

With the patience of a father speaking to his teenager, Ike tried to calm Patton down. He told him that his ambitions were fine, but he said, "The enemy must never be allowed to cross the Meuse."[29] The group settled on a strategy of holding the line and then counterattacking. Patton would lead a charge toward Bastogne, where the 101st was surrounded by the Wehrmacht.

Now that orders had been issued, Ike could return to a second, equally pressing fight—getting more troops. Specifically, he needed more riflemen. Even before the Bulge began, the Allies estimated that they would have a deficiency of more than 23,000 riflemen before the month of December ended. Thanks to the German attack, what had once been a concern was now a crisis.

Eisenhower was now performing triage—looking at the battlefield, allocating resources according to need. He was nothing if not a problem-solver. And if ever a problem was crying out for a solution, it was the problem of manpower. To get more men, Ike was now willing to go to great lengths and take great risks. And his answer would surprise many of his colleagues and millions of Americans.

As he racked his brain thinking of where to find more men, an idea came to him. There was one last rich quarry of potential troops. Ike was prepared to mine it. In December 1944, with the Germans on the move and the Allies needing men, Ike for the first time began to think the unthinkable.

CHAPTER TWO

THE DILEMMA

"Our people are being turned away at factory gates because they are colored. They can't live with this thing."

—A. Philip Randolph

FOR THE BLACK MEN wearing green uniforms, World War II didn't always feel like a war of liberation. Then known as Negroes, 300,000 of these soldiers found themselves thousands of miles from home, fighting a war against the murderous racism of the Third Reich. The irony was not lost on them. Even as they fought against the Nazis, they often had to fight for themselves in the Army.

Yet even in the darkest night a few stars, like diamonds, can often be seen gleaming in the dusky distance. And so it was for many heroic blacks during World War II. Earlier in the war, a young football star from U.C.L.A. learned just how hard life as a black soldier could be. He attended Officer Candidate School at Fort Riley, just a few miles down the road from Ike's boyhood home in Abilene. The young athlete was big, strong, talented, and smart. He was also black. In a bold experiment for the Army, he was allowed to attend O.C.S. with whites. One day, the young, black soldier was on the drill field when a white officer called another black soldier a "stupid nigger sonofabitch." The strapping athlete stepped in: "You shouldn't address a soldier in those terms." Growing angrier, the white officer looked over and yelled: "Oh, fuck you; that goes for you, too!" The young black officer-in-training exploded in rage. He went after the white officer. An observer said he "almost killed the guy."[1]

Some biographers later questioned the story. But it certainly seems consistent with the young man's pride and his temper. And it was similar to countless other injustices faced by black soldiers throughout the war. This particular episode might have been lost to history had the young athlete not gone on to fame as the first man to break the color barrier in baseball. Jackie Robinson was saved from a court-martial at Fort Riley by Joe Louis, who intervened on his behalf. Ironically, white America had cheered Louis when he knocked out Germany's Max Schmelling in the ring in the 1930s. Now serving in the Army, Louis was still beloved and was not afraid to use his clout to help black soldiers.

And help they needed. A lot of help. The American Army in World War II was a Southern army. Many of its important bases—Fort Sam Houston and Fort Benning, for example—were in the South. Many of its important leaders—Bradley and Marshall, for example—were themselves Southerners. The South has always had a martial tradition, dating back to George Washington, continuing with Andrew Jackson, and personified by Robert E. Lee and "Stonewall" Jackson. Indeed, General Simon Bolivar Buckner, an Army commander in the Pacific Theater of World War II, was the son of a famous Confederate general of the same name.

Most of the World War II generals identified with their Southern ancestors. After all, hadn't the Confederates been outmanned and outgunned? Yet through their brilliant generals, they stayed alive for four years and won some amazing victories. Even Eisenhower, who consciously used Grant's strategy, still idolized Lee. This was the cold environment in which black soldiers were forced to adapt.

For black Americans, the war front was really just an extension of the home front. Segregation had followed them from Dixie to Europe. In the America of the 1940s, segregation continued to exist throughout the South. There were separate drinking fountains and restrooms. At theaters and on buses, blacks were ushered to the back. And at the voting booth, a poll tax kept many from voting. And as if that weren't enough, blacks could, and did, still experience lynchings. In these and other ways, black Americans were reminded that they weren't considered complete Americans, that they weren't considered complete humans.

Toward the end of World War II, a young seminary student from Georgia spent the summer working in Connecticut. On his way home, he freely sat in the dining car with other passengers, regardless of color. But once the train reached the South, the young man was asked to take his meals at a rear table. There, a curtain was pulled down in front of him to divide him from the same white passengers with whom he had eaten earlier during his trip. More than outraged, young Martin Luther King, Jr. was humiliated. "I felt as though the curtain had dropped on my self-hood," he said.[2]

In the early 1940s, the evil of racism still hung like Spanish moss across America and its army, blanketing black soldiers in a net of injustice. If some Americans failed to see the evil, more failed to see the irony of fighting against racism abroad while it still existed at home. Part of the problem was the civil rights movement itself. It was hardly a movement at all. Still in its infancy, it seemed awkward and helpless as it tried to stand and then walk.

In the early twentieth century, blacks found little hope in the leadership they were offered. On one extreme, Booker T. Washington urged blacks to "let down your buckets where you are" and take care of themselves. To many blacks, this sounded like appeasement. On the other end, Marcus Garvey suggested blacks take flight. Literally. He gave up on the black experiment in America and recommended a return to Africa. To many blacks, this felt like abandonment.

Then, in 1905, W.E.B. DuBois, harking back to Frederick Douglass, convened a conference whose delegates pledged to "assail the ears" of whites "so long as America is unjust." Four years later, DuBois became a charter member of the new National Association for the Advancement of Colored People. At last, black Americans had an organization to fight for them.

Still, one of the most perplexing problems facing the fledgling civil rights movement of the early twentieth century was not so much white animus as white apathy. Ironically, the Jim Crow laws that segregated the South after Reconstruction were not native to the region. To a large extent, they were imported from the North. The Southern historian C. Vann Woodward observed that "the system was born in the North and reached an advanced age before moving South in force."[3] After slavery had been abolished in the Northern states early in the 1800s, Northern whites were not eager to exist on equal terms with free blacks. A separate system of rules and laws was set up in Northern cities. Before the Civil War, blacks in the North were "excluded from railway cars, omnibuses, stagecoaches, and steamboats or assigned to special 'Jim Crow' sections.'"

Meanwhile, in the South, slavery created a very different co-existence for black and white people. Slavery was many things, but one thing it was not: separate. The slaveowner and his slave often lived side by side, sometimes in the same house. Southerners in the antebellum period had no concept of separating the races. So long as they were the masters, they had no problem living with blacks.

After the Civil War, the South, reeling from defeat and destruction, looked for ways to win the peace without bullets. They found it by glancing North at their conquerors. They adopted Jim Crow laws of their own. And after the Supreme Court sanctified segregation in the *Plessy v. Ferguson* ruling in 1896, the South entered the twentieth century with its racial caste system intact. And while the Northern states no longer officially sponsored legal segregation, many Northern people were sometimes not entirely sympathetic with the cause of social equality.

During World War I, many blacks moved northward to fill jobs offered by manufacturers. More than a decade later, millions more headed north as the Great Depression wrecked the economy in the 1930s. Faced with much racism and little hope for employment, millions of blacks began migrating to the mighty industrial cities of the North. And as often happens, their economics impacted their politics. By the time of Franklin Delano Roosevelt's presidency, blacks in the North were breaking away from their Republican roots and voting for the New Deal. Republicans did little to stop the exodus. Indeed, they seemed to welcome it. With the Catholic Al Smith as the Democratic presidential nominee in 1928, Republicans were surprised by how many Southern votes they won almost by default. They would begin to court Southern votes for the first time since Reconstruction. This marked the beginning of the original Southern strategy for the party of Lincoln.

For his part, Roosevelt was willing to court black voters, but he wasn't particularly interested in taking up their cause. Like a river, he would join forces with converging streams; but he would not change the direction of his flow. All joining waters had to yield to his current.

There were limits to the Roosevelt Revolution. FDR was eager to keep the Democratic coalition together. This included Southern Democrats. Indeed, in 1937, FDR nominated Hugo Black to the Supreme Court. Black was a senator from Alabama and a former member of the Ku Klux Klan. When this was pointed out, Black vigorously defended himself on national radio by insisting that he had excellent relations with Catholics and Jews. Noticeably, he said little of blacks.[4]

Still, the civil rights movement continued to move forward, slowly but with a growing steadiness. It was the looming prospect of world war that finally brought the civil rights movement onto the national stage. Just as Dwight Eisenhower's star was beginning to rise, so too black Americans were beginning to be seen and heard. America was gearing up for a massive war-mobilization effort. No able-bodied person could be spared. The economics of the war was about to challenge the politics of race.

<>

No one realized this more than A. Philip Randolph. As an emerging leader of the civil rights movement, he was a man on a mission. As the storm clouds of war appeared over the distant horizon, he was a man to be reckoned with. For years, mainstream politicians had been able to dismiss black leaders like Marcus Garvey as irrelevant. But now, a new leader was stepping up and speaking out for black America. Sophisticated and urbane, Randolph was well-spoken and well thought of by both blacks and whites. He had once dreamed of being an actor. His leadership skills, matched by his sense of drama, served him well as he entered the national stage of politics.

In September 1940, Randolph scored a minor coup when his labor organization, the Brotherhood of Sleeping Car Porters, hosted First Lady Eleanor Roosevelt. Like Randolph, Mrs. Roosevelt could also see that war was coming. And she shared his desire that the war might not only change Europe, but also America. With her help, a meeting was arranged at the White House to talk about black participation in the military.

One week later, on September 27th, Randolph joined Walter White, of the NAACP, and Arnold Hill, formerly of the Urban League, in calling on the president. FDR also invited the Secretary of the Navy, Frank Knox, and the Assistant Secretary of War, Robert Patterson. Inside the quaint quarters of the West Wing, the men discussed the huge problem of blacks in the military. As the military began to expand, many blacks saw the opportunity to escape the Great Depression while serving their nation and the cause of freedom.

The military did not reciprocate their feelings. By 1940, the U.S. Army had half a million soldiers. Fewer than one percent were black, even though the nation's population was nine percent black. Indeed, a grand total of two blacks served as officers in the entire Army.

During the meeting at the White House, Randolph urged Roosevelt to fully integrate the military.[5] FDR read the concern on his guests' faces. But he could also read the calendar. In just over a month, voters would pass judgment on his quest for an unprecedented third term. Now was not the time for a dramatic overture on race. Instead, FDR offered a more gradual approach. "You have got to work into this," he told the men even as he seemed to agree with their aspirations.

As is often the case with meetings at the White House, the participants later disagreed about what was said. Competing versions were trotted out by both sides.

Walter White was adamant that the president had agreed to the "immediate and total abolition in the armed services of segregation based on race or color." FDR did urge his military chiefs to look into the problem, at least. But Army chief of staff George C. Marshall told his boss he would not commit to "critical experiments which would have a highly destructive effect on morale." Not to be outdone, Secretary Knox vowed to resign if forced to desegregate the Navy.

Adding to the confusion, FDR's press secretary, Steve Early, an unreconstructed Southerner, released a statement claiming that the black leaders supported the president's policy. Outraged, Randolph, White, and Hill issued a rejoinder that called the administration's misrepresentations a "stab in the back." Roosevelt then attempted a clarification. He seemed to agree with both the black leaders and the War Department. First, he insisted that the administration's policy of segregation in the military was not a permanent one. Then, he declared that "we dare not confuse the issue of prompt preparedness with a new social experiment, however important and desirable it may be." Civil rights may be a good thing, FDR essentially argued. But not now. Not with war on the horizon and elections in the balance.

If FDR thought he had diffused the issue, he gravely miscalculated.

◇

Politics has a certain flow to it. Once a dam has been opened even slightly, the force and energy streaming forward can seldom be reversed. History is filled with great men who thought they could appease the disaffected through personal charm or symbolism. Yet these men often didn't realize that the powerful momentum that had been created would only grow in intensity.

The civil rights community had now had a meeting with the president of the United States. They were ready for more. Far from ending the conversation, FDR's meeting had only encouraged more.

Randolph, in particular, sensed the building momentum. When it became clear that Marshall and Knox had convinced FDR to do little, Randolph took action. Shrewdly, he shifted his focus from those in the military to those who supported the military. This was not only an easier problem to tackle, it also impacted almost every black family in America.

Randolph was particularly upset that black workers would be excluded from important defense contracts that were sure to grow even more lucrative as the war drew closer. As the unofficial leader of black America, he had the vision and the clout to call for a march on Washington to protest the exclusion of black workers from these defense projects. As the head of the Brotherhood of Sleeping Car Porters, he had the organizational ability and connections to pull it off. He saw that war was on the horizon. And he knew that America would need every hand available to succeed. He was ready to make some noise. When Randolph spoke, people listened, including the president of the United States.

On June 14th, 1941, Randolph and White returned for an encore at the White House. Once more, when the curtains rose on the meeting, FDR played the part of the sympathetic, but realistic, friend. He still felt the race issue was too explosive, too complicated, and too sensitive to be solved overnight, especially in the shadows of a looming war. Instead, he hoped for a post-war alliance between progressive Democrats like himself and reform Republicans like Wendell Willkie. A bipartisan coalition like this could help move America into a color-blind future. But it would take time and effort to pull off so sweeping, and yet so delicate, a realignment.

In the meantime, FDR had a war to plan for. And Philip Randolph wasn't helping. The president worried that Randolph might make good on his pledge to take to the streets of Washington in protest. This was the sort of headache that FDR couldn't afford and didn't want. Though he had no intention of meeting Randolph's demands, FDR thought he could win him over with some personal attention. He thought wrong.

As the meeting began, FDR turned on his famous charm. He was determined that this meeting, unlike the last, would satisfy the black leaders. Though he had only met him once before, FDR began the meeting with Randolph by calling him "Phil." In his golden tones, he warmly assured Randolph, "You and I share a kinship in our great interest in human and social justice."

Roosevelt had a way of oozing charm out of his mouth and into the heart of the person he was speaking with. In his presence, the air was soon perfumed by Rooseveltian grace and empathy. A visitor to the Oval Office could not help but breathe it in. FDR was perhaps the most congenitally charismatic man ever to reside in the White House. His magic was legendary. He had once ended a late-night meeting with the king of England by slapping the young monarch on the knee and saying with a smile, "Time for bed, young man!" The king loved it. Most people did.

But not Randolph. And not White. They would not be tricked. "Walter, how many people will really march?" FDR asked White.

"One hundred thousand, Mr. President," White sternly answered.

"You can't bring 100,000 Negroes to Washington," FDR gasped. "Someone might get killed," he warned, perhaps referring to the 1919 race riots in the capital.

But White and Randolph were not intimidated. Randolph interrupted FDR's seduction: "Mr. President, time is running on. You are quite busy, I know. But what we want to talk with you about is the problem of jobs for Negroes in defense industries. Our people are being turned away at factory gates because they are colored. They can't live with this thing."

FDR was rarely spoken to this way. But Randolph wasn't finished: "Now, what are you going to do about it?" Stunned, FDR punted back to Randolph: "Well, Phil, what do you want me to do?"

Randolph urged FDR to "issue an executive order making it mandatory that Negroes be permitted to work in these plants." FDR refused. He urged Randolph to call off the planned march of July 1st. The meeting ended in stalemate. With the warmth in his voice turning noticeably cooler, FDR told Randolph he didn't like having people point a gun at his head. Yet, days later, Roosevelt realized that Randolph was serious about carrying out his threat and had the resources to do it.[6]

FDR caved. On June 25th, the modern civil rights movement scored its first major political victory when the president of the United States signed an executive order banning discrimination in defense contracting and appointed a Fair Employment Practices Committee to help enforce it.

Black America had come a long way from the days of Booker T. Washington and Marcus Garvey. For the first time, the civil rights community had shown it could play hardball politics and win. And it would not quietly go back into shadows of American life.

◇

Pearl Harbor was a day of fire that seared the American soul. Outraged, Americans prepared to fight back. When Hitler joined his Japanese ally in declaring war on the U.S., the stage was set for a two-front war.

FDR galvanized the nation for battle. But he continued to see race as a minor issue in a major war. In 1942, as Roosevelt looked for ways to combat Japanese expansion in the Pacific, he received some advice from an unlikely source: Mohandas Gandhi. The leader of the Indian nationalist movement wrote a letter to the president. While not disavowing his famous policy of nonviolence, he did seem to welcome the idea of Allied troops in India as a way of stopping the Japanese. But he also lectured Roosevelt on the contradiction inherent in the American war effort: "I venture to think that the Allied declaration, that the Allies are fighting to make the world safe for freedom of the individual and for democracy sounds hollow, so long as India and, for that matter, Africa are exploited by Great Britain, and America has the Negro problem in her own home."[7]

FDR probably was in no mood to argue with Gandhi, perhaps because he was in no position to argue with him. Roosevelt himself had personally ordered the internment of 110,500 Japanese-Americans. After Pearl Harbor, these Americans were rounded up, taken from their homes, and sent to camps where they could be monitored.

This was not a knee-jerk reaction by FDR. It was the result of years of thought and worry. As early as 1936, Roosevelt had expressed concern about Japanese-Hawaiians, suggesting they be "the first to be placed in a concentration camp in the event of trouble." The president believed that his internment policy was good for everyone, including those interned. According to Henry Stimson and McGeorge Bundy, the internments produced a "distinctly healthier atmosphere" for the Japanese-Americans and all Americans.

FDR was not alone in wanting to fight a war for democracy in a less-than-democratic way. The attorney general of California helped to bring the internment plan to fruition. Japan's "fifth column activities" must be confronted in California, said Earl Warren.[8]

Still, FDR saw himself as a liberator. He could, and did, urge Churchill to consider giving up imperial possessions. But he couldn't, and didn't, consider ushering in a civil rights revolution at home. Certainly not for Japanese-Americans. And not for blacks either. Japan and Germany were the enemies, not Dixie.

FDR never responded to Gandhi's letter or took up his advice. Throughout the war, Roosevelt would continue a policy of benign neglect on race matters. He was sympathetic to black soldiers and their struggles. But he had a political coalition to hold together and a world war to wage and win. And what an odd coalition it was: Southern Democrats, Northern intellectuals, unions, and blacks. The fabric of this mosaic was carefully stitched together, but it always seemed on the verge of tearing at the seams.

In the meantime, black defense-industry workers were reaping the fruits of A. Philip Randolph's labors. The black men and women who went to work in America's defense industry during World War II helped to produce the weapons that helped produce the victory. Excellent workers, their example would inspire other blacks and encourage whites to reconsider their ingrained notions. Black Americans were beginning to build a momentum: The more they took on new assignments and did good work, the less likely America would return to its segregationist past.

But the black defense workers and the black civil rights leaders were not alone in blazing a new trail. Across the Atlantic, black soldiers were eager for a chance to do their part to stop Hitler. By the time of the Battle of the Bulge, black soldiers had come a long way. So had their commander.

<>

The long river of Dwight Eisenhower's life was filled with deep waters and competing currents. Always flowing forward, it sometimes led him through unpredictable bends to shores he could have never imagined. In December 1944, the commander at Versailles found himself in the tempestuous crosscurrents of war, politics, and race.

Like most white Americans of his generation, Eisenhower had had little interaction with his fellow citizens of color. He had correspondingly scant understanding of the unique injustices they faced. Many Americans of his generation saw the experience of others through the prism of their own experiences. When looking at blacks, these people of goodwill assumed the hardship of being poor was similar to the handicap of being black. Growing up in Abilene, Kansas, an overwhelmingly white town, Ike likely felt the same way. After all, his family was far from the middle class. "Whenever any of us expressed a wish for something that seemed far beyond our reach, my mother often said, 'Sink or swim,' or 'Survive or perish.'"[9] This was the natural, if naïve, thinking that many Americans of goodwill brought to the issue of race. Ike wasn't much different. Hadn't he experienced hard times? Hadn't he prevailed over adversity?

Ike's early life was built around athletics in general and football in particular. "We were raised to be athletes," he remembered. He lived for the gridiron. And he almost died for it. Once, an injured leg kept Ike bedridden for weeks. His parents and his doctor worried when it didn't improve. When the doctor threatened to amputate, Ike feared his days of football glory were over. He asked his brother Ed to join him in the bedroom. "I'd rather be dead than crippled," he pleaded to his brother, "and not be able to play ball." Ike ordered his brother to stand guard by his bed to prevent any amputation. Fortunately, the leg healed. Ike's playing days would go on.

It was there, on the gridiron, that one of Ike's first known encounters with people of color transpired. One day, while playing football, young Ike and his teammates looked across the field and noticed a black player getting ready for the other team. The Abilene boys were horrified. They had no blacks on their team. And they had never played against a black. They weren't ready to start now.

Upon further investigation, the Abilene team was shocked to learn that the black player played center. This meant he would line up directly in front of the Abilene defensive line and be in constant contact with the Abilene players as he blocked on each play. This was too much. Such was the extent of the casual racism of the day that the Abilene players decided they simply would not play in that game.

But young Eisenhower proposed a solution. He loved the sport too much to cancel the game. His solution was to volunteer to play across from the center. This was not normally where he played. But Ike was willing to do it, and the team was willing to accept this compromise. Ike made a point of shaking hands with the young black boy both before and after the game. He felt that he had made his point and that "the rest of the team felt a bit ashamed."[10]

Revealingly, young Ike was less concerned with making things better than he was with making things work. Like a repairman, his first instinct was to fix what was wrong rather than construct something better. He was willing to play a different position because it would solve the problem and keep the game going. And he clearly thought he was doing the right thing. But if he took the time to plead the cause of racial justice, denounce the evils of racism, or discuss the deeper philosophical issues involved, no one recorded it. Young Ike was a problem-solver, not a philosopher.

Indeed, it seems likely that Ike may have shared some of his teammates' preconceived notions. At the dawn of the twentieth century, much of the fabric of American society was saturated with the polluted water of latent racism. Not the kind that burns crosses or whips a man's back with a leather strap, although there was a good deal of that, too. Rather, it was the kind of subtle racism that accepts lazy assumptions handed down from generation to generation. And this generic brand of poison was not confined to the worst of America. Millions of Americans had swallowed it whole.

Around the time of Eisenhower's high-school football career, Theodore Roosevelt was president. He thrilled the black community when he hosted Booker T. Washington at the White House. Then he shocked the black community when he dismissed from the Army 167 Negro soldiers for a dubious charge of rioting in Brownsville, Texas. Not content, TR added insult to injustice when he said: "The colored man who fails to condemn crime in another colored man…is the worst enemy of his own people, as well as an enemy to all the people."[11] There was no trial because there was no evidence. The black soldiers were guilty of being black. Their dishonorable discharges were approved at the White House.

This was the progressive, broad-minded Theodore Roosevelt speaking and acting on race. TR had been educated at Harvard and Columbia. He idolized Abraham Lincoln. He claimed to represent all Americans. And in many ways, he was the very best of America. Yet, as president, he was still capable of callous disregard of the rights of black Americans. This was the America of the early twentieth century; the America in which Dwight Eisenhower grew to manhood.

And a man he was becoming. Tough, muscular, and unafraid. While attending West Point in 1913, Eisenhower went home to Abilene on a thirty-day furlough. One day, he walked down the wooden sidewalks of Buckeye Street. Once he was downtown, he entered a barber shop. His flowing shock of brown hair had to be regularly cut to stay within West Point guidelines. As the barber began shortening Ike's hair, a man entered the shop. His name was Dirk Tyler.[12] He was a local boy with a massive physique. On a few occasions he had fought professionally in Kansas City. But mainly he just liked beating up on Abilene kids. He was a bully. And he was a brute. He also happened to be black.

Tyler had heard about the athletic, young Ike. And he no doubt looked forward to challenging him. As Ike's brown hair fell from the blade to the floor, his eyes fixed on Dirk, looming menacingly just a few feet away. "Anywhere, any time," Dirk announced to the young cadet. Eisenhower, not eager for a fight but not willing to run from one, agreed. "Soon's I get my hair cut."

As the fight began, Dirk tried to overwhelm Ike with brute force. But Ike was too smart and agile. Deftly, he dodged the huge hands that were hurled his way. Quickly and effectively, he counterpunched, catching Dirk off guard. Ike's last punch was a right cross. Dirk fell to the floor. He was out.

"I went out determined to use every bit of skill to protect myself," Ike remembered. "And then to find that the boy didn't know the first thing about fighting! He telegraphed his punches from a mile away." Years later, Eisenhower took time out from the Normandy campaign to reminisce with a reporter. Though time had passed, the shame had not. "Poor Dirk. Honestly, I've never been particularly proud of that scrap."

After graduating from West Point in 1915, Lt. Eisenhower reported for his first tour of duty. Ironically, he was ordered to go to Fort Sam Houston in San Antonio, just north of Brownsville, where the infamous "riot" of 1906 had taken place.

Eisenhower settled into the life of an officer. He had graduated from West Point with a fairly undistinguished academic record. And a knee injury had deprived him of the gridiron glory he had so hoped to achieve at the Academy. But that was all behind him now. He was now an infantry officer in the United States Army. And he was deployed to one of the most desirable posts in the whole Army—San Antonio.

Most of the work at Fort Sam could be done before noon, which left plenty of time for hunting deer or dove. Ike also took time to coach a local football team. He paid off his debts with his winnings at the poker table—another competitive game at which he excelled.

But it was business before pleasure at Fort Sam Houston. Not long after Ike arrived, ominous rumblings could be heard from Mexico, a few hundred miles to the south. These were the days of Pancho Villa, revolution, and anxiety along the border. Could war with Mexico be imminent? Many Americans thought so. President Woodrow Wilson mobilized National Guard units with the intention of securing the border.

Eisenhower was sent to a military camp, where he helped to train National Guard units from Illinois. One was a unit of Negroes. This was to be his first encounter with black troops. He was not impressed. One day, the black unit took part in a shooting competition. They were competing against white regiments. To his horror, Ike soon learned that the black soldiers were terrible shots. Jumping to easy conclusions, he assumed that they couldn't shoot because they were black. "This was my first impression," Eisenhower later remembered, "that they were incompetent and not able really to do things in the same manner that whites were able to do it." Ike simply "took it for granted that black people were stupid."[13]

At the time, Ike didn't consider other factors that might have limited the black soldiers' shooting skills. "It never dawned on me they hadn't been trained...had inferior equipment, and the motivation wasn't there because they'd been kicked around and hounded."

At this stage of his journey, Ike still saw the black experience through his own. He hadn't had money or privileges growing up. But he still knew how to shoot a gun. So why couldn't his black troops? Still, he did his best to make sure all his men got the training they needed, regardless of race. But his first impression of black soldiers was not a favorable one.

Ike's experience during this time was a defining moment for his career. His boss, Colonel Daniel Moriarity, was eager to turn over administrative duties to his young second lieutenant. Ike honed his writing skills as he crafted orders, reports, and memoranda for the colonel's signature. No less important, he now had the time and the responsibilities to develop and display his leadership skills. "I began to devote more hours of study and reading to my profession."

Before leaving Fort Sam Houston, Eisenhower's life was changed forever when he met Mamie Doud. A Colorado girl with dribbles of dark hair protecting her forehead, she typically spent the winter months in Texas with her family. Ike and Mamie spent long and leisurely nights at their favorite restaurant, "The Original."[14] They ate chili, tamales, and enchiladas as they looked out at the San Antonio River and into the future.

Love often has its own cadence and rhythm. It didn't take long for the two to know that it was time. After receiving ten days leave, Eisenhower made his way to Denver. On July 1st, 1916, he married Mamie in her parents' home. In many ways, Ike was a nineteenth-century man living in a twentieth-century world. He was Victorian in his habits and beliefs. This suited Mamie just fine. They both had old-fashioned views about their relationship. He believed that it should revolve around him and his career. She agreed. Her life was her family. And her family was her life. In later years, she would insist she was a professional: "I have a career, and his name is Ike."

The next year, America entered the Great War in Europe. Ike was eager to take part in the "war to end all wars." But he never made it out of the states. Heartbroken at having missed his chance for glory, he feared that his time had passed. But he needn't have worried. His efficiency and talent caught the attention of the military establishment. For the next several years, he served in a number of posts—most notably in Panama, where General Fox Conner mentored him. Eventually, he graduated first in his class at the Command and General Staff School in Leavenworth, Kansas. The young major was finding his way. And people noticed.

In 1933, Eisenhower began work for the Army chief of staff, General Douglas MacArthur. They worked together in the War, Navy, and State Department building on 17th Street, just across the street from the West Wing of the White House. The granite, slate, and cast iron building was a fine structure in the French Second Empire style. As a grand edifice, it was a perfect abode for a grand man. MacArthur was everything Eisenhower was not: vain, egocentric, obsessive, flamboyant, and insecure.

He had a way of speaking of himself in the third person. "So, MacArthur went over to the senator...," he would say to Major Eisenhower in describing a visit to Capitol Hill. Ike was startled the first time he heard MacArthur refer to himself this way. But with time, he found the habit not "objectionable, just odd." Eccentricities aside, MacArthur was extraordinarily gifted. He was heroic, brave, and noble. He was a great general, and he knew it.

As his biographer wrote, he was both the "most ridiculous, and most sublime."[15]

But if MacArthur was blinded by his own lights, he could still make out the image of a fine, young officer in his midst. In one of the fitness reports that MacArthur turned in on Eisenhower, he prophetically stated: "This is the best officer in the Army. When the next war comes, he should go right to the top."[16]

Until then, MacArthur was content to see Eisenhower go right with him on his next assignment to the Philippines. Regarding himself as something of a personal savior to the people of the Philippines, MacArthur preferred a throne to a cross. His father had served as military-governor after the United States took possession following the Spanish-American War in 1900. Douglas MacArthur felt a genuine affection for the people. In 1935, he arrived and began preparing for the defense of the islands in case of war.

For most of the next four years, Ike tried to help train the Filipinos. While his boss "spoke and wrote in purple splendor" about the importance of the mission, Ike "played it down as just another job."

But while Ike shared MacArthur's determination to prepare the Filipinos, he lacked his boss's faith in their military abilities. MacArthur openly talked about his pride in his "friendly relations with the Filipinos." He believed they were ready to be made into a great fighting force.

Eisenhower, who was more closely involved in the daily operations, had his doubts. By the end of 1935, he was again seeing troops of color not measure up to his expectations. It did little to deepen his understanding or challenge his prejudices.

Ike wrote in his diary that he had "learned to expect from the Filipinos with whom we deal, a minimum of performance from a maximum of promise." There was "no lack of intelligence" among the Filipinos. But there was still something missing. They were, "with few exceptions, unaccustomed to the requirements of administrative and executive procedure." After meeting with Filipinos and agreeing on a plan of action, Eisenhower said that often "nothing whatsoever will be done." "These peculiar traits we are learning to take into account," Ike lamented in his diary, "but obviously they impede progress."[17]

While doubting the martial abilities of the Filipinos, Ike harbored no such uncertainty about the Germans. As the decade came to a close, he saw another war brewing in Europe. He wanted in on it. He had missed out on the action in the First World War. He didn't want that to happen again. He paid his respects in a farewell visit to Manuel Quezon, president of the Philippines. Quezon tried to talk him into staying, but Ike wouldn't listen. "My entire life has been given to this one thing, my country and my profession," he said. "I want to be there if what I fear is going to come actually happens."

He arrived back in the States in late 1939, just a couple of months after war officially broke out in Europe. For the next two years, Ike manned jobs from San Francisco to Fort Lewis in Washington to the Third Army in Texas. After the attack on Pearl Harbor, he was ordered to report to Washington.

This was it! He was sure he could and would help win the war. He was not the only one to notice. After bad weather forced his plane to land, Eisenhower took the train to Washington. The railcar was packed. Ike, dashing in his uniform, caught the attention of the passengers. But the brigadier general had nowhere to stand, much less to sleep. Sensing this, a portly gentleman extended his hand to Ike. Would the general like to sleep in his private car? Ike was moved by the offer and grateful for a place to sleep. He would spend the rest of the trip to Washington in the private car of Sid Richardson, Fort Worth oilman and one of the richest men in the world. Richardson admired Ike from the first moment he saw him on the train. And he would remain one of Ike's biggest supporters until the end of his influential life.

After arriving at Union Station, Ike made his way back to his old stomping grounds: the War, Navy, and State Department. There, he worked in the War Plans Division. Within a week of the December 7th attack, General George C. Marshall asked the young officer to prepare a plan of action for the war in the Pacific. He did, urging that a stand be made in the Philippines, even while the main base of operations would be set up in Australia.

Marshall read the plan and told Ike, "I agree with you." America was now at war with both Imperial Japan and Nazi Germany. Ike's star was now ascending.

◇

With little fanfare but much to do, Eisenhower arrived in London in 1942 and went to work. He set up headquarters at Norfolk House on St. James Square. Like an emergency room surgeon, he got right to work to revive his patient; in this case, the weary Allies.

His first goal was to establish a genuine partnership with the British. Balancing the competing interests and egos of the various commanders around him would be an ongoing struggle that would last the length of the war. Still, Ike knew that only a unified team could beat the Nazis.

Eisenhower soon learned that his job required him to address many problems, not just fighting the Nazis. And one of the biggest problems was race.

He had experienced a bit of this dilemma while serving at the War Department earlier in the war. Early in 1942, Eisenhower had been tasked with researching and writing a memo entitled "The Colored Troop Problem."[18] Though he was well-equipped to handle military matters, he was still somewhat clumsy in addressing race.

Too often, he took at face value the words of commanders in the field. Too seldom did he take the time to find out the real story. The memo alternated between naiveté and offensiveness. Ike informed General Marshall that the governor of Alaska fiercely opposed the deployment of black troops to the area because "he feels the mixture of the colored race with native Indian and Eskimo stock is highly undesirable." Even more surprising, Eisenhower's memo listed other overseas destinations that would object to the use of black troops, including Hawaii, Panama, Trinidad, South America, and Liberia. It seems not to have occurred to General Eisenhower that he was getting his information from white commanders in the field. In all likelihood, they, not the native people or native governments, were the ones most opposed to the deployment of black commanders. After all, Hawaii,

36

Panama, Trinidad, Liberia, and the countries of South America were hardly white territories with Anglo-Saxon populations.

Now deployed in London, Eisenhower again faced the race issue. The Army, Southern in its mores, customs, and personnel, was feverishly trying to establish separate, but equal, facilities for its Negro soldiers. The same organization had been struggling to deal with nosey reporters interested in the black soldiers who fought for the freedom of the world even though they were not entirely free themselves.

Revealingly, as Ike set up his operation, he reached out to the press. Traditionally, the military and media have had a contentious marriage. They both need the other. But their relationship is tinged by distrust. Most generals worry about loose-mouthed reporters compromising operational security. Hence, information is rationed.

Eisenhower took a different view. He saw the press as part of his command. Put another way, if he couldn't command it, he might still co-opt it. He began "holding short, informal conferences with the press, for the purpose of discussing our mutual problems and finding common solutions for them." Intriguingly, Ike saw a press conference as a dialogue, not as a monologue. A commander is always looking for information. Why not get some of it from reporters? They are in the field. They talk to troops. What are they hearing? Ike insisted that reporters "occupy positions as quasi-staff officers on my staff, and I respected their collective responsibilities in the war as they did mine."

But Ike was about to learn that working with the press was still a contentious relationship, fraught with challenges. During his very first press conference on July 14th, 1942, in London, reporters asked Eisenhower whether they could have access to Negro troops.[19] Ike said he saw no reason why they shouldn't. Indeed, he was surprised by the question. He was later brought up to speed on what prompted it. Prior to his arrival, the American headquarters had set up a ban on stories regarding incidents of trouble between black and white troops.

As Ike studied the issue, he learned that British citizens lacked the "racial consciousness which is so strong in the United

States." Thus, British girls often went out on dates with black American soldiers. This infuriated some of their white counterparts. Fights sometimes ensued. The press, not surprisingly, wanted to cover this. But the American headquarters said no. Until Eisenhower.

One month and one day later, on August 15th, a reporter asked Eisenhower about the censorship of stories about problems that black troops were suffering. "Take it off!" Ike declared in a quick and decisive veto of the old policy.[20] In July, he had permitted reporters to talk to black soldiers for the first time. Now in August, he was giving the okay for reporters to wire home negative stories about the problems of being black in the green uniform. Ike urged the reporters to not lose a sense of perspective. But otherwise, he felt that the more the American people knew, the better.

Later, some other reporters asked him to reconsider and keep the ban in place. It was suggested to the general that the reports of fights between black and white troops might cause dissension back in the states. Ike listened. But he didn't change his mind. He insisted that the American people could handle the truth.

Not just reporters were curious about the new policy. Admiral Harold Stark went to see Ike in his office on August 17th. According to an aide who sat in on the meeting, the admiral was "much concerned." A few weeks earlier, the Navy had censored a *Chicago Sun* story about white and black soldiers approaching something close to a riot in Londonderry. Did Eisenhower really want to end all censorship? Even of stories like this?

To make his intentions clear, Ike put his policy on paper. Writing to Raymond Daniel of the Association of American Correspondents that same day, he explained that "news involving negroes is no more subject to censorship by military authorities than is any other type."[21] But Ike did hedge a bit, perhaps reflecting the warnings of Admiral Stark. He cautioned:

> If a story attempted to take an isolated case of friction between white and colored soldiers and make it appear that this was typical, I would not only censor the whole story but would consider that it exhibited a far from cooperative attitude on the part of such newsman.

Ike's policy was to allow freedom *for* the media in return for discretion *from* the media. Since the British were his partners, Ike forwarded this letter to Brendan Bracken, Churchill's protégé and his Minister of Information. "I wonder whether you could not transmit to British editors the purport of this letter," Ike wrote in a cover note on August 18th, "with an earnest request that they be guided by the policy expressed."[22]

Around the same time, Eisenhower held another meeting with some reporters, including the legendary CBS newsman Edward R. Murrow. Murrow had access to Ike because of his fame and because Ike's press aide was Navy Captain Harry Butcher, a former CBS staffer. Some reporters asked the general why soldiers fighting for freedom were not free in their own country. Eisenhower sidestepped the politics of the question and dealt with the realities of his theater of operations. He said that in his command all soldiers would be treated equally.

But this did not mean an end to segregation in the Army. Ike reminded the reporters that he did not get to make those decisions; they came from Washington. He did the war. FDR did the policy. And FDR needed all the help he could get from Southern Democrats. It was one thing to fight Adolph Hitler; quite another to take on Jim Crow. One battle was enough, one war at a time — that was the essential message Ike gave to the reporters seeking a more democratic Army.[23]

While most of the media were pleased that Ike had removed the ban restricting reporting on black troops, they still questioned the need for separate facilities for blacks. Changing the media ground rules was one thing. But how about changing the rules by which black troops must abide every day?

Again, Ike, though sympathetic, found himself unable to satisfy the questions. In an interview with A.J. Liebling of the *New Yorker*, Ike pledged equality of treatment but allowed that this might still be handled in a segregated manner. Liebling, correctly sensing that World War II was changing not only the world but also America, predicted that what Ike did regarding race relations would have a profound impact. Ike politely thanked Liebling and said he looked forward to reading his reports.[24]

At this point in his career, Ike possessed the cool mind of a manager and not the bold vision of a leader. He would manage the problem of race relations with equal doses of sympathy and realism. But he would not try and lead on race relations; he would not perform radical surgery.

His policy drew support from a new and important local friend, Winston Churchill. The British prime minister told his war cabinet in October 1942 that he didn't want to "stand between" American officers and soldiers. It was not his business to worry about racial policies of the American troops. He told his team, "We mustn't interfere."[25]

Now that his policy on black troops had been established, Eisenhower went about fighting the Nazis. For starters, he now set himself to the task of "organizing and leading an Allied force into northwest Africa." Operation Torch was about to begin. But as he prepared to send Americans into Africa, the questions about the proper role of black troops would only grow.

◇

Napoleon famously observed that in war, the importance of morale is three times that of material. If so, Ike had a problem. His black troops were dangerously demoralized. It was bad enough that they had to suffer segregation in Louisiana. But now it was following them to London?

That summer, Ike again took up pen and paper to write out policy.[26] He addressed his words to the commander of the Services of Supply, where most blacks were serving. Ike said his policy was that "discrimination against the Negro troops be sedulously avoided." One of the biggest complaints uniformed blacks had was the furlough policy. Ike urged that commanders not attempt to segregate soldiers at social gatherings. Rather, he encouraged the twin goals of "avoiding discrimination due to race" and "minimizing causes of friction between White and Colored Troops." How were commanders to achieve this? "This Headquarters will not attempt to issue any detailed instructions," Ike said. Each commander was on his own.

London, in particular, represented a unique challenge to the Army's furlough policy. Upon receiving leave, black soldiers would invariably head to London for well-deserved and much-needed relaxation. In London clubs, they were treated as equals. But at night, they might stay in Red Cross housing. There, they were segregated.

When the problem was brought to General Eisenhower's attention that summer, he was willing to nudge the Red Cross, but not push it. In July, his office issued a directive to the Red Cross, advising it on how to treat black soldiers on leave in London. The memo read, in part:

> While obviously desirable that whenever possible, separate sleeping accommodations be provided for Negro soldiers; whenever that is not possible, Negro soldiers properly on pass or furlough should be given accommodations in the Red Cross Clubs on the same basis as other soldiers.[27]

As long as it was equal, it was okay with Ike for it to be separate. Still, he had spent a considerable amount of time and effort that summer winning small victories for his black troops. He changed the rules that banned press coverage. And he encouraged nondiscrimination in furlough activities.

But Ike was not ready for a civil rights revolution. And neither was the Army. But he was, perhaps unintentionally, ushering an evolution on civil rights in the military.

The 1942 Army was a metaphor for America's internal divisions over race. Blacks were segregated into their own units, and there were restrictions on when and where they could serve. Essentially, service with other black units was encouraged, while service with white units was not.

The genesis of this policy could be traced back to the War Department. Shortly before the war began, along the time of Philip Randolph's urgings at the White House, a report surfaced that urged the Army to integrate its troops. General George Marshall not only disagreed with the report but established what the policy of the Army would be. "The Army cannot accomplish such a solution [civil rights] and should not be charged with the undertaking." Marshall added that the "settlement of vexing social problems cannot be permitted to complicate the tremendous task of the

War Department."[28] The war, and not civil rights, would be the goal of Marshall and the entire Army.

From the mixed signals coming out of Eisenhower's office, a pattern could still be developed. Where he had authority, like with press coverage of black troops, he used his power for the good and was a leader. Where he didn't have authority, such as the segregation of the Army itself, he accepted the policy and was a team player.

But as is often the case with great figures in history, the public policy was a reflection of private views. Ike wanted to do what was right, but still he held back, his conscience itself at war with his immediate objective.

Eisenhower still suffered from the oldest taboo in race relations: He worried about the interaction between black troops and white women. Before the end of August, the Hollywood movie star Merle Oberon visited Ike's headquarters. The general candidly told the star that he worried about his black troops because they were spending their spare time with English girls.[29]

Still, as the invasion of Africa got underway, forces were at work causing Ike to reconsider. One was the war he was fighting. He despised the Nazi racism. How could he not see the irony in the way his own Army treated people of color? Indeed, Eisenhower believed morale was imperative to his success. And the key to morale, according to Eisenhower, was the justness of the cause.

"Belief in an underlying cause is fully as important to success in war as any local spirit or discipline induced or produced by whatever kind of command or leadership action," Ike later wrote. "Cromwell's 'Ironsides' marched into battle singing hymns," Ike noted. His own black troops sang a very different song.[30]

A second force that was giving Ike pause was the conduct and bravery of black troops themselves. He watched them in action. And he was genuinely pleased and proud of their efforts.

As autumn surrendered to winter, Eisenhower could now focus on fighting the war. He, and his troops, both black and white, were about to engage the Nazis in combat for the first time.

◇

After his troops successfully invaded North Africa and began pushing Rommel's troops back, Ike took some time to catch up on his mail. In early 1943, having moved his headquarters to North Africa, he wrote his son John at West Point. "My office is nothing grand but is perfectly comfortable," wrote Eisenhower.[31] He considered himself blessed to have "a group of darkies that take gorgeous care of me." One of them was Sergeant John Moaney, Ike's personal valet. He was often the first person Ike saw in the morning, and the last he saw at night. As the letter revealed, Ike could still occasionally and carelessly use racially derogatory terms to describe blacks. But the friendship between the general and his valet transcended words. For the next two-and-a-half decades, Moaney would proudly serve his boss.

With most of North Africa recaptured for the Allies, Eisenhower began to plot a bold, dramatic, and new phase of the war. As the North African campaign began to wind down, Ike eyed the mainland of Europe. Churchill said of the successful North African efforts that "it is perhaps the end of the beginning." Much more fighting remained.

Eisenhower wanted that fighting to take place closer to Europe. He began preparing for the amphibious invasion of Sicily. It was a huge, risky undertaking. To prepare the battlefield, the Allies would have to fly bombers from North Africa, across the width of the Mediterranean, and deposit their high-voltage explosives on the mountainous island before assault troops ever arrived.

On July 2nd, 1943, the 99th Fighter Squadron escorted bombers on a mission to Sicily. These were the famous Tuskegee Airmen, an all-black unit that was seeing its first major action. As their planes rode with the wind above the waters of the Mediterranean that warm summer day, suddenly enemy planes could be spotted closing in on them. The mission was at risk. The German planes were one hundred-miles-per-hour faster than those of the 99th. The German pilots tried to interrupt the flight and destroy the bombers. The only things standing in their way were the aircraft of the Tuskegee Airmen.

Suddenly, the 99th pilots turned and engaged in a furious dogfight with the Germans. Lt. Charles "Buster" Hall, one of the

99th's fliers, aggressively went after the Nazi planes and scored a direct hit on one. "I followed him down," Hall said, "and saw him crash." The German planes withdrew. The Tuskegee Airmen had saved the day. Black pilots had done more than puncture German planes; they had punctured the German myth of Aryan racial supremacy.

It was a great moment, one worthy of the commander's attention. One day later, on July 3rd, Eisenhower, along with General Jimmy Doolittle and Air Chief Marshall Tedder, arrived at the 99th Fighter Squadron headquarters in Tunisia. He personally congratulated Hall and his comrades on their courage and combat success.[32] Thanks to the heroism of the Tuskegee Airmen, the invasion of Sicily would move forward.

Ike savored these visits with the troops. Gregarious by nature, he loved nothing more than talking to his boys. He wanted to know where they were from, how they were being treated, what he could do to help. Since a visit to the troops meant a visit to the front, Ike was usually urged by his staff to put on a helmet. But he would invariably refuse, ordering his staff to put "that damn thing" away. He felt that it was an insult to the soldiers at the front to wear a helmet when he was seldom in the line of fire.

The invasion of Sicily was a success. Slogging across the island, Allied troops pushed the Nazis back. Now, the stage was set for the invasion of Europe in 1944. As the firestorm of artillery and gunshots rained down over Europe, a subtle, yet perceptible, difference could now be seen in Ike. No longer did he consider black soldiers "pathetic" in their shooting skills. No more did he write of expecting a "minimum of performance" from soldiers of color. The war was changing Ike. He was now more likely to write that he would "confidently count upon the negro soldier again to write a brilliant chapter in the military history of our country."

He had always been the product of his environment. He had been raised in a mostly white town, in a mostly white state, in a mostly white country. He had attended a mostly white West Point. Professionally, he had served a mostly white army in the mostly white officer corps. But now his environment was changing, and so was Ike.

How could he not be inspired by the heroism of his troops, including those who were black? And how could he not be influenced by the mission, which he now saw in increasingly moral terms?

At the end of the Tunisian campaign in 1942, Eisenhower reversed centuries of military tradition in refusing to allow captured German generals the right to call on him. For Ike, there could be no such relationship with the Nazis. There would be no banquet like the one Washington hosted for Cornwallis. "Daily as it progressed," Ike wrote of his wartime emotions, "there grew within me the conviction that as never before in a war between many nations the forces that stood for human good and men's right were this time confronted by a completely evil conspiracy with which no compromise could be tolerated."[33] Ike saw this as the right war, and he was trying to fight it in the right way.

That meant using every tool at his disposal. Hitler had vowed that his master race was tougher and stronger than any other breed. Yet a Tuskegee Airman shot down one of Hitler's pilots. Ike saw this, took note of it, and took the time to congratulate the pilot in person. He was seeing more of black soldiers and liking what he saw. Interaction often brings inner change.

That did not mean the military as a whole was ready for the age of equality. In 1944, FDR told black newspaper publishers that the reason discrimination existed in the military was because of the officer corps. "It is perfectly true, there is definite discrimination in the treatment of the colored...troops," the president admitted. "The trouble lies fundamentally in the attitude of certain white people—officers down the line who haven't got much more education, many of them, than the colored troops."[34] Though unintentionally condescending and insulting to the black editors, Roosevelt's remarks about the officers were true. Most of the military establishment was not ready to lead the charge on race.

◇

In the spring of 1944, Eisenhower was back in England. He was preparing for the supreme moment of his military career—the invasion of Europe. Shortly before D-Day, Bedell Smith, his hot-

45

blooded chief of staff, thrust himself into the supreme commander's office.

"Oh, my God," Smith blurted out, "General de Gaulle won't go!"[35] The liberation of France was to include a grand entrance by the self-proclaimed leader of Free France. The temperamental Frenchman had been moderately cooperative thus far. Now, he reverted gloriously to type.

"What's the matter?" Ike asked.

"Well," Bedell answered, "de Gaulle says he's not going to go in an American plane—it has to be a French plane." That the French had no planes at the time—indeed, had no country— seems not to have occurred to *le general*.

Eisenhower was accustomed to outrageous behavior from his associates. No small part of his job was finding ways to keep his fractious team happy. He would solve the problem for de Gaulle. "Bedell," he said calmly, "get the general in the *salle d'honneur* at the airport. Then get a sergeant, give him some paint, go out and paint the American stars off that plane, and put the French tricolor on the plane." Bedell promptly implemented these orders.

When the time came for de Gaulle to fly to France, he was led to a plane and told, "General, here's your French plane." General de Gaulle's long frame circled around the circumference of the aircraft.

After spotting and examining the tricolor on the side of it, de Gaulle was satisfied. "Zank you very much," he said as he got onto the plane. It was a small victory for the unity of the coalition.

Eisenhower had a remarkable ability to clear a pathway of common sense out of a thicket of complicated problems. If painting one of his planes would keep an ally happy, then so be it.

But as D-Day drew near, other problems resisted cosmetic solutions.

◇

In the late-night hours of May 5th, an Army technician named Leroy Henry arrived at his lover's house in a suburb of Bath, England.[36] Twice before, Henry had met the woman for sex. Both times, he paid her one pound. But on the night of May 5th, the woman asked for two pounds. When Henry refused, she ran screaming to her husband. She claimed she had been raped by an American G.I. A trial was held, and Henry was found guilty and sentenced to death. Though few people believed he had actually raped her, it was bad enough that he had had sex with her. Henry was a black U.S. soldier. His lover was a white Englishwoman.

The story was a sensationalized scandal that was one of the most publicized racial events of the war. On June 3rd, Cecil King, a columnist for the *Daily Mirror*, wrote that Henry had received a far harsher sentence than a white soldier would. That same day, the NAACP cabled Ike and asked him to intervene in the case. Though swamped with the final preparations for D-Day, Eisenhower did review the case. It didn't take long. On June 19th, after looking it over, he revoked the conviction and the sentence due to lack of evidence.[37] Upon Ike's orders, Henry returned to active duty. And Ike returned to fighting the Nazis. It was a small step for justice.

Building on the success of D-Day, Allied troops steadily moved south and east from the coast across Europe. Yet, there was no single hammer blow upon the anvil to finish off the Nazis. A war of maneuver grew. And so did Ike's need for men. Eisenhower, no doubt reflecting on the heroism of the 99th and other units, saw no reason why black soldiers couldn't be sent to the front alongside their white comrades.

In December of 1944, as Eisenhower sat in his office at the Hotel Trianon in Versailles, he was a changing man, if not yet a changed man. He was different from the young officer who had been at Fort Sam Houston or in the Philippines years before. As he studied the maps on the Battle of the Bulge, he realized that this was a unique war that called for unique innovations.

For Ike, it was time to make a move. For African-Americans, it was time to make history.

CHAPTER THREE

THE REINFORCEMENTS

"I feel that in existing circumstances I cannot deny the Negro volunteer a chance to serve in battle."

—Dwight D. Eisenhower

THE GENERAL was angry. Angry at the horrors of the Nazis...angry at himself for being caught off guard...angry at not having enough troops. Now, as the Battle of the Bulge raged in the dark forests of the Ardennes, he was ready to transform his anger into action.

At his headquarters in Verdun, Eisenhower had met with General John C. H. Lee, now commander of the Communications Zone. On more than one occasion, Lee had been accused of mistaking his first three initials for "Jesus Christ Himself." He was a proud, difficult man, less than likable, but very effective. Lee was convinced that the time had come for black troops to be utilized alongside white soldiers. Eisenhower agreed. After securing Ike's approval, Lee contacted General Benjamin O. Davis, who oversaw Negro troops. Davis immediately set to work on a plan to train black soldiers for service in the field as individual infantry replacements.

On the day after Christmas, General Lee announced Eisenhower's new policy in writing to the troops. Reflecting growing awareness of the Nazis' racial ideology, the letter announced that the "Supreme Commander desires to destroy the enemy forces" by utilizing "every available weapon at our disposal."[1] This included "a limited number of colored troops who have had infantry training." They would be allowed to join "our veteran units at the front." It concluded with a vow that the black troops would be able to fight "shoulder to shoulder" with white soldiers and, reflecting, said that the supreme commander was confident that they would continue "the glorious record of our colored troops in our former wars."

A couple of days later, the formal plan was delivered to the commanders. For black soldiers, the dream of fighting "shoulder to shoulder" with white soldiers was about to become a reality.

But the dream seemed more like a nightmare to Bedell Smith. A chief of staff is always worried about details, while the commander can entertain grand designs. To Smith, Eisenhower was asking for trouble with this new policy. Not only was the new plan ill-advised, Smith thought, it might well be illegal. At least according to the standards issued by the War Department.

Smith's temper was on full display.[2] Like fireworks, his rockets soared one at a time until building to the grand finale. First, he went to General Lee. Smith had once worked at the War Department for General Marshall, and he was fully aware of the rules for black troops. Smith said that he feared a press backlash. The media would likely "take the attitude that, while the War Department segregates colored troops into organizations…the Army is perfectly willing to put them in the front lines. Mixed in units with white soldiers, and have them do battle when an emergency arises."

Lee was unconvinced. The Army needed troops. The Negro soldiers wanted to fight. It made perfect sense to use them.

Smith persisted. Putting his pen to paper, he now appealed to Eisenhower not long after the New Year. He argued that the new policy went against the War Department directives. And he suggested that in the future, no "general circulars" on black troops be issued until "I have had a chance to see them."

Advocates of a losing cause often try to assert a special degree of qualifications. Smith performed a virtuoso demonstration. Having failed to convince Lee that the media would object, Smith now tried to convince Ike that he simply knew best because he knew the most about the issue. He didn't hedge or hint. He was, typically, direct and abrasive. "I know more about the War Department's and General Marshall's difficulties with the negro question than any other man in this theater," he wrote, adding that he did so "with all due modesty."

For his part, Eisenhower had mixed feelings.[3] On the one hand, he really did think the black troops would do a good job. On the other, he was too busy fighting a war to launch a moral crusade against the War Department. He told Smith that he didn't want to "run counter to regulations in a time like this." It was a repeat of what he said to reporters in London in 1942. He was only willing to fight one war at a time. Besides, as the supreme commander, he relied on the advice of his chief of staff. And if Smith—with all of his self-proclaimed expertise on the subject—objected, then Ike was willing to reconsider the order.

What he was not willing to reconsider was the basic principle. He still thought black soldiers should be used. Ike personally rewrote the order. The new version was mischievously given the same date, file number, and subject as the previous one. And a cover note was attached asking for the return of the earlier version.

On January 4th, the new directive went out. It still offered black soldiers the chance to fight at the front "without regard to color or race."[4] However, now the black volunteers would be organized into their own units. Individual black soldiers would not be "shoulder to shoulder" with white soldiers, but black units would be side by side with white ones. It was a step forward, if something short of the bold strides promised by the first circular.

◇

Ike's order made minor history, but it made a major difference to his black soldiers. Prior to this point, most Negro troops were serving in the Services of Supply. They drove trucks or fixed equipment or unloaded ships. Occasionally, they could serve in combat when the circumstances prevented their interaction with white troops. Usually, a vehicle was involved. When shrouded inside the cockpit of a plane or the interior of a tank, no one objected to the presence of black soldiers. The Tuskegee Airmen, flying thousands of miles above the ground, exemplified this. Another example was the 761st Tank Battalion. This was a black outfit that was assigned to Patton's Third Army in 1944.[5] Patton doubted they could help him in his race across France. He feared that "a colored soldier cannot think fast enough to fight in armor." But they had fought well and disproved Patton's fears. Most important for white commanders who were worried about race mixing, they had fought from inside their tanks.

On January 7th, Eisenhower wrote to explain the new policy to Marshall.[6] Like any staffer eager to avoid upsetting his boss, Ike downplayed the significance of his order. He started by reminding Marshall of the manpower crisis. He spoke of "combing out able bodied men" for combat service. Then he pointed out the obvious solution of using black soldiers. "We have more than 100,000 Negroes in the Com Zone, and they will have to be distributed to do as much of this heavy work as possible," he tactfully told Marshall. He made his appeals on the firm foundation of practical need: "I feel that in existing circumstances I cannot deny the Negro volunteer a chance to serve in battle."

Eisenhower also anticipated a large number of black volunteers. He had a plan to deal with it. "If volunteers are received in numbers greater than existing Negro combat units I will organize them into separate battalions for temporary attachment to divisions and rotations through front line positions," he wrote to Marshall.

Eisenhower was, first and foremost, a military man. But he was demonstrating a politician's shrewd ability to split the difference. Like a chemist in the lab, he would mix and match the different elements to produce an effective solution. He would take the black volunteers and use them at the front, but he would organize them into their own units. "This will preserve the principle," he wrote, "for which I understand the War Department stands and will still have a beneficial effect in meeting our infantry needs."

Eisenhower was soon confirmed in his expectations. The descendants of the 54th Massachusetts and the Buffalo Soldiers were eager to storm their own Fort Wagners and charge up their own San Juan Hills.

But it would take weeks to retrain the men for service in the field. In the meantime, the momentum in the Battle of the Bulge began to shift. Ike's strategy of holding the line and pushing back was beginning to work. In the center of the Bulge, the 101st continued to hold out against the German attack at Bastogne.

By December 26th, elements of Patton's Third Army had reached Bastogne. "Lovely weather for killing Germans," Patton happily announced upon his arrival.[7] By the middle of January, the German thrust had been stopped and reversed. Between December 16th and January 16th, more than 120,000 German soldiers were killed or captured. Hitler had paid dearly for his gamble in the Ardennes.

Eisenhower, in between visits to the front and meetings with his commanders at Trianon, never kept his eye off of the long-term objective. The Bulge, once a distraction, was now a springboard. "All during the Battle of the Bulge we continued to plan for the final offensive blows," he wrote, "which, once started, we intended to maintain incessantly until final defeat of Germany."[8]

Meanwhile, Negro troops realized that the great battle in the Belgian woods was winding down. But if they had missed out on the Bulge, the new black volunteers did not want to miss out on the rest of the war. By the end of February 4th, 562 Negroes had volunteered for combat. By March, they were being assigned to the field in platoons. Many of these men were non-commissioned officers who took a reduction in grade and pay because only privates were eligible for the offer. Such was their desire to get in on the action.

Even as the volunteers began their training, it became clear that there was neither the time nor the facilities to fulfill Ike's vision of independent black battalions. On February 9th, Eisenhower informed Marshall of the latest evolution in his policy. He wrote, "it appears I'll have to use negro volunteers by platoons." But he still preferred to "make them independent battalions, and as time goes on, perhaps we can accumulate them into such formations."[9]

But most creatures of the Earth do not easily change stripes. And so, not everyone was sure these reinforcements were worth it. In February 1945, Henry Stimson wrote in his diary of Marshall's critique of black soldiers during the First World War.[10] Marshall said the only place where black soldiers "could be counted on to stand would be in Iceland in summertime where there was daylight for twenty-four hours."

Marshall was wrong. By March 1, 2,253 soldiers graduated from a crash course on training and were sent into thirty-seven platoons. These platoons were then spread out among the Sixth and Twelfth Army Groups. Typically, once these troops were in the field, they carried out all the assignments just like their white colleagues, from patrolling to outposting to assault.

Three platoons were assigned to the 1st Division. Far from being unable to "think fast," these soldiers proved to be somewhat "over-eager and aggressive." Likewise, the platoon assigned to the 393rd Infantry went immediately into battle and was credited with "killing approximately 100 Germans and capturing 500." These achievements took place on March 18th during fighting at the Remagen bridgehead, not far from Eudenbach. The official battle report credited the 393rd Infantry with being "particularly good in town fighting" and praised them for their frequent assaults. The black soldiers were unafraid of the vaunted Wehrmacht and undoubtedly took out their anger on them.

Overhead, the Tuskegee Airmen had more than earned their wings in battle. They soared like eagles and they pursued the enemy like hawks. By the end of the war, they had destroyed 111 enemy aircraft in air combat. Another 150 enemy planes were destroyed on the ground. From North Africa to Italy to Northwest Europe, the Tuskegee Airmen flew 1,578 missions and earned one hundred Distinguished Flying Crosses.

With each mission completed, each Nazi captured, each act of bravery, black soldiers were indeed writing a new and "brilliant chapter" in military history. But more important than what they did in battle was that they were in battle at all.

The levees of racial equality had been breached. And the floodtide would crest years later back in America.

◇

By April 1945, the scarlet roses outside the White House were breathing a naturally perfumed aroma upon the fresh, spring air. Yet inside, it was the darkest of winters. Franklin Delano Roosevelt's war had at last come to an end. Twelve years in the White House—four of them at war—had finally overcome the great warrior. Stricken by a heart attack at Warm Springs, Georgia, his staff and his nation mourned the loss of the great man.

Thousands of miles away, Eisenhower was awakened by Generals Patton and Bradley with the news. Though he later admitted he hadn't "known the president very well," Ike nevertheless felt genuine grief. "I knew him solely in his capacity as leader of a nation at war—and in that capacity he seemed to me to fulfill all that could possibly be expected of him."[11] Eisenhower was certain "there would be no interference with the tempo of the war." He would finish the job.

As the country mourned Roosevelt, the Allies continued to pound the Nazis. The end was now in sight. True to his convictions, Eisenhower refused to play gracious host to the vanquished as the war was winding down. He hated the Nazis more than ever. His anger had only been reinforced a few days earlier, when he had visited his first concentration camp near the town of Gotha. He was outraged. "I visited every nook and cranny of the camp" Ike said.[12] He wanted see first hand just how evil the Nazi camps were. He later said that he simply couldn't find the words to describe the "brutality" of the Holocaust. To the end, and to the Nazis, he would bare an iron fist.

On the evening of May 6th, Eisenhower awaited the arrival of Field Marshall Alfred Jodl at the Allied headquarters in Reims. Late that night, Jodl arrived. The surrender itself was handled by Ike's deputies.[13] During the negotiations, the Germans asked for a forty-eight-hour postponement. Eisenhower knew what they were after. After D-Day, as the Allies moved closer to Germany, many German officers had sent their families into Czechoslovakia, where they thought they would safe from Allied bombing. But now, the Soviets were overrunning Czechoslovakia.

The Nazis were stalling for time, hoping to get as many Germans as they could back into Germany, and out of the reach of the Soviets. But they were also trying to delay the inevitable surrender as long as possible. A forty-eight-hour delay could be followed by another delay and then another.

During the negotiations, one of Ike's deputies, General Ken Strong, rang and asked about delaying the surrender. Eisenhower was not amused by the tactic, and not fooled by the request. He called their bluff.

"You tell them that forty-eight hours from midnight tonight, I will close my lines on the Western front so no more Germans can get through," Ike shot back, his voice tinged with anger. "Whether they sign or not—no matter how much time they take." He hung up the phone. Eisenhower would give his enemy forty-eight hours to save their friends and family. But he would not give them one second more to save their cause. The time to surrender was now. The clock was ticking.

Defeated at the bargaining table, as they had been on the battlefield, the Germans finally yielded. In the early morning hours of May 7th, Field Marshal Alfred Jodl signed the instrument of surrender. After signing it, he asked to see Eisenhower. It would be the first and last time Eisenhower met directly with a Nazi general during the war. If Jodl had counted on a generous and gracious victor, he had counted wrong.

At 2:41 a.m., May 7th, 1945, Jodl was led from the War Room through the hallway, up the stairs, past the secretary's desk, and into Eisenhower's office. Ike had been pacing in his office, smoking cigarettes, when he heard Jodl coming down the hall.

Upon entering, Jodl spotted a simple, wooden desk. Behind it, engulfed by a plume of white billowing smoke, stood the Supreme Allied Commander. He was perfectly upright, simply clothed in his service dress uniform. He bore no gun and wore no sword. He was also devoid of any goodwill to his supplicant. One look at Eisenhower's hardened face, and Jodl knew he would receive no special treatment. The Nazi stood at attention, defiant but powerless. Eisenhower glared, purposely.

He had no time for smalltalk and no use for Jodl. Speaking through an interpreter, the conqueror informed the vanquished: "You will, officially and personally, be held responsible if the terms of this surrender are violated." Eisenhower's presence and voice, which routinely commanded respect and awe from his colleagues, were now pointed aggressively at the German. His face seething with contempt; his eyes piercing as they coldly stared down the Nazi. Jodl said, "Ja" when asked whether he understood the terms of the surrender. "That is all," Eisenhower said. The meeting was over.

For three years, Eisenhower had directed the Allies. Now even the Nazis took orders from him. He dismissed Jodl from his presence. The German saluted and left. As he did so, Jodl passed by Ike's secretary's desk, beneath which the supreme commander's Scottish terrier, Telek, was posted on duty. Perhaps sensing the mood of his master, Telek growled menacingly. The war in Europe was over.

To memorialize the occasion, Ike asked his staff to pose for a picture. Then he entered the War Room, where Captain Butcher had arranged for some cameras. Earlier in the day, Ike had complained that the "damned war room looks like a Hollywood setting." Now, he looked into the lenses and spoke of the "armistice." Butcher interrupted him. He urged Ike to use the word "surrender" instead. Ike started over, this time announcing the "surrender."

Eisenhower looked on as his staff debated the wording of an official statement. Reaching for rhetorical heights, the staffers tried to outdo themselves with soaring, lyrical tributes to Allied effort. Growing tired, Ike thanked them for trying. Then he dictated the victory message:

"The mission of this Allied force was fulfilled at 0241 local time, May 7, 1945."

◇

Dwight Eisenhower was now one of the world's most famous people. World War II would forever define his life. In the coming years, those seeking guidance in regards to his character, belief, or style of leadership only needed to look at his war years. Here, Ike's full bloom could be seen in all its rich and varying splendor: bold but cautious, patient but persistent, more practical than philosophical. And even the issues he faced during the war—the unity of the Allies, the security of the free world, and even the dilemma of race relations—would return.

For the time being, his military legacy had been chiseled by the fires of battle and christened by the blood of his soldiers. Ike knew that D-Day would be studied, the Bulge written about, and the overall war discussed for the rest of time. But there was another part of his legacy that was largely hidden, even from Eisenhower himself. It was unintentional, unexpected, and probably undesired.

Like the country that now idolized him, his decisions regarding black soldiers showed Ike to be a man in conflict.

To be sure, he had taken positive actions on behalf of black soldiers. He had changed the media rules on covering black troops. He had encouraged his commanders to fight discrimination. He had personally visited and congratulated black soldiers. He had single-handedly saved an innocent black soldier from the gallows. And, in a crucial moment of the war, he had made history in sending black troops to the front.

Yet he could not easily shed the skin of his rural Kansas upbringing. He could still refer to blacks as "darkies," privately worry about their fraternization with white women, and when challenged by his staff about utilizing them in the Bulge, hesitate and then modify his orders.

By the standards of his time, Eisenhower's policies were fairly progressive. But his personal views were more conventional. His dilemma formed the intersection between the high road of morality and the hardened streets of realism. If it was the first time this inner conflict had been exposed, it would not be the last. Eisenhower and the country he served would be forced to grapple with race; to treat America's birth defect.

Eisenhower's decisions during World War II would have lasting consequences. Like a pebble cast into a pond, the ripples of his orders sending troops to the front would spread and deepen and roil the waters of postwar America. If blacks could die freely in Europe, they should be able to live freely in America. But that was a debate for another day.

For now, Eisenhower was content to look out over the scorched battlefields of Europe and reflect on what had been gained, while regretting all that had been lost.

Perhaps he could not yet say, with Henley, that he was the master of his fate, and the captain of his soul, but he certainly knew that he had defeated a ferocious enemy and made the world safe…at least for now.

At age fifty-four, he had seemingly conquered the world.

◇

On June 12th, Eisenhower, like a triumphant gladiator of yore, rode into London in a horse-drawn carriage. Crowds lined the streets to get a glimpse of their ally and savior. The procession took Ike past the ruins and rubble of much of London—inflicted by the Luftwaffe.

At Guildhall, the Lord Mayor of London, Sir Frank Alexander, swathed in immaculate robes of crimson and gold, met the supreme commander. He presented the hero of D-Day with the gold-encrusted sword that Wellington had carried as he vanquished Napoleon at Waterloo. It was a temporary gesture until Ike's own specially designed sword arrived from the manufacturer.

Eisenhower delivered a formal speech of appreciation. Having written for generals as a young officer, he was fully prepared to match the meaning of his words to the majesty of the moment. He stood ramrod-straight, handsome in his olive uniform. His words were noble, his tone was modest.

"Humility must always be the portion of any man who receives acclaim earned in the blood of his followers and the sacrifices of his friends," Eisenhower told the assembly. "I come from the very heart of America," he said.[14] As the crowd watched the general, they no doubt appreciated that he wasn't just talking about where Abilene is located. Much more than the physical heart of the country, Ike spoke its spiritual heart. And who better to speak for America's heart? He was so very American in the way he talked, looked, and acted.

Like any good communicator, Ike explicitly linked himself with his audience. He compared himself to Londoners and spoke of the "real treasures free men possess" and that are worth fighting for. And he deliberately made a moral case for the war he had just fought and won:

> To preserve this freedom of worship, his equality before law, his liberty to speak and act as he sees fit, subject only to provisions that he trespass not upon similar rights of others—a Londoner will fight. So will a citizen of Abilene.

Eisenhower paid tribute to the team effort behind the Allied victory. "Had I possessed the military skill of a Marlborough, the wisdom of Solomon, the understanding of Lincoln, I still would have been helpless without the loyalty, vision, and generosity of thousands upon thousands of British and Americans."

This was Eisenhower at his finest: noble, grand, sublime. He revealed his deepest convictions. He gave credit to others for his success and took responsibility for the blood of those who had died. He praised the work of his team, emphasized the importance of unity and consensus, and located his work in the context of a broader struggle for freedom and equality. He painted the war in Europe with broad strokes on the canvas filled with the bright colors of hope and promise.

It was one of the greatest speeches of his life. As Ike finished, his Naval aide, Henry Butcher, peered through his damp gaze at the British Prime Minister. Churchill's eyes, too, were moist with tears. The next morning, the *London Express* headline praised Ike's "Immortal Words."[15] And on the front page, Eisenhower's text was placed next to the text of Lincoln's Gettysburg Address. To many, the comparison seemed apt.

Later, at a luncheon in Ike's honor, Churchill led a toast. As the descendant and biographer of Marlborough, perhaps the greatest figure in British military history, Churchill was uniquely qualified to speak to Ike's achievements. He predicted that Ike would continue to influence world events. And then he memorably praised Eisenhower's vision and courage in planning and executing the D-Day invasion. "Not only did he take the risk and arrive at the fence, but he cleared it in magnificent fashion," Churchill metaphorically saluted.[16]

He led Ike to the balcony. The crowd below stretched to the horizon. As far as Ike could see, the people of London stood ready to see him, hear him, experience him. "I've got just as much right to be down there yelling as you do!"[17] Ike yelled, thrilling the joyous mass of people.

The London throng foreshadowed what life would be like. Eisenhower was now master of all he surveyed. In the military constellation of 1945, his star glittered above all others.

But with cloudless glory came heavy burdens. For the rest of his life, with rare exception, Ike would be the most celebrated person in any room he entered, the most important leader in every meeting he attended. Anywhere he was, and everywhere he went, people looked upon him as the hero of Normandy, the man who had saved the world from Hitler. Every word he uttered would be remembered by the recipient. Every action he took would be watched by the world.

Cautious by nature, Ike would now learn to measure carefully every syllable his mouth gave voice to, and to consider thoughtfully every step in which his life might take him. Despite his frequent protestations, he could never again be a simple farm boy from Kansas. Now and forever, he would travel along a very public road where his every move was watched.

His power was not limited to the adoring and roaring crowds of London. For the rest of his life, he would inspire awe and reverence at all times from all people. Years later, Norman Rockwell was invited to be a guest at a private dinner with Ike. The famous artist was overwhelmed with awe, so much so that he feared meeting Ike. He sought from his doctor a prescription of barbiturates to relax his excited nerves in the presence of the great Eisenhower. Eisenhower would have been surprised to know that he impacted people this way. But he did. And he would.[18]

As Ike looked out at the London crowd that glorious, sun-soaked day in June, he could be forgiven for thinking, and hoping, that his days of conflict were over. But they weren't. Churchill had correctly prophesied that Eisenhower's role on the world stage was only beginning. A man who could destroy Hitler was not a man to go into the gentle shade of a quiet retreat.

His leadership, on full display in World War II, would be needed again. He was disciplined and organized, stressed teamwork and unity, focused on big items and delegated authority, and worried about fighting the enemy rather than fighting the War Department. When confronted with tricky personnel issues like race, he chose simply to solve the problem rather than address the root causes. He was already a superb manager, but he was still learning to be a great leader.

Like Alexander the Great, he had shown himself capable of cutting the Gordian Knot with a shear of common sense and realism. But could he untie the disparate cords that had created the knot in the first place? All his life, he had focused on solving problems, not on resolving their underlying issues. In the coming years, he would have to grapple with both; he would have to both cut and untie.

But for now, Eisenhower had much to be proud of. And so did his troops—*all* of his troops. It would be three more months before peace would come to the Pacific as well. But as World War II came to a close, night fell on a very different world, and on a very different America. Beneath the lilac veil of dusk, new life was preparing to be born. A new day and a better nation were about to dawn.

Forces of change had now been set in motion. They would take on a momentum of their own. Historic changes in battlefield tactics and weapons were dwarfed by a social revolution in embryo. A precedent had been set. An honorable battle record had been established. The myth of black inferiority on the battlefield had been shattered. The Second World War was, in fact, the beginning of a second American revolution.

One small harbinger: an explosion in the membership of the NAACP. At the start of the war, the organization had claimed 50,000 members. After the war ended, that number mushroomed to 350,000. Black workers in the defense industry who had helped beat back Adolph Hitler weren't going to back down from Jim Crow.

And the black soldiers who had gone to the front of the line in battle weren't eager to go to the back of the bus in Birmingham. No sooner had the battles of World War II ended before the battle for equality in America took on a new urgency.

It was to be a battlefield on which Dwight Eisenhower sometimes appeared a reluctant warrior. But it was a fight that he— and the country—could not avoid.

CHAPTER FOUR

THE AFTERMATH

"I'm a soldier....I have no political ambitions at all."

—Dwight D. Eisenhower

ON JUNE 18, 1945, the United States Congress convened a special joint session to honor the hero of Normandy.

As General Eisenhower entered the august House Chamber, he was engulfed in a torrent of cheers. Senators and congressmen competed with each other as they reached to shake the general's hand. Most were content simply to touch the great man.

Wearing his service dress uniform, Ike waded through the flood of well-wishers and admirers. Above and behind the rostrum at the front, reporters, like birds on a limb, leaned forward in the press gallery, peering down at the spectacle below, ready to record the momentous event. At last, Eisenhower arrived at the well of the House. He stood erect and waited. But the ovation only grew. After two minutes, Eisenhower did what he did best—he took command. He raised his arms to ask for silence. And the members of the House and Senate obeyed him. They sat down, and many gazed with wonder upon the man who had destroyed Hitler. In the pre-television age, some in the Chamber that day had never seen Ike speak before. They focused intently on him, waiting for him to begin.

If his speech that day did not rise to the rhetorical heights of his Guildhall triumph a few days before, it was still pure Eisenhower: humble, gracious, patriotic, and, in its own way, inspiring. "In humble realization that they [his troops], who earned your commendation, should properly be here to receive it," he said to his congressional fan club, "I am nevertheless proud and honored to serve as your agent in conveying it to them."[1] The citizens populating the galleries lustily applauded, their cheers raining down until they became one with the sea of praise coming from the dignitaries on the House floor.

To Ike's left and behind him, on the wall of the House Chamber, was a portrait of his hero, George Washington. Behind him on the right was Lafayette, the pivotal ally who helped win the Revolution. The symbolism was perfect. America was born thanks to an allied effort. And now, Eisenhower had just led the greatest allied effort in history.

Clairvoyants might have seen an omen in the grand room that great day. All around him in the House Chamber, Ike could see engraved portraits of history's great lawgivers—from Moses to Maimonides, Justinian to Jefferson. Napoleon also is represented in the Chamber. Did Eisenhower notice the Corsican's image? Did he, too, think about translating military greatness into political power? He didn't say. But many wondered.

One who could be forgiven for wondering was the president. That afternoon, President Harry S Truman hosted a reception for Ike at the White House. The two men had never met before. Together, they formed a study in contrast. Truman was a career politician: often bitter, angry, fierce when fighting political battles. He gave no quarter and asked for none. He wore wire-rimmed glasses, which were appropriate because he loved books. Above all, he loved books about military history. He was well-read, hard-working, and well-meaning. And, like his countrymen, he was quite star-struck about the man from Abilene.

Eisenhower, on the other hand, was the anti-politician—his views on politics were unknown, but his wartime leadership could not be denied. As a soldier, he stressed consensus and cooperation. He spoke in the broadest terms, giving much to comfort those who admired him, and little offense to those less inclined. Above all, his personality was his politics. He was warm, gracious, and vibrant. He was all-American. He cut a statuesque military figure that Truman could admire. For the time being, the two men seemed to get along fine.

The South Lawn of the White House gazes over the Ellipse and the National Mall—democracy's front yard. This sweeping panorama of emerald is accented by the majestic, white marble of the Jefferson and Lincoln Memorials, and offset by the vertical dignity of the Washington Monument. With this spectacular backdrop, Ike stood at attention as the commander in chief pinned an oak leaf cluster on the general. Mamie stood close by, wearing black and decorated by a glistening pearl necklace.

During the ceremony, Truman told the general that he himself would rather have the medal than the presidency. Later, in a letter to his wife, Bess, Truman wrote what everyone was thinking: "They are running him for president."[2] Still, the Missourian professed no concern. "I'd turn it over to him now if I could." A few weeks later at the Potsdam Conference, Truman told Ike he would support him in any endeavor. "That definitely and specifically includes the presidency in 1948," he pledged to the general. But Eisenhower didn't seem interested.

Ike may have thought he could avoid the aftermath of his wartime success. But by the time he arrived in his hometown of Abilene a few days after his White House appearance, he knew better. Crimson and azure bunting dressed the brick and stone buildings along Buckeye Street. Thousands filled the streets and stood on building tops to welcome home their favorite son. It was a day of parades, pride, and subliminal politics. After addressing the throng, Ike spoke to reporters. He could no longer ignore the rumors. "I am a soldier," he told them, "I have no political ambitions at all." Less than a Shermanesque refusal, it would not end the speculation.

Thanks to World War II, a star had been born that would not easily recede with the dawn of a new day.

◇

Not everyone returning from the war received a hero's welcome. While Ike was being feted in Washington, black veterans were again being beaten in Dixie. Minorities coming home were sometimes attacked, often times spit upon, and many times cursed. A grateful nation was not so grateful to the hundreds of thousands of black veterans.

The anger did not subside with time. In July 1946, George Dorsey was near Monroe, Georgia.[3] Dorsey and his wife, Mae, were met by a crowd of local whites. Dorsey might have thought the crowd was there to greet and thank him. After all, he had worn the uniform and served in World War II. But the crowd was there to bury Dorsey, not to praise him. He and his wife were shot. And if shooting them once was good, shooting them repeatedly was even better. A coroner later detected 180 bullet holes in one of the bodies. So much for gratitude.

But George Dorsey did not die in vain. The Army was beginning to rethink its rules and regulations on the use of black soldiers. Like water flowing downstream, the prospect of change was gaining force. Many in the South stood on the banks, blind to the accelerating current.

Even before the war ended, signs pointed to a different Army and a different America. On April 9, 1945, Truman K. Gibson, civilian aide to the secretary of war, declared that the policy of using black and white troops together was a success. In a statement released to the press, Gibson described his efforts to investigate the effectiveness of the policy changes brought about by the exigencies of war, including the Battle of the Bulge. Gibson was satisfied that the commanders with whom he had spoken believed that the policy had worked. Indeed, it gave "lie to any charge that Negroes cannot and will not fight."[4]

Not content merely to inform the press of the success of these ad-hoc measures, Gibson was ready to make them official policy. To do so, Gibson pushed for, and got, an official War Department review. Popularly known as the "Gillem Board," the three general officers reviewed the facts and prepared a list of possible policy recommendations.

In January 1946, the Gillem Report was issued, calling for the eventual goal of creating an Army "without regard to antecedent or race."[5] To reach these lofty heights, however, the report offered some fairly modest steps. Gillem urged that the Army establish a 9.5 percent quota for black soldiers. Still, even this was too much for some Southerners. Many of the same senators who had cheered Eisenhower the previous June in Congress now demanded that the Army chief of staff veto the Gillem Report.

As it happened, the new Army chief of staff was Eisenhower. Truman, still fawning over the general and his talents, thought Ike the perfect replacement for Marshall, who would now complete his life's work as secretary of state.

The irony of it all may have escaped Ike. His decisions on black troops in World War II helped to spur the Gillem Report. The Report helped to create debate in Washington over segregation in the military. And the debate in Washington focused attention on Eisenhower, who had taken the job of Army chief of staff just weeks before the Gillem Report was published.

Ike received its findings at his new office in the Pentagon. During the war, out of the dank swampland of Northern Virginia, a pale-colored, five-sided building, threaded with nearly eighteen miles of corridors, had been constructed as the military's new home and nexus. On his first day as Army chief of staff, Eisenhower promptly found himself lost. Having nearly exhausted himself by walking around and around inside the building, Ike finally stopped and asked for directions. "Can you tell me where the office of the chief of staff is?" he asked a group of female stenographers.

"You just passed it about a hundred feet back, General Eisenhower," answered one, giving directions to the instantly recognizable figure.[6] Ike was embarrassed, especially when the story that the chief of staff had gotten lost in the Pentagon made it into the newspapers.

But if the Pentagon was a maze, the issue of race in the military was a minefield. As he had in World War II, Ike would continue to walk carefully.

Neither idealistic nor, strictly speaking, pragmatic, Eisenhower was at heart an empiricist. His response to the Gillem Report was characteristic: a mix of sympathy for his black soldiers, and caution over how best to proceed. He endorsed the report but added the caveat that his support was "subject to such adjustment as experience shows is necessary."[7]

His support for the report came in part from his own practical needs. As Army chief of staff, Ike was once again fighting the battle for more men. Entombed inside the "labyrinth of corridors" at the Pentagon, Ike toiled away to create the post-war Army. America could never again see itself as an island protected by oceans on either side. Two world wars had taught the nation a hard lesson: Protecting America meant projecting power. America would need to station troops in Europe and in Asia. Freedom's frontiers were global now and required substantial troops.

To that end, Eisenhower recommended that the Gillem Report did not go far enough in recommending a 9.5 percent quota for black troops. Why not "an even 10%" quota? When this proved inadequate, he went further and abolished quotas altogether for blacks serving as enlisted soldiers. One year later, in 1947, on Ike's orders, black companies of soldiers integrated into National Guard units (although they were still restricted from serving in all-white companies or platoons).

To black visitors who entered the general's sanctum in the Pentagon, Ike seemed cooperative and committed to the goal of a desegregated Army. Walter White of the NAACP left one meeting with the chief of staff and subsequently wrote that he was "certain you [Eisenhower] agree that no really democratic Army will ever be achieved as long as such racial demarcations resulting in discrimination and segregation continue."[8]

As with the Bulge, Eisenhower was almost overwhelmed by the response of blacks to his policy. Volunteers poured in. By July 1946, blacks made up sixteen percent of the Army. Some predicted this number could rise to twenty-four percent.

The War Department pulled back. In July, black enlistments were halted. Philleo Nash, an advisor to President Truman, talked to the Army chief of staff to see what he thought of the decision. Eisenhower complained that the ban on black enlistments was a bad idea. He suggested that the War Department "water down" the new policy to allow at least some enlistment for blacks.[9]

Nash reported this to the White House, where the president was beginning to feel the winds of change.

◇

Harry Truman was a Southerner. Born and raised in Missouri, he had admired Confederate heroes like Lee and Jackson since he was a boy. He often used the rugged language so common—and shared the rugged views so prevalent—among Southerners of his ilk. Even as president, he was a very Southern man.

Once, Congressman Adam Clayton Powell asked President Truman to intervene when his wife, the noted black singer Hazel Scott, was denied a performance at Constitution Hall, operated by the Daughters of the American Revolution (DAR). To add insult to injury, Bess Truman was to be given a tea by the DAR at Constitution Hall around the same time. Powell asked Truman to denounce the DAR.

When Truman refused, the already chilly relations between the two burst into a bitter squall. Powell took to calling Bess the "last lady." Enraged, Truman responded in a staff meeting by calling the congressman a "damn nigger preacher."[10] Congressman Powell, one of only two black congressmen and a member of the president's own party, was never invited to the Truman White House.

Still, though Truman didn't see blacks as equals, he did see them as humans. This was no small achievement in the 1940s. To his credit, Truman was genuinely disturbed by reports of atrocities committed against black veterans returning home from the war.

When Walter White and other black leaders visited him at the White House in the fall of 1946, they told the president of lynchings that were still taking place in the South. With gripping, vivid details, they described the horror that it was to be a black Southerner. "My God," Truman exclaimed, "I had no idea it was as terrible as that! We've got to do something."[11]

Doing something meant, ultimately, setting up a committee. Truman was a politician down to his fingertips. Though genuinely offended by the crimes described to him, his instincts told him to move cautiously. He had inherited the great coalition carefully pieced together by FDR. It still included Northern liberals and Southern Democrats. Like his predecessor, Truman would have to walk a fine line between doing what was right morally and doing what was smart politically. With an eye toward the 1948 elections, he needed both Brooklyn and Birmingham on his side.

The committee Truman set up was chaired by Charles Wilson, president of General Electric. Less than a year later, the committee issued its report, *To Secure These Rights*. It recommended thirty-five proposals for ending segregation in society, including the desegregation of the military.

Truman didn't quite know what to make of the Wilson report. In a press conference on November 6th, 1947, he admitted that he hadn't "read it carefully yet."[12]

Truman's hesitation as president was not unlike Eisenhower's hesitation as Army chief of staff. Both were sympathetic to black Americans yet questioned whether the country as a whole was ready for drastic change. And in a democracy, as Lincoln famously observed, the will of the majority cannot easily be ignored.

Exactly that point was made by a seminal scholarly book that found a mass audience when it appeared as the post-war era began. In *An American Dilemma,* Swedish researcher Gunnar Myrdal studied the plight of black Americans. The thesis of the book could be found in its subtitle: *The Negro Problem and Modern Democracy.* In essence, Myrdal argued that modern democracy *was* the Negro's problem. "It is thus the white majority group that naturally determines the Negro's 'place.'"[13] After all, if most people are white, and the majority rules, then blacks are going to be at a disadvantage. The book placed the black issue squarely within the context of the larger political culture. Myrdal predicted that eventually enlightened white Americans would have to find the solution to the "Negro problem."

The black novelist Ralph Ellison took exception to this point in a review of the book. "For the solution of the problem of the American Negro and democracy lies only partially in the white man's free will," Ellison had written years before *Invisible Man* made him famous and made Americans think harder about race.[14] Anticipating the modern civil rights movement, Ellison argued in his critique of Myrdal's book that the "full solution will lie in the creation of a democracy in which the Negro will be free to define himself for what he is and, within the large frame-work of that democracy, for what he desires to be."

Meanwhile, Truman didn't have time to read Myrdal or Ellison. He was busy reading the political tea leaves. Nineteen forty-eight was fast approaching and it was an election year. After losing four presidential elections in a row, the Republicans were primed for victory. Truman's numbers were low. GOP hopes were high, especially after they had stormed back in 1946 to take control of Congress for the first time in sixteen years. Truman's survival depended on keeping his fragile coalition together.

It was no accident, then, that Truman was increasingly reluctant to hold meetings like the one he had had with Walter White in 1946. In late 1947, A. Philip Randolph appeared again on the scene. Having failed years before to convince FDR to change the racial policy of the military, Randolph now set his sights on Truman. He was now national treasurer of the Committee Against Jim Crow in Military Service and Training.

Randolph was particularly concerned about the proposal to create universal military training for all young adults, something supported by both Truman and Eisenhower. Randolph objected on the grounds that young black men would be drafted to serve in a military that was still segregated. The White House shied away from any meetings between Truman and Randolph, notwithstanding Randolph's insistence that the issue was "so serious and urgent as to require a personal conference with the president."

On the other hand, members of Truman's own party in the South were threatening to oppose his plan for universal military training unless the segregated military was preserved. Truman was in a bind.

As the new year began, Truman tried to split the difference. Like all great politicians, he hoped to navigate a passage to victory in the broad, diffuse area between the comforting words of today and the vague promises of tomorrow. In February, he promised that he would issue an executive order to end discrimination in the military. But no one knew when or whether that executive order would come. And Truman seemed not to be in any hurry to carry it out. Since a Gallup Poll had told him that only six percent of the American people supported civil rights, Truman's gradual pace soon slowed to a near stop.[15]

But the river of momentum continued to build and flow, irresistibly, undeniably.

<><

Now, the president of the United States was on the record. Whatever his intentions, Truman had announced that a desegregated military was the official policy of the government. For members of Congress, it only made sense to find out what America's greatest soldier thought.

In April 1948, Dwight Eisenhower appeared before the Senate Armed Services Committee. It was a performance that would haunt him for years.

Like Truman, Eisenhower acknowledged the complexities of the issue. Seated behind a wooden table, with a bouquet of microphones in front to record and broadcast his words, Eisenhower recalled his experiences with black troops during the war. His philosophy was that a gradual, education-based approach was the best way to go. Drawing upon his war experience, Ike suggested placing segregated platoons into larger, all-white units.

"I do not mean to say that I have any final answer to the problem," he told the senators, "and I believe that the human race may finally grow up to the point where it will not be a problem." Foreshadowing themes he would sound in the coming years, Ike called for knowledge and cooperation as the ultimate weapons against bigotry. "It will disappear through education, through mutual respect," he said of the cure for racism.[16]

As the senators looked on, they couldn't help but admire the witness. Three years removed from his battlefield glories, Ike still looked every bit the conquering hero. True, his features were weathered a bit by experience; the sides of the head covered in ever-graying, ever-thinning wool; the smile still incandescent.

Still, Ike believed that change was coming and that change was good. He just didn't think this would happen quickly or easily. "But I do believe that if we attempt merely by passing a lot of laws to force someone to like someone else, we are just going to get into trouble."

He even opened his soul on the issue: "I do not by any means hold out for this extreme segregation as I said when I first joined the Army thirty-eight years ago." Perhaps Ike remembered his encounter with the black troops of the Illinois National Guard at Fort Sam Houston. He had been wrong about them. On civil rights, he was still trying to get it right. But like most Americans, he was still struggling. Ike's testimony, however, was a failure. Despite the balance he had sought to achieve, his words were largely interpreted as an endorsement of segregation in the military.

Not that Truman was any more eager to desegregate the ranks. Weeks turned into months, with no executive order as promised.

Outside Washington, Truman's words were rippling downstream, creating a current that was felt on faraway shores like Minnesota. Near the end of April, the mayor of Minneapolis, Hubert Humphrey, wrote to the defense secretary after the reorganization of 1947 unified the armed services under the National Military Establishment. Humphrey saw no reason why the state-run National Guard units in Minnesota should not be immediately integrated. But he feared, in the absence of a clear policy from Washington, that such a move might result in the loss of federal funds. "I can see no moral, legal, or practical reason which would justify the federal government in withholding funds from the State of Minnesota" if its National Guard units were desegregated.[17] Humphrey had been encouraged by the words of Truman's February announcement. But he wasn't sure why there was still no policy to back up the promise. Humphrey, like all Americans concerned about the issue, was in limbo until further notice from Truman.

That further notice finally came. And it was created by, of all things, politics. After Southern Democrats bolted the Democratic Convention that summer and announced plans to run Strom Thurmond as the Dixiecrat candidate, Truman realized that FDR's grand coalition had officially ended. No longer was there any need to split the difference with the South. On July 26th, 1948, he issued Executive Order 9981, outlawing racial segregation in the military.[18]

That he was hesitant to act, yet cognizant of the politics of the issue, should not detract from Truman's achievement. The dream born at the Bulge, of black soldiers fighting "shoulder to shoulder" with their white colleagues, was measurably closer to becoming reality.

◇

Ironically, Truman might never have gotten the Democratic nomination if Eisenhower hadn't turned it down. In the America of the mid-twentieth century, there were two parties, each with two wings. There were liberal and conservative sections of both the Democratic and Republican Party. In those days, many Americans were less into ideology than they were party.

As Democrats had become increasingly nervous about the president's re-election prospects, both liberals and conservatives began to search for an alternative. Both fixed their gaze on the conquering warrior whom all Americans loved to call "Ike."

As the election year of 1948 began, Ike tried once more to quash the rumors about a potential candidacy. He wrote a public letter to the *Manchester Union-Leader* announcing his decision to "remove myself completely from the political scene."[19] In the *Washington Post*, the famed cartoonist Herblock responded with the image of "Mr. American Public" reading the news of Ike's refusal to run, and weeping.

But not everyone was so resigned. Some believed that Ike was still their man. As winter faded to spring, many Democrats increasingly believed that the bloom was off Truman's flower. They feared he would lead the party to defeat. They needed an alternative. Both liberal and conservative Democrats saw Ike as the answer.

How could people on both ends of the spectrum see Ike as their man? In the *New Republic* that spring, Dale Kramer wrote that the answer was simple. "Democratic politicians are not concerned about Eisenhower's views," he informed readers. "What they want is a winning candidate...."[20]

Leading the liberal wing of the "draft Eisenhower" movement was James Roosevelt, son of FDR. Roosevelt would chair the California delegation to the Democratic Convention that summer. And he, along with his brothers, was convinced that only Ike could save the party from disaster. James Roosevelt was convinced that Truman "couldn't be elected."[21] Even his mother, Eleanor, "called several times" to discuss prevailing upon Eisenhower, recalled Hubert Humphrey.

Truman was outraged by the Roosevelt family's actions. He angrily confronted James Roosevelt in person and said, "If your father knew what you were doing to me, he would turn over in his grave."[22] Roosevelt was perhaps surprised by Truman's anger—it was well known that the president himself had offered the nomination to Ike years before. But that was ancient history to Truman. He was becoming increasingly alarmed by what he saw as the vagueness of Ike's refusals to stay out of it. This marked the beginning of the end of the warm relations between the two men.

But the Roosevelts weren't alone in recruiting Eisenhower. Ike's Southern friends saw him as a conservative alternative to Truman. Nearly two years before, in the fall of 1946, Ike had been laboring away at his desk in the Pentagon one day when he was visited by Douglas Southall Freeman. Dr. Freeman was a renowned newspaper editor who wrote definitive biographies of Washington and Lee in his spare time. He was an enormously influential opinion leader whose editorials and books were read by countless Americans throughout the South. Eisenhower was familiar with his work and had carried on a warm friendship with the author since the war.

As Freeman entered Ike's office, his crisply pressed suit was fitted snugly around his lean frame. The bald-headed, short man didn't wait for Eisenhower to greet him. Moving swiftly toward Ike until he reached the side of the desk, Freeman bowed on his knees just as Ike stood up. He told the general that he had come to talk to him about the importance of his running for the presidency. "And before I speak to you on this subject, I feel I should pray." His baritone voice was textured by his Virginia accent. He looked and sounded like a throwback to the era of the Southern Cavaliers. As Freeman silently prayed, Ike solemnly bowed his head until Freeman began to rise.

Having talked to God, Freeman now talked to Ike. "I believe the hand of the Lord is upon you and that you must accept the presidency and clean up this mess here in Washington."[23]

"God forbid!" Ike responded, startled to hear that Yahweh wanted him in the White House. As Freeman settled into the leather chair opposite Ike's desk, the general explained his old-fashioned views about the separation between military and political power. "The Army may suffer," Ike said, if anyone suspected its leader of being "a partisan." But Freeman was persistent, and persuasive. Surely, a man like Ike could not refuse the will of the people. Ike did seem to leave the door slightly ajar. If the country was to demand that he was the only one who could do the job, he might be willing to consider it. He had always responded to duty.

The two men shook hands. It was a warm embrace between two friends. Freeman had made his point. Ike had heard him out. How could he not listen to Washington's biographer? Freeman left the meeting satisfied. "I think I made a dent," he told a friend.

In the period leading up to the 1948 election, Freeman had worked behind the scenes to get Southern conservatives to draft Ike. Freeman's friend, Virginia's senator Willis Robertson, after talking to Freeman, paid his own visit to Eisenhower. Ike had left the Pentagon by then and was living in New York. He told Robertson that he wasn't interested. But again, he seemed to leave the door open to a draft movement. Robertson was convinced that Ike's sense of duty would compel him to answer such a call.

No one accepted Eisenhower's refusals. Even his old boss, Douglas MacArthur, thought he would run. During a discussion one night in MacArthur's Tokyo's headquarters, Ike professed that he had already received all the honor and glory he could ever want. MacArthur reached over, patted his former protégé on the knee, and smiled: "That's all right, Ike. You go on like that, and you'll get it [the presidency] for sure."[24] The condescension barely masked MacArthur's own jealousy. Seething with envy at Ike's popularity, his displeasure would only grow with time. MacArthur wanted to be president; Ike didn't. This only made Mac's jealousy rage ever more fiercely.

And so the groundswell for Ike continued to build. By the time the Democrats gathered in Philadelphia in July 1948, the *New York Times* reported that Eisenhower had significant support from every region of the country. The reporter, Jim Hagerty, wrote that in view of such evidence, "President Truman is facing a hard and possibly losing fight for the nomination."[25]

On July 5th, Eisenhower issued yet another public refusal, saying that he could not "accept nomination for any public office."[26] Undeterred, Democratic senator Claude Pepper of Florida proposed that Ike lead a national movement, not just the Democratic Party. This prompted a third and final denial: "No matter under what terms, conditions or premises a proposal might be couched, I would refuse to accept the nomination." At last, Eisenhower had ended the speculation about the 1948 campaign.

Truman went on to face the governor of New York, Thomas E. Dewey, whom he defeated partially because his civil rights policies attracted substantial support from Northern blacks and organized labor. Eisenhower settled for a different kind of presidency.

◇

In the summer of 1948, Eisenhower traded in his military uniform for academic robes. He became president of Columbia University in New York City. From the start, he was miscast. Moving about the neoclassical structures on Morningside Heights, Ike breathed a rarified air of importance and even condescension. Even at home, he and Mamie felt out of place in the grandiose and palatial home reserved for the president of Columbia. New York wasn't really their kind of town, either. Ike admitted that he was still a Kansas farm boy who liked the "green grass better than the paved streets."

But it was the culture of the university that was the most difficult to adapt to. At one meeting, an esteemed faculty member assured the new president that Columbia was home to "some of America's most exceptional physicists, mathematicians, chemists, and engineers."

Eisenhower responded by wondering whether they were "exceptional Americans" as well. When the professor brushed this off, Ike was angered. "Dammit," he raged, "what good are exceptional physicists...unless they are exceptional Americans?"[27]

Ike wanted to bring Columbia more into the mainstream of American values. The faculty and staff were equally determined to see Columbia remain true to its sublime status as an elite institution.

Ironically, Ike's views were not as naïve and simplistic as they may seem in retrospect. A few hours' car ride to the north, his friend, James Conant, was attempting something similar on an even grander scale at Harvard. For fifteen years, Conant had served as president of the hallowed institution on the Charles River in Cambridge. Now, in the aftermath of the war, he decided that America's oldest, most renowned college could do more to serve its nation. To match the mission of Harvard with the meaning of America, Conant oversaw the publication of the "Redbook." The book sought to provide a quality liberal education guide not only for Harvard but for other colleges and even secondary schools throughout the nation. "Our purpose is to cultivate in the largest number of our future citizens an appreciation both of the responsibilities and the benefits which come to them because they are American and free," Conant wrote in words that Eisenhower would have agreed with. Indeed, in his own slightly less lyrical way, Eisenhower said he wanted Columbia to be a "more effective and productive member of the American national team."

Conant had success in pushing his program at Harvard largely because he was accepted by the Harvard community as an academic man of the first order. Ike, in contrast, was viewed as something worse than a fish out of water: a general in the academy. Still, Ike always believed that education should teach citizenship. And he would later remember Conant's role in successfully promoting that belief at Harvard.

Columbia could have afforded to listen to Ike on the importance of civic values. But he had some things to learn from Columbia, too. One day, in the spring of 1950, Ike was handed a list of names the university planned to honor with honorary degrees. One of the names was that of Ralph Bunche, scholar and diplomat, who had recently won praise for his United Nations work in the Middle East. Bunche was the only African-American on the list. By tradition, the Columbia president hosted a reception for all those receiving honorary degrees.

Ike wondered aloud whether the other recipients would be comfortable at a reception attended by Bunche. When he was assured that there would be no problems at an enlightened institution like Columbia, Ike proceeded with the event.[28] At the reception, he sought out the Bunches and congratulated the diplomat on his award. Eisenhower later remembered that the Bunches were well received and the entire event was a big success.

Ike was pleased, but somewhat surprised, at the hero's welcome that the Columbia faculty gave to Bunche. Coming from a career in the military, he could not have imagined that an important part of society—the academy—held very different views on race from the Southern commanders he was used to dealing with. Still, his personal sympathies were in the right place. He genuinely admired Bunche, even if he was a bit nervous about a public event for him.

Ike's main contribution to Columbia—and his major passion—was the creation of the "American Assembly." Again, as he had in the war, Ike demonstrated a desire for consensus on contentious issues. Ike's friend Averell Harriman had given the university an estate on the Hudson River called Arden House. There, Ike brought together various leaders from various segments of society, including business and education. The idea was to get these leaders to deal with tough national issues and to develop commonsense ideas on ways to deal with them. Many of the Columbia community dismissed the project as a conservative think tank designed to repeal the New Deal. It wasn't. It was yet another example of Ike's commitment to consensus and his use of teamwork. It was consistent with the way he operated during the war and predictive of the way he would operate later.

But Columbia was not where Ike belonged. Soon, he could notice the fast-moving clouds that were beginning to eclipse the sun and spread dusk over Morningside Heights. It was time to leave. Night had fallen. He must prepare for a new day. War in Korea and nervousness in Europe were demanding the attention of America. When President Truman asked him to return to active duty to command NATO in Europe, Eisenhower was ready. Duty was something he never resisted.

<>

Ralph Bunche wasn't the only African-American making headlines in post-war America. On April 15th, 1947, the Brooklyn

Dodgers made history when they started the first African-American player in Major League Baseball history. Jackie Robinson, who had almost been court-martialed at Fort Leavenworth during the war, faced death threats and hostile opponents when he stepped onto Ebbets Field. Like many of the icons who would later make a huge impact on the civil rights movement, Robinson was carefully chosen, and was perfectly prepared, for his role. He was a war veteran, an articulate man, and a terrific athlete.

Branch Rickey, the president of the Brooklyn Dodgers, studied Robinson and decided he would be the pioneer who would break the color line in the sport known as America's pastime. But there was one worry: As Robinson had shown at Fort Leavenworth, he had a temper, and a justifiable sense of outrage at the way African-Americans were treated.

When Rickey told Robinson of his plans to integrate baseball, he warned the player that much venom would be spewed at him and that he should not respond. Robinson was indignant. He asked Rickey whether he was looking for a man too scared to fight back.

No, Rickey answered. He was looking for a player "with guts enough not to fight back."[29]

Jackie Robinson took to the diamond and focused on baseball. He ignored the insults, the taunts, and the cleat spikes that opposing players deliberately planted into his shins as they slid into the base. Each time he was angered, he would remember Rickey's words.

By doing so, he won a massive following among African-Americans. In the South, a young Henry Aaron was so inspired by Robinson that he would set out to make his own baseball history. But perhaps more important than what black America thought was what white America thought. Robinson was impossible to dislike. He was all-American. And his example and his courage soon made him a hero to millions of Americans of all backgrounds. Outside of Joe Louis, it would have been inconceivable a few years earlier that white Americans would cheer a black athlete. Now they did. Indeed, in some ways, Robinson's achievement was more impressive than Louis's. In the run-up to

World War II, Americans cheered Louis because he pummeled a German. Americans cheered Robinson even as he beat white American athletes. Times were changing.

And so, one of the most important civil rights victories was won on the baseball diamond. And one of the civil rights movement's most endearing and enduring leaders for the next twenty years would be Jackie Robinson.

Meanwhile, the NAACP was also winning victories in other venues. While A. Philip Randolph and other black leaders sought influence with political leaders like Truman, the NAACP sought victories in the courts. Specifically, the NAACP began to target an area that seemed ripe for court intervention—education.

Under the leadership of a brilliant young lawyer named Thurgood Marshall, the NAACP began to challenge the constitutionality of *Plessy v. Ferguson's* separate-but-equal doctrine as it applied to public schools.

The grandson of a slave, Marshall wore dark-rimmed glasses and a neatly trimmed mustache. His sharp legal mind was evidenced every time he spoke. He was spirited and humorous, idealistic but realistic. Above all, he had a keen sense of politics and where issues and events were leading. He had the prophet's gift for seeing over the horizon, of imaging today what tomorrow would look like. In the post-war era, Marshall could sense that change was coming. And he was ready to help speed it up.

Marshall shrewdly reasoned that many Southerners cared most about keeping children in segregated schools. They were less concerned about the oldest students—graduate students. So, it was there that Marshall began the attack. "Those racial-supremacy boys somehow think that little kids of six or seven are going to get funny ideas about sex and marriage just from going to school together," Marshall explained, "but for some equally funny reason, youngsters in law school aren't supposed to feel that way. We didn't get it, but we decided that if that was what the South believed, then the best thing for the moment was to go along."[30]

And so, Marshall and the NAACP went along. Marshall's first big victory came when the NAACP joined the suit of Ada Lois Sipuel, who had been denied entry into the University of

Oklahoma Law School. Her case went all the way to the U.S. Supreme Court, where, in 1948, a unanimous court ruled in her favor. Still, the court refused to rule on the constitutionality of separate educational facilities, mainly because Oklahoma hadn't bothered to set up a black law school. It was an easy call to order the admission of Ms. Sipuel.

Marshall continued to rack up impressive victories as the 1940s came to an end. Many colleges read the writing on the wall and began to desegregate voluntarily, lest they, too, face litigation. Momentum for desegregation in graduate education was building.

Still, the fundamental issue posed by *Plessy* was still unresolved. Marshall began to consider shifting his focus to America's elementary and secondary public schools. He began to consider forcing the issue. By challenging public schools, the courts would have to issue a ruling on the constitutionality of *Plessy*. No one outside the NAACP knew it at the time, but the battle lines were being drawn for the epic struggles of the 1950s civil rights movement.

As Marshall contemplated the future, a young seminary student named Martin Luther King contemplated the past. King was the son and grandson of preachers. Even at this young age, he had shown that he possessed the magical ability to use scriptures and metaphors to change the minds and touch the hearts of his listeners. He also possessed a brilliant mind, and he was remarkably well-read. A conversation with King was like a communion with the past: Hegel, Bonhoffer, and Neibuhr were all likely to show up.

In his graduate studies at Crozer Seminary in Pennsylvania, young King had, for the first time, discovered Ghandi. It was to be a love that would last his lifetime. In his research of the Indian, King marveled at how Ghandi used good to overcome evil and preached nonviolence as a weapon against violence. "He was probably the first person in history to lift the love ethic of Jesus above mere interaction between individuals to a powerful effective social force on a large scale."

Never again would King see preaching as something to be done only in the pulpit on Sundays. As he graduated from Crozer in the early 1950s and headed to Boston for his doctorate, King was a changed man—he believed that sermons were to be lived, not preached. And he was convinced that the cancer of hate could be overcome with the radiation of love.

<>

As the New Year of 1952 dawned in Paris, the NATO commander's eyes were fixed across the Atlantic. For some time, Eisenhower had been watching the domestic political scene in America. He didn't like what he saw.

Truman had lost control. America again found itself at war, this time in Korea. A bitter row had erupted between President Truman and General MacArthur. Truman correctly realized that in the nuclear age, total wars could no longer be fought. MacArthur correctly realized that this meant a stalemate in Korea. When the general wrote a letter bordering on insubordination to House Republican Leader Joe Martin, Truman had had enough. He fired the American Caesar, but at a huge political cost. Truman's numbers plummeted and were never to recover completely .

Closer to home, Truman's domestic problems were different but no less. Early in 1952, Truman was angered by the steel industry's price increases. In a time of war, with the Department of Defense their largest customer, the steel companies' decision to raise prices struck many as unfair. It struck Truman as un-American. He was outraged. And on April 8th, he signed Executive Order 10340, federalizing all steel plants. "They are trying to get special, preferred treatment," Truman said in a nationally televised address. "As president of the United States it is my plain duty to keep this from happening."

Thanks to the Korean War and the MacArthur fiasco, Truman was already treading in rough waters. Now, he was overwhelmed in a hurricane of public outrage. *Newsweek* lamented Truman's "talent for trouble." And The *Washington Post* complained that "nothing in the Constitution" gave Truman the right to take over the steel plants. The courts quickly agreed and ordered Truman to stop his actions. The president was humiliated. His presidency, for all intents and purposes, was over.

But who would replace him in the White House? More than ever, the eyes of the nation turned east, across the Atlantic, toward

Paris. Even when he had issued refusals in 1948, Ike had always seemed to leave the door open to a draft. If the people really wanted him, how could he resist, given the chaos otherwise known as the Truman administration?

But the thought of the hard road that lay ahead still made him uneasy. And he hesitated before making his decision final or public. "When I was a boy," Eisenhower wrote to a friend in early 1952, "I had one pastime that was rather fascinating to me. I would go out to the corral in the morning and watch one of the men trying to get a loop over the neck of a horse. I was always pulling for the horse but...he was always caught—no matter how vigorously he ducked and dodged and snorted and stomped. Little did I think, then, that I would ever be in the position of the horse!"

With Korea and Soviet communism dominating the headlines, Ike hoped that if he were to run, his campaign and his presidency could focus on foreign policy. But he would soon learn that the domestic front was just as contentious as the war front.

As Eisenhower began to make his plans, he must have thought over the hard gravel road that he had always traveled. Tough work was always his lot. From Abilene to West Point, from World War II to NATO, Ike's life had been refined by the fires of harsh experience. Now, the presidency seemed his for the asking. What a remarkable journey his life had been!

He could not have known then what would happen in the coming weeks, months, and years. He could not have known the profound social changes that Thurgood Marshall and the NAACP had planned for America in the 1950s. He could not have known that a young seminarian named Martin Luther King was learning theories that he would apply on America in the coming years.

No, Ike could not have known that his journey and the journey of the civil rights movement were on a collision course.

THE CANDIDATE

"Eisenhower's heart was in the right place...but...he would not lead the charge to change race relations fundamentally in the United States."

—Herbert Brownell

THE LITTLE MAN had big plans. And it had all started on the worst night of his life.

Before the 1948 election, Thomas E. Dewey was a legend. He was a little engine that was always in motion: prosecuting gangs, putting criminals in jail, and serving as an effective governor of the nation's biggest and most important state. Short in stature, the New Yorker was long on results. Indeed, Hollywood movies were made based on his successful investigations of crime rings.

As the Republican presidential nominee in 1948, he had been expected to defeat Truman easily. But the fiery president had gone on the offensive. Hell hath no fury like a politician running scared. And Truman proved it in '48. Like a wounded lion fighting for his life, Truman flailed all around him. First, he accused Dewey of harboring plans to establish a "Wall Street economic dictatorship." Then, attacking his opponent from both sides, went on to say, "If anybody in this country is friendly to the Communists, it is the Republicans." How Dewey and company could simultaneously favor the free market and a Communist dictatorship, Truman did not explain. But the roar of the bleeding lion was beginning to rouse the voters with chilling memories of the Great Depression.

Senator Robert A. Taft, the Republican leader in the Senate, worried that Dewey wasn't doing enough to fight back. The only way to handle Truman, he said, was to hit him "every time he opened his mouth."[1] But Dewey refused. He thought people would see through the attacks. Curiously, Dewey even allowed Truman to get to his left on a number of natural Dewey issues, including civil rights. While Truman as president had a mixed record, Dewey as governor had pushed for historic anti-discrimination laws in his state. But now, with his eye on Southern states that Herbert Hoover had carried, Dewey let Truman claim the mantle as the civil rights candidate.

By the time Election Day arrived, Truman's pandering had turned off the pundits. "If there had been any formidable body of cannibals in the country," columnist H.L. Mencken acerbically observed, "he would have promised to provide them with free missionaries fattened at the taxpayers' expense." The voters felt differently. On November 2nd, 1948, Truman scored an historic upset, defeating Dewey by more than two million votes.[2]

An elder statesman now, Dewey had no intention of retiring to private life to lick his wounds. Instead, he decided that if he couldn't restore the Republican Party to power, he knew just the man who could.

He wasted no time in getting started. Dewey wrote to the president of Columbia University and asked for an appointment. One hot July morning in 1949, the governor of New York entered Ike's study on Morningside Heights.

Even after the devastation of 1948, Thomas E. Dewey still exuded a gangbuster's confidence. Short and stocky, his dark hair was tightly clipped, and he always seemed to wear finely tailored suits. The firmly held mustache was the final touch. He more than justified Alice Roosevelt Longworth's famous put-down likening him to the little man on the wedding cake.

Still, Eisenhower could not help but be impressed with the thorough and lawyerly presentation made by his guest. Dewey possessed the ability to enter a thicket of issues and open a clearing that was easy to see.

On this day, Dewey swiftly sliced through the politics and went to the heart of the matter. Ike had to run for office. It was his duty. He was the only one who could save the country's future.

Dewey acknowledged, "I know you disclaimed political ambition" in the run-up to the 1948 election. "But that was when you were just a soldier," he said in dismissing Ike's disavowal of political interest.

Dewey urged Ike to consider running for governor of New York first to give him some experience. Ike refused. He told Dewey that the thought of staying out of politics appealed to him. "Not if you want to preserve democracy," Dewey sternly answered. Simply put, Ike was a "logical nominee" for the Republican Party.[3] The meeting ended with the men shaking hands. Ike would give the matter some thought.

Dewey appointed himself the prime mover in the campaign to draft Eisenhower for the Republican nomination in 1952. Like a maestro, he would conduct his symphony by building it to a crescendo, adding new instruments and new voices until the sound was music to Ike's ears.

For three years, Dewey devoted himself and his formidable organization to convince Ike to run and to be prepared once he did. He worried when Ike didn't run for governor in 1950, believing that he needed a high-profile preparation job before seeking the presidency. But the next year, when Truman appointed Eisenhower as commander of NATO, Dewey was thrilled. This was even better: a nonpartisan job on the international stage that raised Ike's profile and reminded Americans of his leadership skills. The stars were neatly aligning themselves for 1952.

In the meantime, America found itself waging a Cold War with the Soviets. Yet many Republicans seemed mired in 1930s-style isolationism and were lukewarm about the Marshall Plan to rebuild Europe and NATO to fortify Western Europe's defenses. When Senator Taft, speaking for millions of Republicans, opposed NATO, Dewey knew that Eisenhower was paying attention.

Without Ike's knowledge or consent, Dewey continued to step up his campaign to draft Ike. By 1951, an unofficial Eisenhower organization was in place. It included Dewey, General Lucius Clay, and Massachusetts Senator Henry Cabot Lodge, Jr. Setting up at the Commodore Hotel in New York, these men continued to build the groundswell of support that they hoped would carry Ike from Paris to Washington.

Since money is momentum in politics, a separate fundraising group was also established in New York. Led by publisher Bill Robinson, it included many of Ike's business friends. After the war, Ike had become friendly with a number of corporate titans. In return, they were enamored of him. He admired these business leaders for their skill and success. They admired him for saving the world from Hitler.

Perhaps the most important of these men was Cliff Roberts.[4] The two men became acquainted during a golf trip to Augusta National in 1948. Roberts was a New York investor who had a genius for playing the supporting role to a leading man. For years, he had been Bobby Jones's right arm, making the golf champion's dream of a world-class course in Georgia a reality. Now, in Ike, Roberts prepared to do everything he could to make Eisenhower president. For the rest of Ike's life, Roberts would handle all of his financial affairs. He would become one of Ike's best friends. And he was an important part of the unofficial Eisenhower operation in 1952.

So was Bob Woodruff. As the head of Coca-Cola, this Georgian also became friendly with Ike after the war. During the fighting, Woodruff was thrilled to receive a telegram from the Supreme Commander, asking for cases of Coke to be sent to the troops. Woodward framed the message and hung it in his office. He, too, was enlisted to help out Ike's nascent presidential campaign.

Others came on board, as well. Peter Jones of Cities Service Oil Company took part, as did Sid Richardson, the Fort Worth oil man who had first spotted Ike on the train to Washington after Pearl Harbor. George Allen was a personal friend of Truman's. But he liked Ike, too. He was living proof of Robert Frost's often-quoted lyric that good fences make good friends. After all, Allen owned land in Gettysburg adjacent to the Eisenhower property. All of these men gave the growing Eisenhower movement the financial resources needed for success.

As 1952 began, Eisenhower was still unwilling to enter the race. But he was starting to come around.

If it was acclamation he wanted, he was about to get it. Jacqueline Cochran went to see him in Paris. She was a famous pilot and was married to financier Floyd Odlum. Cochran took with her a film that had been taken of an Eisenhower rally at Madison Square Garden on February 8th. It was quite a show. An overflow crowd chanted the general's name and held placards announcing, "I Like Ike."

America's most beloved songwriter was in the film, too. Irving Berlin supported Ike with his voice. The author of one of Ike's favorite songs, "God Bless America," produced a campaign jingle for the general. As he sat on his couch with Mamie watching the film, Ike saw Berlin take center stage and lead the Madison Square Garden throng in singing Berlin's tribute to Eisenhower, "I Like Ike."

Eisenhower was persuaded. After the film ended, his eyes filled with tears. "I'm going to run," he told Cochran, his first such admission.[5]

But it was a private admission. Publicly, he still refused to comment. He had met several times with Dewey. He realized that the momentum was building, exactly as Dewey's team had planned. Aware of the unofficial campaign operation that Dewey had set up at the Commodore Hotel in New York, he did little to discourage it. But if he meant to make good on the promise he had made to Jacqueline Cochran, he needed to get started.

In these crucial months in early 1952, General Lucius Clay, an old comrade in arms from World War II, took the lead in nudging Ike to the precipice of presidential politics. Clay urged him to talk things over with an expert. He had in mind Herbert Brownell, a superb lawyer and a shrewd member of Dewey's brain trust. He had largely escaped any blame for the 1948 debacle. And he was ready to help out the next Republican presidential candidate.

In March 1952, Brownell entered his office on Broadway in New York and sat down at his desk. Going through his mail, he opened a letter postmarked from Paris. "I understand that there is a prospect of my seeing you over here very soon," he read. "This note is just to assure you of a warm welcome."[6]

Eisenhower was ready to talk politics. Brownell was ready to listen. He made plans for a secret mission to Paris, complete with an alias and an unannounced meeting with the commander of NATO.

◇

By 1952, NATO had constructed a series of headquarters buildings at Rocquencourt in Versailles. Ike had now returned to the uniform, and to the city of his 1944 World War II headquarters. It was there, on the morning of March 24th, 1952, that a car arrived bearing Herbert Brownell.

Twice before, their paths had crossed. Like almost everyone else who entered the general's presence, Brownell had liked him. But today was to be no social gathering. The stakes could not be higher. Brownell wanted to find out whether Ike was serious about running. And if so, what were his views? No one really knew. After all, both parties had recruited him in 1948.

Brownell was immaculately dressed in a business suit. The top of his craggy head, unadorned by hair, gave him the look of a distinguished and experienced man of affairs.

Eisenhower, in his Army uniform, warmly greeted his visitor. He led Brownell into his office and sat him down in a chair juxtaposed to his desk. Behind Eisenhower were the flags of the NATO countries. Yet Brownell fixed his attention on his host. He felt both impressed with Ike and completely at ease.

Perhaps feeling a bit too at ease, Brownell tried to open the conversation with some smalltalk. A refined man of high culture and aristocratic manners, he mentioned that the night before he had gone to the Folies-Bergère. Eisenhower stared at him. Brownell later realized that Ike was uninterested in idle talk unless it pertained to golf, hunting, or fishing. For the most part, he was all business, all the time.

And he certainly was that day with Brownell. For ten hours, the two men sat alone, talking, listening, feeling each other out. A transplanted New Yorker, Brownell was a native Nebraskan, and his Heartland accent perhaps had a familiar ring to Ike's ears. The two men hit it off.

Eisenhower began by describing his ambivalence about politics. Then, he stunned Brownell with a story about Robert A. Taft. Eisenhower said he had told Taft that he would not run for president if Taft would embrace NATO and endorse the internationalist wing of the party. Taft had refused. And Ike was concerned that the Republican Party, in the hands of such men, might still refuse to learn the lessons of World War II. Brownell had been unaware of this meeting. But he was heartened at the strong stand Ike had taken on Europe in his meeting with Taft.

Though he agreed with most of the Republican domestic agenda, Eisenhower worried about the isolationist tendencies he saw in the party.

Ironically, in speaking with Brownell, Eisenhower turned the conventional wisdom about his potential candidacy on its head. Many experts at the time imagined Eisenhower running to save the party from extinction. Dewey appeared to believe this as well.

But Ike told Brownell that America was ready for a change after twenty years of Democratic rule. A Republican would win in 1952, he believed. If he were to run, it would not be to save the party from imminent demise, but to save the country from an isolationist Republican White House.

Around noon, a knock on the door was heard. It was an enlisted soldier bringing in two trays with lunch. As the two men ate, the conversation continued. And Brownell's pleasure only grew.

The general seemed to be a mainstream Republican. Though encouraged, Brownell pushed Eisenhower on one specific issue. "I asked about his position on civil rights," Brownell remembered.

Revealingly, Eisenhower began by discussing World War II. "He described his actions during the war in breaking down racial barriers in the Army." Having established his credentials on the issue, Eisenhower pledged to continue on this path as president. "He stated flatly that if elected," Brownell recalled, "as a first order of business he would seek to eliminate discrimination against black citizens in every area under the jurisdiction of the federal government." Though he probably didn't go as far as Brownell wanted him to, his interviewer was satisfied that Ike "clearly stood on what was then the progressive side of the issue."

But a few moments later, Ike gave Brownell pause. The visitor asked Eisenhower about the party split between liberal and conservative factions. Taft Republicans were complicit in accepting the Southern strategy that dated all the way back to Hoover. Meanwhile, Ike's main supporters, most notably Tom Dewey, were progressives who had been pushing for civil rights. Whom would Ike side with?

The general told Brownell that many Southern Democrats were also supporting him. He left it at that. Combined with Ike's previous comments, in which he talked with pride about his leadership in utilizing black troops during the war, Brownell shrewdly concluded that "Eisenhower's heart was in the right place" but that "he would not lead the charge to change race relations fundamentally."

As the meeting ended, Brownell told Ike that his views were firmly in the mainstream and that he could win. But, he warned, he would have to get moving. He would have to fight Taft for the nomination. Brownell later said that this frank admonition seemed to "surprise him, and I believe it was an important turning point in his thinking about running."[7]

Brownell had indeed given Ike much to think about. And talk about. Throughout his time at NATO, Eisenhower had entertained a number of dignitaries at golf and dinner. These guests were often privy to his thoughts as he discussed domestic and foreign policy issues. One such visitor was C.L. Sulzberger, who headed the *New York Times* Foreign Service. Sulzberger had known and covered Ike for years.

One day on the golf course, he asked Eisenhower about racial tensions in America. In between swings, the general related the Ralph Bunche incident at Columbia. Far from being impressed, Sulzberger was shocked that Eisenhower had hesitated to host the dinner for Bunche. "I am sure Ike felt he was doing a good thing and was very charming to the Bunches," Sulzberger later wrote in his diary. "I must say any thought of hesitation would never have occurred to me. I consider Bunche one of the finest Americans of our time."[8]

Ike told Sulzberger that race relations were steadily improving in America. Sulzberger was unconvinced. "Ike unquestioningly has some bias against Negroes although I fancy he considers himself fairly liberal in this respect."

During another outing with Sulzberger, Ike reflected on race relations during World War II. Perhaps recalling his conversation in 1942 with A.J. Liebling, he told Sulzberger that it had been suggested to him that he could improve race relations in America by taking action to promote equality during the war. Sulzberger recalled that "Ike felt it was not the role of any army or its commander to spearhead social reform in the government to which it was responsible. Any American general who conceived his duties as such should be fired."[9] Ike had used black troops because it made sense in fighting the war, not because it made a difference for civil rights.

Eisenhower's use of his World War II experiences was revealing. He exhibited a chameleon-like ability to show slightly different colors to different audiences. In his NATO office, Ike spoke with pride to Brownell about having led by example on race. On the golf course among friends, he spoke of his decisions on black soldiers as merely a duty to be performed.

Eisenhower, like the nation he served, was ambivalent about civil rights.

About running for president, however, he had reached an unambiguous conclusion. He had no choice but to accept his duty and make the race. It was General Clay who finally forced the issue. "Goddamn it, Ike," he told him, "it's time to do this."[10]

Eisenhower first sought to notify the president of his intentions. His reward was a terse, handwritten note from the Oval Office: "I hope you will be happy in your new role."[11] Truman would have a lot more to say about Ike in the coming months. Relations between the two men would never be warm again.

Before he announced his decision, Ike lunched with a group of his favorite reporters in Paris. Pastries of ham curls stuffed with goose liver were on the menu, washed down with wine. And warm memories were recalled.

Eisenhower loved these gatherings with friends. He was a natural storyteller, with the narrator's gift for luring the listener in and then surprising him with an unforeseen ending or punchline.

As the reporters asked Ike about his plans, he was candid in describing the sense of duty he felt to resign and return home to run for president. When a reporter asked him whether he felt lucky about running, Ike answered with an anecdote. He told a story about a young officer named McElroy, with whom he had once played poker. The young man loved playing poker with Ike, but he invariably lost. Ike felt bad knowing the meager wages the junior officer was making. So, he went to the officer's superior, his friend George Patton. Together, they came up with a plan to save McElroy from himself. They agreed that Patton would order the young man to play one more round of poker, and then it would be a forbidden game in the unit. On the night of the last round, Ike finally managed to make himself lose so that the young officer could win back some of his money.

"And do you know what McElroy said to me when we got him out of the game?" Eisenhower paused for effect, then delivered the punchline: "'Damnit, Patton ordered me to stop playing poker—just when my luck started to change.'" Eisenhower waited as the laughter grew around him. When it died out, he spoke fondly of the man. "He had two of the finest boys you ever saw. Made wonderful officers during the war. Still are wonderful officers."

As the lunch ended, a fresh-faced reporter named Theodore White stood up and gazed across the table at the general in his uniform: "We knew we had a candidate." And White was starting to think he might have a new career. "I certainly cannot say that from the moment Ike rose and left us…I knew I was on the way back to America to pursue presidents on the trail of power." But, he added, "the lunch was a turning point."[12] He was fascinated by the idea of Eisenhower leaving the military to enter politics. For a literary-minded reporter like White, this was drama of the highest order. He would spend the rest of his life writing the popular *Making of the President* books that chronicled presidential elections.

Like Washington and Grant, Ike would now seek to become only the third American to hold in his lifetime both supreme military and political power. He resigned his commission. And he returned to the United States on June 1st, 1952. It was time to run for president.

◇

While Dwight Eisenhower had been pondering his options about 1952, Thurgood Marshall had been racking up legal victories. Throughout the late 1940s and into the early 1950s, the river of Marshall's lawsuits and court cases continued to roll forward, slowly eroding the bedrock of segregation.

In 1950, the eyes of Texas were on Marshall. There, the NAACP had decided to strike closer at the heart of segregation. Heman Marion Sweatt was a military veteran and postal worker in Houston. He was also a college graduate who had done graduate work at the University of Michigan. He contacted the local NAACP about applying to the University of Texas Law School. Marshall was a bit alarmed about Sweatt's Communist sympathies. But he decided to go ahead and have him apply to the law school. Sweatt was clearly qualified for entry to U.T.

Marshall had his man. And when Sweatt was turned down by the school on account of race, Marshall had his case. A lower court overturned the admissions decision but gave the school six months to build a black law school. Marshall doubted that the school would spend the money necessary to build an entirely separate law school for one black student. Marshall understood what many Southerners did not: Segregation was an expensive policy.

When the six-month deadline passed and no black law school had been built, Marshall made his move. During a court hearing, Sweatt took the stand to say that he wouldn't go to a separate law school even if it were built. Throughout his testimony, he was poised and persuasive. At a break, Joe Greenhill, the Texas Deputy Attorney General, approached Marshall to compliment him on his client. "We went out early this morning and filled him full of gin," Marshall joked.[13] The lawyer always retained the ability to make people like him, even his adversaries.

A trail of rulings and appeals led to the steps of the United States Supreme Court in 1950. The Truman Department of Justice filed a brief on behalf of the NAACP position, arguing that segregation challenged the "vitality and strength of the democratic ideals to which the United States is dedicated."[14]

In his remarks in front of the Supreme Court, Marshall spoke of the same weakness that Gunnar Myrdal had written about in *The American Dilemma*. "The rights of Sweatt to attend the University of Texas cannot be conditioned on the wishes of any group of citizens," he said in arguing that the majority may not deny the minority its rights.[15]

In response, the attorney general of Texas, Price Daniel, gave the classic Southern defense: "All we ask in the South is the opportunity to take care of this matter and work it out," he paternalistically said to the court.[16]

Here, in almost perfect forms, were the arguments that would define the school-desegregation issue in the coming years. Marshall argued that separate was unequal and that the rights of the minority should not be subject to a tyranny of the majority. Daniel argued that the South was not racist, just realistic. They could best solve the problem if the federal government would stay out of the way.

Majority rule versus minority rights; the federal government versus local control. Different actors would enter the stage in the coming years. But the storyline and the script remained remarkably intact. As the decade of the 1950s began, only the ending of the story was unknown.

In June, the Supreme Court handed down its ruling on the Sweatt case. "We cannot find substantial equality in the educational opportunities offered white and Negro law students by the state," Chief Justice Fred Vinson wrote for a unanimous court.[17]

History had been made. Tradition had been overturned. A white law school would now have to admit a black student regardless of the separate-but-equal precedent. The court had moved a step closer to reversing itself on the infamous *Plessy* ruling. Marshall, realizing what this portended for the future, told his client, "We won the big one." It was then that Marshall at last set his sights on elementary and secondary schools. It was time to overturn *Plessy* itself. "We now have the tools to destroy all governmentally imposed racial segregation," he said.[18]

Preparing to launch his assault, Marshall chose his first battleground: South Carolina. And he filed suit. Twenty parents attached their kids' names to the suit, which alleged that their separate black schools were unequal and unconstitutional. A trial was scheduled for May 1951.

Meanwhile, Marshall spotted an even better case that he could take to court. It came from, of all places, Topeka, Kansas, a town not far from Ike's boyhood home of Abilene. There, in contrast to South Carolina, the black schools were quite good. This was exactly what Marshall wanted. He wanted to force the courts to rule on the legality, not the equality, of separate facilities.

By 1952, both the Kansas and South Carolina cases had been ruled on by lower courts. Marshall lost both times. Now, he could appeal to the Supreme Court. The stage was set for one of the greatest legal showdowns in American history.

That same year, the Supreme Court announced that it would consider five different segregation cases at once. Marshall's long road was beginning to bring him within sight of his destination. At last, he would stand before the Supreme Court to challenge the very essence of *Plessy's* separate-but-equal doctrine.

In the most important Supreme Court case in decades, Thurgood Marshall would ask the court, and the nation, to revolutionize race relations in America.

The case even had a name. It was now formally called *Brown v. Board of Education of Topeka.*

<>

While Marshall was fighting in the courts, Eisenhower was settling down in Denver. There, at the elegant Brown Palace Hotel, Eisenhower established his campaign office. In his typical fashion, he set out to run an orderly, efficient campaign. And he intended to win.

So did his staff. They revered their boss and worked tirelessly to help him win the White House. One of these was Ann Whitman. She was a lifelong Democrat who nevertheless loved the hero of Normandy. She was a bright, charming, and hardworking woman. Her chocolate-colored, densely massed hair bordered her graceful face and hazel eyes.

She first volunteered at the New York office of the Eisenhower campaign. She was a great secretary. Her work was good, and her work was noticed. In June of 1952, she was sent to the Denver office. Proximity is power in politics. Ann might not have known it, but getting sent to Ike's personal office was a sign that her star was rising.

After a few days of work in Denver, she arrived at her desk one morning and was asked to report to the "Executive Office." When she did, she learned that the general's personal secretary was ill. Could Ann fill in for her? Certain that this would only involve answering the telephone, she agreed to do so.

But just a few minutes later, her anxiety grew into fear when she was told that the general wished to dictate a letter. Shaking with nervousness, she entered the office of the man she so admired. Eisenhower's sanctum was a long conference room with his desk located at the far end. As Ann entered the room, Ike, sharply dressed in a civilian business suit, stood and walked toward her.

Ann's joyful nervousness soon yielded to Ike's demeanor. He shook her hand and extended his welcome to "Mrs. Whitney." Ann didn't dare correct him. She sat down and went right to work. Ike paced the room and dictated letters and speeches while Ann typed, her hands still shaking a bit.

Before long, Ann had taken over as Ike's full-time secretary. It was the thrill of a lifetime. "He's been darling to me," she wrote to her husband.[19] She was particularly taken by Eisenhower's policy of open access to his top staff. And Ike made clear that definitely included Ann.

Early on, he told Ann that when she approached his office she should "barge right in and sit down."[20] She shouldn't worry about knocking. When Ann responded that she was somewhat afraid of him, Eisenhower laughed and alluded to the masks a leader is required to wear. "All that bluster doesn't mean a thing," he reassured her.

Ann didn't know it at the time, but she would remain Ike's personal secretary for the next ten years. She would spend more time with him than virtually any other aide. For now, she was content to sit guard outside his Denver office, answering phones and typing speeches and letters. She also got to witness the parade of celebrities who came to wish the general well or offer him advice.

That summer, Sid Richardson arranged for a young minister named Billy Graham to pay his respects. Graham had first come onto the scene during the Truman administration. Though he couldn't endorse Eisenhower, he clearly admired the general and hoped he would win.

During previous conversations, Eisenhower had asked Graham whether he would submit religious language that could be used in speeches. "Of course I want to do anything I can for you," Graham answered. But he added, "I have to be careful not to publicly disclose my preferences or become embroiled in partisan politics." Eisenhower appreciated Graham's honesty and decency.[21]

In their Denver meeting that summer, the conversation turned to Eisenhower's faith. Though raised in the fundamentalist River Brethren Church, the general now rarely attended church. "General, do you still respect the religious teaching of your father and mother?" Graham asked him.

"Yes, but I've gotten a long way from it," Ike confessed.[22] He went on to explain that he was disillusioned by organized religion, specifically by the church. He didn't understand why they spent more time preaching on current events than teaching eternal truths. Still, he believed he should set a good example as president. "I don't think the American people would be happy with a president who didn't belong to any church or even attend one." He promised Graham that after the election he would join a church. He pointed out that Mamie was Presbyterian, and asked the minister for a recommendation. Graham suggested National Presbyterian in Washington. And he promised to pray for the general as the campaign heated up.

With the approach of the Republican convention, he would need a lot of prayers.

<>

That summer, thanks to the growing phenomenon of television, millions of Americans watched their first presidential convention. The Republicans gathered in Chicago. It was quite a spectacle. Eisenhower was leading a rebellion against the ruling class. In storming the gates of the fortified Republican garrison, he would have to abandon traditional tactics in favor of a guerrilla attack.

He had no choice. Most of the party establishment, including former President Hoover and Ike's old boss General MacArthur, were squarely on the side of Mr. Republican, Robert A. Taft. Taft was the son of William Howard Taft, who was still revered for resisting the progressive heresies of Theodore Roosevelt. The younger Taft owned the conservative base.

At sixty-two, Taft still seemed vibrant and vigorous. His waistline now showed a bit of a paunch. And the salt-and-pepper threads vainly stretched across the top of his head. On most days, he wore dark, three-piece suits. And with his ever-present glasses he could zero in on an issue with great skill, great insight, and great knowledge.

Ironically, Mr. Republican held fairly conventional Republican views on domestic issues. It was in foreign affairs that he most resembled the Republicans of the past. Starting with Wendell Willkie (a former Democrat) in 1940 and continuing with the two Dewey nominations in 1944 and 1948, the party had attempted to enter the political mainstream by offering an internationalist foreign policy. Now, in 1952, the base of the party hoped to revert gloriously to type. Millions opposed the Marshall Plan and NATO. Taft spoke for them when he argued that America should not "interfere in the affairs of other nations" and criticized Washington for trying to play the role of "demigod and Santa Claus to solve the problems of the world."[23]

Not only were conservatives against NATO, they were also against Ike. The attacks were sometimes vicious. The movie star John Wayne, a Taft supporter, was in a particularly foul mood when he encountered an Ike supporter one day. Wayne angrily asked the man why he didn't "get a red flag."[24] As the convention opened, Taft claimed that he had 607 delegates, just enough to secure the nomination.

To win, the Eisenhower team needed to force the action. Like any political operation, it made deals. Specifically, one very important deal. In an effort to keep the field cluttered with candidates and prevent Taft from grabbing the California delegation,

General Clay urged Governor Earl Warren to stay in the race. In return, Clay, tendering the "only commitment we ever made," promised that Eisenhower would support Warren for any federal office he desired.[25]

Shrewdly, the Eisenhower forces gambled that television would change the whole dynamic of the convention. The days of the smoke-filled back rooms were over. From their living rooms, Americans watching the proceedings would demand fair play.

And so Ike's strategists, led by Henry Cabot Lodge, Jr., pushed for a "Fair Play Amendment." The idea was to settle a dispute over contested delegates from Texas. Before the convention, pro-Eisenhower delegates had held precinct meetings in Texas in May and elected delegates to the convention. The state party, on the other hand, had chosen its own pro-Taft delegates. The "Fair Play Amendment" was designed to prevent the pro-Taft Texas delegation from putting Taft over the top. Thanks largely to television, many of the convention delegates didn't want to be seen voting against "Fair Play." When the Eisenhower forces won the fight over "Fair Play," they had essentially won the nomination.

Eisenhower immediately went to Taft's hotel room to enlist his vanquished competitor. It was the first, but hardly the last, time he would try to bridge the gap between the Dewey and Taft wings of the party. This was the question that Brownell had posed to him in Paris. Which side would he choose? Now, his actions provided the answer: Ike would accommodate both, as much as possible.

Further accommodation was evidenced by his choice of a running mate. Eisenhower found the right balance in Senator Richard Nixon of California. Nixon offered many virtues: He was young, a Westerner, a firebrand on fighting Communism, and he possessed an intense and gifted political mind. Curiously, he was also quite progressive on some social issues, including civil rights. His jet-black hair and ski-jump nose had first become familiar to Americans when he successfully took on the Communist spy and cause célèbre of the American Left, Alger Hiss. At a brief meeting in Eisenhower's suite at the Blackstone, Ike asked Nixon to join him in the campaign. "I would be happy and proud to," Nixon answered.

After the convention, Eisenhower, ever the manager, picked his campaign team. Two of the most important choices were chief of staff and press secretary. Ike asked Governor Sherman Adams to serve as chief of staff. Adams was in many ways the political version of Bedell Smith, Ike's World War II chief of staff. He was tough, disciplined, and abrasive. His thin frame, short hair, and nervous demeanor only added to his aura. When he spoke, people listened...often in fear.

In the new age of television, Ike would need a good press assistant. He found it in Dewey's old press secretary, Jim Hagerty. The son of a former *New York Times* reporter, Hagerty himself had become a *New York Times* reporter. And he certainly looked and acted the part. His dark hair framed an intense face. His rumpled suits emitted a nicotine odor that came from the packs of cigarettes he consumed each day. He drank hard, lived hard, and worked hard. Though he appeared disheveled, he was not disorganized or dysfunctional. He was extremely capable and was ready to make Ike the first television-age president.

During August, the high command mapped out Ike's strategy. And like he had been during the war, Ike was intimately involved in the planning process. He welcomed input, but he gave the final orders.

From the beginning, Ike was in charge. One of the first decisions he made was to wage a national campaign. And this meant not writing off the South, even though the Democrats had a Southerner, Senator John Sparkman of Alabama, on their ticket. His staff urged him to avoid the minefield of Southern politics and to stay in the safe and secure confines of Republican regions. Ike overruled them. He truly wanted to represent all Americans. A series of Southern stops were planned, including Atlanta, Jacksonville, Miami, Tampa, Birmingham, and Little Rock.

Ironically, at the same time his campaign was scheduling a Southern swing for the fall, Ike himself was getting ready to meet with the NAACP. They had asked for the meeting. In return, he would ask for their support. The conundrum that Brownell first spotted in Paris was about to play out before the eyes of the nation. Ike would seek to dance around the controversial issues of racial politics and win both Southern votes and black votes at the same time.

It called for some fancy footwork.

◇

Adlai Stevenson met with the NAACP first. As the Democratic nominee for president, he was the anti-Truman. For that matter, he was the anti-Ike. Urbane, sophisticated, and, above all, eloquent, Stevenson spoke in complete paragraphs, each lyrical sentence perfectly giving way to the next. He was perhaps the first politician to master the modern art of the sound bite. He was forever telling audiences that he wanted to be "the man who put candid in candidate" or reminding them that "we must look forward to great tomorrows." He was a walking, talking slogan of a man.

His long face and receding hairline gave the appearance of the intellectual that he was. He loved ideas and debates. And as governor of Illinois, he also brought a formidable amount of government experience to the task. But he was a better public servant than he was a politician. When told by a supporter on the campaign trail that all thinking people would vote for him, Stevenson responded: "That's not enough. I need a majority." Though his candor won him lifelong adherents who sometimes proclaimed themselves "Madly for Adlai," it did not always play well with the mass of voters. Under the best of circumstances, Stevenson would have had a hard time winning. But it was his unhappy fate to run against America's beloved war hero.

Known as a liberal, Stevenson sought to balance his ticket in 1952 by naming Senator Sparkman of Alabama, whom Truman had suggested to him. This was enough to alarm the NAACP. But it got worse at a press conference in Springfield, Illinois, in late July. The NAACP had successfully petitioned the Democratic Platform Committee to include a plank supporting a Fair Employment Practices Commission with the authority to act against segregation in the private sector. This was the new frontier in the expansion of civil rights beyond the schoolhouse and the courthouse. No longer content to haggle over government contracts as

A. Philip Randolph had done, the black community now demanded equal treatment even in the private sector.

On July 30th in Springfield, Illinois, Governor Stevenson, with one eye on the reporters in front of him and the other on the Southern states he needed to carry in November, suggested that he supported state fair employment practices commissions (FEPCs), rather than a federal one.[26] This was news to the NAACP and not what had been promised in the Democratic Platform.

Concerned by this retreat, the NAACP convened a meeting with Stevenson. Roy Wilkins was chosen to meet the Democratic standard-bearer. The handsome and talented man had first been hired at the NAACP by Walter White in 1932 to help deal with the eccentric W.E.B. DuBois. DuBois was widely believed to be running the NAACP magazine, *The Crisis,* into the ground. Wilkins ran DuBois out of the office and into retirement. Now, twenty years later, Wilkins was the number-two man at the NAACP, behind his boss and friend, Walter White.

When Wilkins met with Stevenson that summer, the Democratic candidate reversed himself. He claimed he had seen the light and that he now supported legislation for a federal FEPC. He also pledged that he would support a change in Senate rules to end filibusters. On civil rights, he vowed that his goal was to "get something done." He didn't want to "just talk about it."

Still, he warned Wilkins against underestimating the importance of consensus and compromise in politics. He called the NAACP's approach a "whole loaf" one and encouraged it to work with him even if, as president, he had to settle for a "half loaf" or a "quarter loaf."

Wilkins left with a favorable impression overall. In a report filed with the NAACP Board of Directors, he called Stevenson a man who "understands the whole broad background on civil rights, who needs no kindergarten explanation of philosophy and objectives."[27]

On August 26th, Wilkins met at the Hotel Commodore in New York with General Eisenhower. For forty-five minutes, the men discussed General Eisenhower's views on civil rights. It was perhaps his most detailed exposition yet on the subject. But the meeting did not begin well. It was a hot August day, but inside the room the temperature plummeted.

Wilkins asked Ike about a federal Fair Employment Practices Commission. Reflecting his belief in a limited federal government, Eisenhower flatly stated he "could not support" what he termed "compulsory" federal legislation.

Wilkins bristled at the use of the word "compulsory." Most civil rights leaders of the era regarded the federal FEPC as essential. They feared that without a federal stick, the carrot would not work. Wilkins told the general that a commission without compulsion would have the effect of offering "merely good advice."

But good advice appeared to be exactly what Ike had in mind. He suggested that perhaps a commission could be established that would study the problem and give advice to state governments on ways to combat employment discrimination. He went on to complain that the federal FEPC legislation had become the litmus test that a candidate must pass in order to be seen as a civil rights candidate. He supported civil rights. But he did not support the federal FEPC legislation. Why should he be labeled an enemy of the cause?

Eisenhower then returned to the themes he had first stressed to Herbert Brownell in Paris, and the policies he had first pursued in World War II. Where he had authority, he would take action. He would start in the District of Columbia. He would end segregation in the Capital. He would also end segregation in employment within the federal government.

To reassure Wilkins of his commitment, Ike spoke with pride of his use of black troops during the Battle of the Bulge.

In reporting back to the NAACP board, Wilkins said that Eisenhower appeared "honest and sincere in his declared opposition to discrimination, but he speaks always in general terms." On employment in the private sector, Wilkins concluded that the Republican candidate "wants merely to survey discrimination...not enact a law to correct the condition."[28]

Ike's views might not have pleased the NAACP, but they were very much in line with those of most Americans at the time.

A Gallup Poll that July showed that most Americans thought employment discrimination was an issue for the states to resolve.

In Thoreau's terms, Ike and the NAACP were in harmony, but perhaps not in melody. Not for the last time, they would find themselves singing different parts.

<><

Eisenhower began his fall campaign with a stop in every Southern state save Mississippi. Like Dewey and Truman in '48, he waged an old-fashioned whistlestop campaign aboard a nineteenth-century train. In the back of the train, a red, white, and blue sign read, "Eisenhower Special" with the words "Look Ahead, Neighbor" down below. At each campaign stop, Ike would emerge from the train and deliver a speech that had first been written in New York by C. D. Jackson and Emmet John Hughes, both fine writers who had come from *Time* magazine.

Still, as always, Ike's final words were his own. He used a blue pencil to edit every text and to add many of his own phrases. Hughes, who was hardly an uncritical observer, later wrote that Ike insisted on an adherence to the truth in all his statements. He was the anti-politician. No golden promises for him; no grandiose plans to save the world. He would simply describe the problem as he saw it and discuss what he could do about it. Nothing more. Nothing less. Nothing else. Ike told his staff that he would not pander to the American people. "If they don't want me, that doesn't matter very much to *me*," he matter-of-factly stated. "I've got a hell of a lot of fishing I'll be happy to do."[29]

But elections are won by fishing for votes. And not even Ike could avoid baiting his hook. So he set out to explain himself and his views to the American people. The most important stop on the Southern swing was in Columbia, South Carolina. There, Eisenhower's team orchestrated a political masterstroke. The governor of South Carolina, Jimmy Byrnes, was a national figure who had served Democratic administrations. He had been a Supreme Court justice and later the secretary of state. At five-feet-seven and 140 pounds, his appearance was deceiving. He may have been physically small, but politically he was a heavyweight. And like all politicians, he had an agenda.

Governor Byrnes was worried over the most important issue in his state—race relations. Blacks were becoming restless, demanding more and accepting less. Specifically, Byrnes was concerned that Thurgood Marshall and the NAACP had targeted the South Carolina low country with a lawsuit challenging segregation in schools. Byrnes was at least smart enough to realize that he had better provide equal resources to both black and white students. "It is our duty to provide for the races substantial equality in school facilities," he said in response to Marshall's maneuvers.[30] He did so not because he supported integration, but because he opposed it. By setting up decent black schools, he hoped the courts would preserve the *Plessy* doctrine.

Not surprisingly, Byrnes had become increasingly nervous about the drift of his native party since 1948. Byrnes had always admired John C. Calhoun, the South Carolinian who long before the Civil War had taken the cause of states' rights to absurd levels in arguing that a state could nullify a federal law it disliked. Byrnes, too, felt that states' rights must be preserved. And the Democratic platform of 1952 worried him. Its support of a federal FEPC was enough make Byrnes consider the unthinkable—supporting the Republicans. When looking over the platform adopted by the GOP in Chicago, Byrnes was pleased to read that "power, reserved to the states, is essential to the maintenance of our federal government."

Not only did he like the platform, he also liked the candidate. Byrnes and Ike had first met during the war. At the time, Byrnes had been working for FDR and had been sent on the presidential plane, the *Sacred Cow,* to confer with the Supreme Commander on logistics at the war front. Byrnes came away impressed.

Now, eight years later, he hadn't lost his initial regard for Eisenhower. Though Ike was a Republican, Byrnes believed that this was a man with whom he, and the South, could do business.

When the *Eisenhower Special* pulled into Columbia that September, Byrnes insisted on hosting Ike and his entourage at the governor's mansion. The Eisenhower team was impressed. "The mahogany did gleam," Ann Whitman wrote to a friend, "the flowers were almost too real, the staircase a beautiful thing, and the trees were magnolias."[31]

At a public rally on the steps of the South Carolina State House, Byrnes warmly greeted Ike as the crowd roared its approval. As the ceremony began, the band played "Dixie." Eisenhower stood at attention until the song ended. When he began his remarks, he explained himself to the crowd: "I always stand up when they play that song."[32]

Eisenhower made a few of his listeners nervous when he sounded the vague and distant call of equal rights: "We will move forward rapidly to make equality of opportunity a living fact for every American." Since no specifics were attached to this rhetoric, most in the crowd dismissed it. Why should they be concerned? Byrnes wasn't.

Rather than leave the Democratic Party formally, Brynes decided to establish a regional movement called "Independents for Eisenhower." The goal was to bring home Dixiecrats who had left the party in 1948 and voted for Strom Thurmond. By rallying independents and Dixiecrats under the Eisenhower banner, Byrnes believed the GOP might win several Southern states. This operation, almost singularly planned and led by Jimmy Byrnes, was the central organization that the Eisenhower campaign used in the South. No one would be more responsible for the success or failure of Ike in the South than Byrnes, a fact that Byrnes would remind Eisenhower of later on. Byrnes was a consummate politician. He was available, but he wasn't a cheap date.

In the meantime, Adlai Stevenson had problems of his own. He was now sounding an almost Eisenhower-like tone on civil rights. Before a New York audience, he argued: "The fight for equal rights must go on every day in our souls and our consciences, in our schools and our churches and our homes, in our factories and our offices as well as in our city councils, our state legislatures and our national Congress." He added that progress could already be seen: "Things are taking place in the South today that would have seemed impossible only a few years ago." And he further confused his position on a federal FEPC by stating that he would support such legislation "particularly, I assume, when states fail to act and inequalities of treatment persist."[33]

Progress would come with time, step by step. This was not the fighting oratory of Truman pledging to end segregation in the military. It was closer to the soft phrases of gradual progress that Eisenhower routinely used on matters of race. Why would Stevenson allow himself to mirror Ike's position on civil rights so closely?

He was in a bind. Personally, he was to the left of Eisenhower on civil rights, but his running mate, John Sparkman of Alabama, was well to the right of both men. Stevenson would have to split the difference. He would talk about civil rights in general terms that were acceptable to Northern liberal crowds and inoffensive to Southern white crowds. But in so doing, he ended up sounding a lot like Ike. In the short days and long weeks of the campaign, the battle lines on civil rights became slightly blurred.

In October, Eisenhower went to Harlem. Offering his most elaborate explanation of his civil rights policy yet, the candidate began by specifically relating his views on race to having viewed the Holocaust as a soldier. "I have seen the broken bodies of men and women and children which are the sure results of bigotry," Eisenhower said in directly linking his racial views to his tour of the Nazi concentration camp at Gotha in 1945. He was a changed man because of the experience. He could never see race the same way again.

Once more, he spoke of eliminating discrimination in the public sector and of discouraging it in the private sector. "We will end the disgrace of our national capital," Ike said in vowing to desegregate the city that Woodrow Wilson had resegregated nearly four decades earlier. He went on to pledge that he wouldn't stop until "unfairness and discrimination are wiped out in every area where the federal government operates." But once Ike ventured into the realm of the private sector, he had far fewer assurances for his audience. "Beyond that, we will use the information, the resources, the influence of our federal government to see to it that this problem is kept before the American people."

Since it was a political campaign, Eisenhower was not above assailing his opponents on the issues. And in John Sparkman, Ike found an easy target. He used the perennial campaign tactic of directly quoting his opponent. "'I am against the civil rights proposals,' says the vice-presidential candidate of the party in power, 'always have been and always will be.'"[34]

Still more revealing was Eisenhower's attack on an opponent he didn't name—Harry Truman. As the campaign wore on, Ike was increasingly focused more on Truman than on Stevenson. Almost from the moment Ike returned from Paris, Truman had been on the attack.

Perhaps worried that his party might lose, and that he might be blamed, Truman had attacked Eisenhower and had helped turn their relationship from warm and friendly to hot and angry.

In addition to a thin skin, Truman possessed a short fuse. It was only a matter of time before a match was lit and an explosion took place.

That October day in front of Harlem's residents, Ike implied that Truman was a grandstander: a man more interested in the *politics* of the issue than in the *principle* of the issue. Ike laid down a blistering line of attack on those who "play politics with your problems or try to buy your votes with false promises." He said that civil rights were too important for politics. "I do not propose to say anything before this election which I am not prepared to make good on after the election." Unlike the Democrats, Ike said that he took pride in not knowing how to "talk out of both sides of my mouth."

The inference was obvious. Not only did Stevenson talk about civil rights while his running mate denounced blacks, but Ike believed that Truman himself had used the issue to score points rather than to make progress. In 1948, Truman spoke of integrating the military and then held off on executing the plan until after he had already lost the Dixiecrats and, presumably, the South. Indeed, the military remained significantly segregated even as Ike spoke that day in October 1952.

Eisenhower and Truman were both sensitive to criticism. They were also both fiercely competitive. It was all but inevitable that their friendship would not survive a political rivalry. With each attack from both men, more kindling was added to the fire, causing it to rage ever more fiercely.

Around the same time as Ike's Harlem speech, Truman had attacked Eisenhower for his 1948 testimony in which he defended a gradual elimination of segregation in the military. Ike responded by pointing out that Truman had supported the poll tax as a senator.

When Eisenhower made a campaign appearance with former Republican senator Chapman Revercomb of West Virginia, Truman at last exploded. Revercomb had supported strict immigration quotas for Catholics and Jews. This gave Truman an opening. He charged in with little subtlety, and even less accuracy, accusing Eisenhower of accepting "the very practices that identified the so-called 'master race.'"[35]

Thus, the cycle repeated itself, only with a slightly different turn of direction. Four years earlier, Truman had compared Dewey to the Communists. Now, he compared Eisenhower to the Nazis.

But Dwight Eisenhower was no Tom Dewey. He knew how to fight back. Rather than launch a frontal assault, he outflanked Truman. He mournfully lamented that the president had debased himself and his office by accusing Ike of being "anti-Catholic, anti-Semitic, and anti-Negro." When spoken by the man who had liberated Europe from the Nazis, these words provided a resounding and effective rebuttal to the hyperbolic Truman.

It only got worse. By the end of the campaign, Truman was telling audiences that "the Republican candidate is not qualified" to be in the White House. For his part, Eisenhower always got a roar from the crowd when he dismissed Truman and his staff as "too small for their jobs, too big for their breeches, and too long in power."

◇

If the black issue was an important factor in the campaign, the red issue was the deciding one. With Communists on the move in Korea and in the news in Washington, few doubted which issue would decide the election. Eisenhower instinctively played to his strengths. His whole career had been one of working with allies, confronting global powers, and winning wars. Not surprisingly, he made foreign policy the centerpiece of his campaign. After all, the campaign was ultimately about Ike. The American people knew him, liked him, and trusted him. He was the issue. He was the campaign. People were not so much voting for Ike's principles as they were voting for Ike's judgment.

And what exactly would his judgment be on foreign policy? He was typically shrewd in his approach. In his nomination-acceptance speech, rather than directly discussing the intricacies and complexities of geopolitics, Ike had used proxy issues and symbolic language. He reminded Americans that he knew "something of leading a crusade." It was not lost on anyone that the "crusade" he spoke of had been one of the greatest military operations in history. Here was a man who knew how to confront world problems the hard way, if necessary, and through diplomacy, if possible.

On September 12th, at his Morningside Heights home, Eisenhower met with Senator Taft to iron out their differences. Much was later made of the "surrender" that occurred that day. "Taft lost the nomination," Adlai Stevenson crowed, "but won the nominee."[36] But sound bites could not hide the substance of the meeting. And taken as a whole, Ike fared quite well.

Eisenhower agreed to Taft's positions on domestic issues: a $60 billion budget, a tax cut, and labor reform. But a surrender occurs only when one party gives up his position to another. Ike was largely comfortable with Taft's domestic agenda. What he really wanted to do was to lead on the world stage. Here, Taft offered little resistance. At the conclusion of their two-hour breakfast meeting, Taft told reporters that on foreign policy, "our differences are differences of degree."[37]

With those words, decades of Republican orthodoxy instantly crumbled. A structural flaw had doomed the house of conservative foreign policy in the mid-twentieth century: While demanding the boldest outcomes, conservatives opposed many of the necessary tools. *Eastern Europe and China must be freed from Communist rule,* they would demand. *But we don't need NATO, and we won't venture far beyond our own shores,* they would add in the next breath. The dilemma of how to simultaneously engage, and withdraw from, the contested field of the Cold War seemed not to bother them too much.

Thus, it was a significant shift in Republican philosophy to embrace Ike's muscular foreign policy. Yes, Eisenhower spoke the language of liberation that was so soothing to his party's base. But he also matched the talk of liberation with the harsh realities of global commitment. Eisenhower's party would now accept a more active American role in the world. And while denouncing the Communist takeover of sovereign countries, his party would be realistic about what could be done to reverse it. This was a sea change in thought. If any surrender had taken place, Taft had yielded to Ike on foreign policy.

The most pressing question in the campaign involved Korea. What could be done about Korea? Still, most Americans were willing to trust Ike's judgment on this one. Who better to end the stalemate than the hero of World War II? Back in the summer, Ike had promised Jim Hagerty that when the time came he would vow to visit Korea personally. Later on, when he did in fact promise the American people, "I shall go to Korea," the election was over. Here was America's greatest warrior vowing to inspect and confront the Korean nightmare himself. It was one of the most powerful campaign pledges ever uttered.

Through it all, Ike journeyed 51,376 miles, visited forty-five states, and stopped in 232 cities and towns. As if to prove that his age was no handicap, Ike carried on a schedule that was longer and harder than Stevenson's. Privately, however, he was exhausted. "Those fools at the National Committee!" he roared on the train. "Are they trying to perform the feat of electing a dead man?" Yet, on he went. "Okay," he would say the next morning after a night of restorative sleep. "Fire away. Whatever they want, I'll try."[38] By feeding on the energy of the crowds, he carried on, town after town, day after day.

One of those days, he was joined on the train by E. Frederick Morrow. Morrow was a World War II veteran and an attorney. He was a tall, handsome man whose short, pepper-colored hair was flavored by a touch of salt. He was immaculately dressed and had just left a stint working at CBS News.

Morrow also stood out because he was now the first and only black campaign staffer on the train. After a campaign event one night, Ike invited his staff into his train car to discuss the speech and the event. When Morrow entered, Ike turned to him and said, "Oh, you must be the new man on the staff."

Morrow confirmed that he was. Ike then shook hands with him and introduced him around the train. Then, he asked his new staffer, "What did you think of the speech?"[39]

Nervous, but not intimidated, Morrow spoke his mind: "Sir, I didn't think it was very good." Eisenhower appeared surprised to hear the new man speak so candidly. But he was not offended. He had long ago learned that hearing bad news is often the precursor to better tidings. Ike welcomed Morrow's frank input. A friendship was born that night.

Morrow stayed through the duration of the campaign. He was even given that rarest of political commodities that staffers compete and fight for—face time with the boss. On one such occasion, Morrow sat with Ike in his train car as they left an event at West Point. Ike, having just been home again at his alma mater, was in a spirited and reflective mood.

As the train rolled alongside the Hudson, Morrow spoke up as he watched the great river arch gracefully south. "General, you expect me to go out and stand on platforms all over this country and make speeches in your behalf," he said as Ike turned and looked at him, "but I have to be armed with information about questions that are going to be asked me that only you can answer."

Eisenhower looked closely and listened intently. His young, black aide feared questions about Eisenhower's testimony before the Armed Services Committee in 1948, when he was seen as siding with segregation in the Army.

"Why," Morrow boldly asked, "did you testify against integrating the armed forces?"

The general's always-expressive face turned fiery red. He stared at Morrow for more than a minute. The men were silent as only the sound of the train's steel wheels, rumbling on the tracks, filled the air.

Finally, Ike spoke. "Son, your father's a minister, isn't he?"

"Yes, sir," Morrow said, relieved to see the face of red softening a bit.

"Did your father ever teach you anything about forgiveness?"

"Yes, he did," Morrow assured Ike, surprised but touched by the general's candor.

"Well," Ike said softly, "that's where I am now." He explained that in preparing for his testimony, he had asked "field commanders to let me have their viewpoints. Their viewpoints were negative. I never, never questioned them. I just thought that...commanding these men...they had a responsibility, they ought to know." Only after the fact, Ike admitted, did it dawn "upon me that most of these men had a Southern exposure."

Morrow could already feel a bond of honesty being built between himself and his boss. His whole being focused intently on Ike. The general revealingly described one of the crucial turning points in his journey on race. "The thing that I will never forget," Ike explained, "is the sacrifice that black soldiers made at the Battle of the Bulge when I had to call for every able-bodied man, no matter what his situation or position in the Army, to help stem the tide."

Ike acknowledged that the men's eagerness for combat had not been matched by their training. "[S]ome of them would die with a rifle in their hands they'd never fired before," he lamented. "They came off the trucks and out of the kitchens and out of the labor battalions ...." Ike's eyes wandered away from the train and back to the bloody forests of Europe. "[T]hey fought nobly for their country," he said with genuine, emotional pride. "And I will never forget."[40]

I will never forget! Morrow was overwhelmed. At first, he worried that maybe he shouldn't have brought the subject up at all. Now, he was glad that he had. He was indeed a preacher's son. He did know about forgiveness. He also knew about redemption: the lifelong journey of people to make things right. All humans make mistakes. But the hope of redemption is that people can change, people can grow, people can learn.

It was the last time Morrow would ever doubt Ike's sincerity on race relations or the origins of his evolution on civil rights.

Years later, he would say that that conversation on the train "gave me the inner strength that I needed" in standing up for Eisenhower in front of black crowds. He wasn't always satisfied with Ike's decisions. But he never questioned Ike's commitment and never doubted that he was heading in the right direction. He also never worried about Ike's affection for him personally. He would later call his personal relationship with Ike "a beautiful thing."[41]

As October surrendered to November, and the campaign wound down with victory in sight, Morrow joined the other members of the staff one last time in Ike's private train car. It was a memorable, emotional scene. Mamie sat with the thirty-odd staffers as they serenaded the night away. Ike ordered drinks for his staff as they sang "Battle Hymn of the Republic" and "You'll Never Walk Alone." For three hours, the staff was converted into a chorus, the train car into a rolling music box.

They sang well into the night.[42] When they got to Irving Berlin's "God Bless America," several of the staff looked over at Ike, who was lustily crooning along.

Twenty years. Five elections. Countless heartbreaking moments. After one of the longest droughts in American political history, a Republican was certain to win the election and move into the White House. The long, hard days of wandering in the wilderness were over. At last, the Promised Land was at hand. It was an emotional, unforgettable night for everyone on the train.

Fred Morrow added his voice to the chorus. He was proud to serve Ike, touched by his honesty about his journey on race, and certain that he would be a great president for all Americans, including black Americans. He was honored to be a part of the Eisenhower team. "It was a big family group, gathered in a spirit of camaraderie and fellowship." And most important, it was a team that was about to win, a team that was about to make history.

◇

It was a landslide. Eisenhower won by more than six-and-a-half million votes. In the South, Governor Byrnes's strategy paid off with wins in Texas, Tennessee, Virginia, Florida, and Oklahoma. Byrnes's own South Carolina went to Stevenson, but just barely. Still, it was quite an achievement for a Republican to do well in the South. It was the beginning of the end of the Democratic Solid South. Byrnes deserved some of the credit. And a bill would come due at some point in the future.

But if Ike's efforts to win some Southern states paid off, it came at the expense of black votes. Ike joined the long line of Republican candidates since the New Deal who had failed to win a majority of the black vote. FDR and Truman's inroads into the black community continued to lead most blacks home to the Democratic Party. Indeed, when the *Afro-American* published its list of Man of the Year finalists for 1952, Adlai Stevenson was at the top, ahead of Thurgood Marshall.

Ironically, one black family who did not vote Democratic was the King family in Georgia. Martin Luther King, Senior, was a lifelong Republican and minister of the Ebeneezer Baptist Church who voted for Ike. So did his son, who was still studying Gandhi and the power of peaceful protest in his doctoral program at Boston University.

Thurgood Marshall was less impressed with Ike. He doubted the president-elect was committed to genuine civil rights. Not that he had time to worry about elections. Chief Justice Fred Vinson had scheduled the first oral arguments in the *Brown v. Board of Education* case. They would be heard on December 9th, 1952. It was the moment that Marshall, and the entire civil rights community, had been waiting for.

And while Marshall was preparing to confront *Plessy* in court, California governor Earl Warren waited to collect his prize for helping Ike get the nomination. He didn't have to wait long. In late November, the president-elect sent word to the governor: "I want you to know that I intend to offer you the first vacancy on the Supreme Court."[43]

The signs all pointed to an eventful decade in the 1950s. Ike was headed to Washington; Warren was waiting on a Supreme Court appointment; Byrnes was emboldened by his relationship with Ike; Marshall was ready to end legal segregation; and a young Martin Luther King was just starting to find his voice. The seeds had now been planted...and at some point in the future, there would be both bitter and sweet fruit to harvest. But all of that lay in the future.

For now, most Americans seemed content that the political season had ended and that Ike had won. Perhaps few had even noticed a foreshadowing campaign event that Ike had held in Little Rock, Arkansas, on September 3rd.

"Free government is the attempt to translate into the political world a deeply felt religious faith," the candidate had said that day to cheers from the crowd. "This country is, I believe, going to remain great by acknowledging the brotherhood of man under the Fatherhood of God." As the warm, September sun rained down him, Ike told the crowd at MacArthur Park that, as president, he would pursue a racial policy based on "the equality of man."

These were not familiar words to the ears of Little Rock citizens. Most candidates didn't go into Arkansas to talk about civil rights. But Eisenhower didn't tarry long in this terrain; he moved on to the safer ground of less controversial topics.

But not before taking a shot at Truman's attempt to federalize the steel industry. Most of the Little Rock audience resented Truman's attempts to nationalize a private industry. The crowd cheered when Ike criticized Truman over the steel dispute. And they went wild when he expressed gratitude for the people who had been most responsible for ending it. "Thank God," he prophetically said, "for the Supreme Court."[44]

Almost five years later to the day, brimming crowds would again fill the streets of Little Rock. This time, however, few cheers would be heard.

PART TWO

THE CHARGE

"I do believe; help me overcome my unbelief."

—Mark 9: 24

CHAPTER SIX

THE PRESIDENT

"Whatever America hopes to bring to pass in the world must first come to pass in the heart of America."

—Dwight D. Eisenhower

A FEW MINUTES after noon on January 20, 1953, Dwight D. Eisenhower and Harry S Truman stepped out of their car and into the United States Capitol. Not a word was spoken as they entered the cast-iron-domed building, where the atmosphere was scarcely less frigid than outside. They proceeded through the Rotunda, whose frescoed canopy depicted George Washington ascending into clouds of glory.

At last, they reached their destination. In those days, inaugurations were held on the East Front of the Capitol. Eisenhower and Truman made their way down the stairs and to the front of the stage. The sound of applause filled the icy air. And, as if on cue, the sun cut though the overcast sky, its winter rays pronouncing a warm benediction on the ceremony about to begin.

Even still, Heaven breathed down a brisk wind that chilled the atmosphere, which seemed fitting, given the relations between the two men at center stage.

At 12:32, Chief Justice Fred Vinson administered the oath of office to Dwight David Eisenhower as the thirty-fourth president of the United States. The crowd roared; the new president smiled; the band played "Hail to the Chief."

After leading a short prayer that he had personally crafted, Eisenhower laid out his dreams and goals for the country. His would be a presidency focused on world affairs. He would take the helm of state and steer it firmly through the stormy winds and harsh seas of the Cold War.

His overcoat that day was dark blue and double-breasted. His white scarf encircled his neck. His uniform may have changed, but Eisenhower was still very much in command. He had put on a few pounds since the world first came to know him in World War II. The lines on his face were more pronounced. And the cluster of white tufts on his head had receded. But he was still Ike. And his presence, as much as his words, captivated the crowd.

"We are called as a people to give testimony in the sight of the world to our faith that the future shall belong to the free," Eisenhower proclaimed. Painting with broad, bold strokes, he described the progress of freedom as "man's long pilgrimage from darkness toward the light."

Not only did Eisenhower play up foreign policy, he played down domestic policy. "Great as are the preoccupations absorbing us at home...each of these domestic problems is dwarfed by, and often even created by, this question that involves all humankind." The central question of the time, indeed of all time, was how best to foster freedom around the world, he argued.

Eisenhower didn't entirely neglect the domestic landscape. But he did clearly see it through the wide lens of world affairs. Near the end of the speech, he linked the promotion of freedom abroad with the protection of freedom at home. "For this truth must be clear before us," he said, "whatever America hopes to bring to pass in the world must first come to pass in the heart of America."[1]

He didn't have to look far to see how far America would have to go before it was truly a beacon to the world. As he peered out at the huge throngs of people in front of him, Eisenhower perhaps didn't notice that he was facing in the direction of Anacostia, a neighborhood just a few blocks past Capitol Hill. The dynamics of the largely white community were already beginning to change. Increasing numbers of blacks were moving into the neighborhood in a steady stream that would one day transform it into an almost exclusively black enclave.

If Ike's sixty-two-year-old eyes couldn't see as far as Anacostia, they could certainly see across the street. He couldn't help but make out the majestic steps and ivory pillars of the nation's highest court that were sitting there on First Street. Inside, the nine justices of the Supreme Court were already mulling over the most important civil rights case of the century.

<>

A few weeks earlier, the Supreme Court had begun hearings on the school segregation case. Many players would take part in the great drama that was unfolding at the Supreme Court; none mattered more than Ike's friend and ally, South Carolina governor Jimmy Byrnes.

Behind the scenes, Governor Byrnes was busy orchestrating every move. He even went so far as to hand-pick the man to defend segregated public schools: John W. Davis. The silver-haired Davis sported a Southern accent and an immaculate pedigree. He was once the Democratic presidential nominee. But he was first and foremost a lawyer. And his venue of choice was the Supreme Court. In a career spanning more than five decades, he had either written or argued more than 250 cases before the nation's highest court. No other attorney could match this record.

When Byrnes asked Davis to take on the school segregation case, he claimed that the case had little to do with race. No, it had to do with local control. Washington, D.C. should not decide public school policy, Byrnes insisted. That should be left to the local folks. Byrnes's sermon wasn't necessary. Davis was already a true believer. He not only agreed to take on the case, he also refused to take any pay. This was to be a labor of love. Davis would make one last great stand before the Supreme Court. He would fight to defend his native region from what he and Byrnes saw as the overreaching hand of Washington.

Having picked the lawyer, Byrnes moved skillfully to repackage the case. Ever-mindful of the stigma that would attach itself to a case with a Southern name, Byrnes decided to gloss it over with a friendly-sounding name from the heart of America.

He called officials in Kansas and urged them to file a brief defending their segregated schools. Byrnes also knew what Thurgood Marshall knew—the separate schools in Kansas were fairly equal in resources. Thus, while Marshall hoped to use this fact to argue that separate was inherently unequal, Byrnes hoped to use it to uphold the status quo.

On December 9th, oral argument began in *Brown v. Board of Education of Topeka.*

In golden tones, Davis told the nine justices that "if conditions have changed so that segregation is now considered unwise, it is a matter for the legislature to decide." He waxed philosophic about how "the Court has no right to read its ideas of sociology into the Constitution."[2]

His choice of words was intentional. In the NAACP brief, Marshall had saturated the text with research and data emphasizing the sociological harm done to children who were told they must attend a certain school because of their race. Shrewdly, Marshall shifted the focus away from the quality of the separate facilities to the mere injustice that separate facilities existed in the first place. Marshall called these separate schools a "humiliation" to black children. He further argued that separate facilities were responsible for "destroying their self-respect."[3] This was a whole new legal approach that Marshall was arguing. In response, Davis quoted W.E.B. DuBois that black children would benefit from being "where they are wanted."

Three days later, the arguments ended. The fate of school segregation now lay in the hands of the Supreme Court.

◇

"I read it far more for your blue pencils than for your applause," Eisenhower had rebuked his Cabinet in December after his reading of the draft inaugural address was greeted with thunderous applause.[4] Inside the regal corridors of New York's Hotel Commodore that cold, winter day, Ike established the first and most important rule for his Cabinet: They were there to advise, not just assent.

Early in his career, he had learned the importance of listening to others. As a young infantry officer, Ike had longed to attend the prestigious Command and General Staff School. But the chief of infantry vetoed his nomination, virtually guaranteeing that Ike's career would not advance to the higher ranks of leadership. But his mentor, Fox Connor, had a solution. He helped to get Ike transferred out of the infantry so that the chief of infantry could no longer veto Ike's nomination. Eisenhower reported to Command and General Staff School at Fort Leavenworth in 1925. He finished first in his class. Thereafter, he never failed to marvel at Connor's creativity in overcoming obstacles. Eisenhower made a lifelong commitment to taking the advice of those who know.

"Always try to associate yourself closely with and learn as much as you can from those who know more than you, who do better than you, who see more clearly than you," he later wrote to young people.[5] It was a principle that had served him well in war. He hoped it would serve him just as well in politics.

As his presidency began, Ike established an operational pattern. And it involved not just working with his team but also working differently from his predecessors. In many ways, his leadership style was a reaction against not only Truman, but also FDR. Eisenhower privately complained about the imperial presidency that his predecessors had established. He told speechwriter Emmet Hughes that FDR, in particular, had "usurped" the powers of Congress.

More to the point, having spent decades in uniform, Ike wanted to bring some military discipline to the White House. FDR had gloried in the disorganized chaos of his White House. "The left hand doesn't know what the right hand is doing," he joked. To FDR, the more chaos and competition among staffers, the better. It gave him flexibility and freedom.

Eisenhower saw disorganization as an invitation to disaster. Like a perennial gardener, he believed in carefully planting flowers in separate rows, giving each room to blossom.

And so he organized the staff like a military headquarters, complete with the first presidential chief of staff, former New Hampshire governor Sherman Adams. And he refused to engage in pandering to Congress, trying to outdo his opponents with bigger programs and more money. Indeed, Eisenhower sought to work with Congress. In many ways, he was a throwback to the Whigs of the nineteenth century. He saw himself as the executive who enforced the laws that originated in Congress.

On policy matters, a sharp distinction could be seen in Eisenhower, one that was hinted at in the campaign and in his inaugural address. On foreign policy, he had a firm hand; on domestic policy, an open mind.

In waging the Cold War, Eisenhower was in command: decisive, determined, and demanding. During one early Cabinet meeting, a presentation was made about the French strategy for holding on in Vietnam. Ike the president soon gave way to Ike the general. "What the hell does the goddam" French Army think it's doing? he roared.[6] He was bewildered by the mindless tactics and strategies being used by his wartime allies. Eisenhower had strong and pronounced views on the military, foreign relations, and the Cold War. After all, he had spent his entire career dealing with these issues.

On domestic policy, Ike deferred to his Cabinet, asked questions, listened closely, and sought consensus. This reflected his unfamiliarity with many domestic issues, but also his desire that the country be as one. Fighting the Cold War brought people together; refighting the New Deal tore them apart. In 1953, most of America would support President Eisenhower on anything involving the world scene. But divisions over domestic policy made national consensus much harder. "It just wasn't natural to him, in terms of his whole background," one staffer later remembered, "to have to stand up and pose as an expert...on a whole range of issues that were unfamiliar to him, especially domestic issues."[7]

And so on world affairs he would try to lead; on domestic matters, he would try to manage. Nowhere was this difference in approach more evident than on the explosive domestic issue of race.

◇

As his presidency began, Dwight Eisenhower showed little interest in the school desegregation drama brewing at the Supreme Court. He was busy with the world. Eisenhower's primary concern—foreign policy—was beginning to evolve in profound ways that would impact the nation for years to come.

He had campaigned on a platform of liberation for those en-slaved by Communists. But how was he to make good on the promise? Since the Communists had no intention of liberating their own empires, America must promote a rebellion. Eisenhower un-derstood what his old boss, MacArthur, never quite had: that in a nuclear age, military action must be the last option.

This left him in a bind. He supported liberation and wanted to fight the Communists. But he couldn't do so with only military measures. He was also in a bind financially. As a Republican president, he was committed to balancing the budget and to spending no more than necessary on defense.

How to liberate enslaved peoples without starting a nuclear war or breaking the budget? This was Ike's seemingly impossible task. And yet, he began to formulate a way out of the morass.

His "New Look" defense posture would depend less on con-ventional weapons and more on nuclear weapons. The latter were more powerful; just as important, they were cheaper. Though Ike had no intention of using them, he felt it was impor-tant to act like he did. Having made his pilgrimage to Korea and surveyed the battlefield, he decided it was time to get the atten-tion of the Communists. In the spring of 1953, he announced that if the war in Korea did not wind down soon, he would be forced to respond "under circumstances of our own choosing." The Communists got the hint. Soon, negotiations for peace in Korea were under way. Ike's strategy was working.

But with the stick came the carrot. On April 16, 1953, Eisen-hower spoke eloquently of world peace to the American Society of Newspaper Editors at the Statler Hotel in Washington. True to his campaign pledge, he castigated the Soviets and demanded the "full independence of the East European nations." Should the Soviets accede to his demands—which he knew they wouldn't do—he would engage in arms-limitation talks. This was an easy offer to make because America would be negotiating from a posi-tion of tremendous nuclear advantage.

But the speech was most remembered for Eisenhower's ideal-ism and passionate eloquence. Bemoaning the nuclear standoff, he lamented that his and other nations spent vast sums on the military. "This is not a way of life at all, in any true sense. Under the cloud of threatening war, it is humanity hanging from a cross of iron."[8]

The address was a huge hit with the press and with allies who were worried about nuclear tensions. Now that Ike was publicly on the high road of idealism, he could turn his attention to the back roads of realism.

Well aware that he couldn't fight a nuclear war, and knowing that he was pledged to help the people behind the Iron Curtain, Eisenhower would increasingly rely on his intelligence services to fight the Cold War. Begun under Truman, the CIA would take on new life under Eisenhower. Their aggressive—and secret— operations were the perfect prescription, in the president's eyes, to the disease of Communism in a nuclear age.

◇

Eisenhower found it impossible to disentangle the issue of race from his global agenda. As the president fixed his eyes on the Soviets, his ambassador to the United Nations, Henry Cabot Lodge, Jr., told him that segregation in America was the "Achilles heel" of American foreign policy.

True to his campaign promises and his long-held beliefs, Eisenhower prepared to lead by example on race. He knew that much of the battle in the Cold War was the battle for public opinion. America would look better in the eyes of the world if it did better in its treatment of all citizens.

Like he had in World War II, he sought to take modest steps that would help solve the problem. He was still not much interested in the philosophical underpinnings of the civil rights movement. And like he had as a military commander, he sought action only where he had authority. And that meant the first battlefield would be the District of Columbia, which remained one of the most segregated cities in America.

Racism had long found a home in the nation's capital. After the Civil War, a series of desegregation laws were passed to ensure fair and equal treatment in Washington. But as Reconstruction ended and a racial caste system replaced slavery, the D.C. desegregation laws ceased to be enforced. They would become known as the "Lost Laws." By the turn of the century, Washington was again becoming a Southern town whose laws were separate and unequal.

Perhaps no one in the twentieth century did more to give blacks less than President Woodrow Wilson. The champion of the New Freedom created new restrictions on black residents in the District. A native Southerner, surrounded by Southerners in his Cabinet, Wilson wasn't so much insensitive to racial issues as he was indifferent. With his approval, several Cabinet agencies became resegregated for the first time since the end of the Civil War. Wilson wholly approved, saying that the new policies would be "to the advantage of the colored people themselves."

Wilson set not only the policy but also the tone for the capital.[9] In 1915, he viewed the premiere of the film *The Birth of a Nation* at the White House. The movie was based on a book written by Thomas Dixon, one of Wilson's former students. The thought of the president watching a movie about the Ku Klux Klan in the White House could not have encouraged black residents of the nation's capital.

By the time of Eisenhower's inauguration, black residents in Washington were treated very much like those in Birmingham or Montgomery: separate water fountains, separate public schools, even separate seating arrangements in movie theaters.

A century earlier, another Republican, Abraham Lincoln, saw Washington, D.C., as a showplace and a test. People noticed what happened in the capital; it behooved the nation to try and put on its best face there. In 1849, Congressman Lincoln drafted legislation that would have emancipated slaves in the District. He failed to submit the bill, but he never failed to see the wisdom of having the nation's capital reflect the best in the nation's values. In 1862, President Lincoln signed legislation to do just that.

Eisenhower now championed a similar philosophy. He had told the country that it must "give testimony in the sight of the world" about the power of freedom. One way to do that might be to actually practice freedom in the capital. And since the Constitution gave authority over the District to the federal government, Ike had the power to act.

But how best to act became his first civil rights test as president.

As Eisenhower prepared to move forward on desegregating the District of Columbia, his leadership skills on domestic policy could be fully seen. He began by working closely with his staff and his Cabinet. Dating back to his Army days, Eisenhower had always depended on good staff work. In front of his team, he could be himself. His magical bond with people—particularly those closest to him—almost never left him. Once, during a trip to Taiwan, the president had hoped that the official dinner he was attending would serve Chinese food—one of his favorite cuisines. Instead, steaks from Kansas City had been flown in. Afterward, back in his hotel room with his staff, the president fumed: "Goddammit, I want some Chinese food!"[10] His staff got it for him and never stopped laughing about the incident. Even as president, Ike's barracks language only endeared him to his team.

On more serious and more difficult issues like civil rights, Ike preferred listening to talking. Inside the administration, that meant Attorney General Herbert Brownell. He asked Brownell to figure out how best to make good on the campaign promise to desegregate D.C. Brownell was glad to do so. Ever since his meeting with Ike at NATO Headquarters in 1952, he had believed that Ike's "heart was in the right place" on race. At the same time, he knew that the president didn't want to lead a social revolution. Desegregating Washington, D.C., was a perfect place to begin. It was a federal responsibility. And it was an issue that Ike had explicitly told campaign audiences he would address. Here, Eisenhower could make a statement about civil rights; more important, he could make a difference.

Brownell quickly got to work. He soon rediscovered the "Lost Laws" and began making legal maneuvers to get the statutes enforced once more. He urged Eisenhower to apply some friendly peer pressure on local D.C. leaders to do the right thing and desegregate.

Inside the Cabinet, Brownell led the charge for racial justice. Others had their own opinions. Secretary of State John Foster Dulles had opinions on nearly everything. Dulles was a devoted Christian and a top-rate corporate lawyer whose abilities were matched by his aggressiveness. Indeed, his lack of subtlety would lead Winston Churchill to compare him to a bull who carried his own china shop around with him. Dulles's sour face was topped by white hair and accentuated by his wire-rimmed glasses.

For his part, Dulles feared that segregation in America left the U.S. open to charges of hypocrisy from the Soviets. But he also understood the importance of working with key Southerners who chaired key committees in Congress.

Others in the Cabinet had an interest in the issue, as well. At Treasury, Eisenhower had appointed George Humphrey, a Cleveland executive who owned a plantation in Georgia. Humphrey and Ike were destined to grow close. The first time they met, Eisenhower reached out his hand to the balding businessman and said, "Well, George, I see you part your hair the same way I do." And for the newly created Department of Health, Education, and Welfare, Eisenhower chose Oveta Culp Hobby, a Democrat and a Texan who had worked with Eisenhower during World War II, when she had headed the Women's Army Corps. Not surprisingly, Humphrey and Hobby were more cautious on civil rights than Brownell was.

But Eisenhower often listened to people outside his Cabinet, as well. In the early weeks of the administration, a stream of concerned citizens flowed into the Oval Office to voice their opinions on race relations. Merlyn Pitzele of the New York State Board of Mediation had conferred with Ike before the inauguration. Ike asked Pitzele to think about proposals to attack segregation in the District without resorting to legislation or even executive order.

On February 12th, Ike met at the White House with Bishop Ward Nichols of the African Methodist Episcopal Church to discuss ways of creating "first-class citizenship for all of the people." And Senator Francis Case was asked to suggest language on civil rights that could be inserted into the upcoming State of the Union Address. To a person, all must have felt that Ike was sincere, if not impassioned, about the issue.

Having now studied the terrain of the battlefield, Ike began to order his troops into action. At his command, his staff developed a list of civil rights proposals that could be achieved without legislative action. Still, his zeal for executive action was tempered by his desire to cooperate with Congress, which was largely influenced by key Southerners. More to the point, Ike wanted to approach civil rights in a way that was different from his two predecessors' actions. As he saw it, both FDR and Truman had "exerted the bulk of their effort on securing civil-rights legislation—antilynching, anti-poll tax, and FEPC measures, for example—which habitually met defeat from opposition led by members of the Democratic party itself."[11]

Thus, as Ike began to articulate a civil rights plan, he did so with a slightly muffled voice.

On the one hand, he wanted to cooperate with a Congress that didn't much care for civil rights. On the other hand, though he felt that executive action might be the answer, he was concerned about exercising these powers and "usurping" Congress like his predecessors had.

The result of this procedural dilemma, combined with Ike's modest campaign promises and his meetings with Brownell and other civil rights leaders, was a measured statement on equality in his February 2nd State of the Union Address. Speaking from the same rostrum where he had appeared in June 1945, after his return from Europe, Ike gave his most explicit description to date of his civil rights policy.

"We know that discrimination against minorities persists," he admitted to the members of Congress. "Such discrimination—confined to no one section of the Nation—is but the outward testimony to the persistence of distrust and of fear in the hearts of men."

Yet, in the next breath, Ike harked back to his 1948 Congressional testimony about how to handle Army desegregation. He urged America to move forward on civil rights by taking the slow, but steady, road of gradual progress. "Much of the answer lies in the power of fact, fully publicized; of persuasion, honestly pressed; and of conscience, justly aroused."

Having established the policy goal, he gave a specific example of where and how he would act: "I propose to use whatever authority exists in the office of the president to end segregation in the District of Columbia, including the Federal Government, and any segregation in the Armed Forces."[12]

Two weeks into his presidency, Eisenhower had drawn his battle lines on race. He would seek to eliminate discrimination where the federal government was in charge. But he would do so carefully. He would lead by example. He would reason. He would listen. And he hoped others would follow his example. To Ike, this was leadership. To others, it wasn't nearly enough. And Ike soon heard from them.

<>

If Eisenhower had hoped his goodwill and good words about civil rights in his State of the Union would be enough, he was wrong.

On March 19th, 1953, the president held a press conference in what was then referred to as the Executive Office Building. Eisenhower had officed there earlier in his career, when it had been called the State, War, and Navy Building. The fourth floor of the building still housed the Indian Treaty Room. No Indian treaties were ever signed there, but the room still sported a beautiful, cast iron railing on the balcony and the original English Minton tile floor. The ornate decorations were complete with French and Italian marble panels and an engraved stream of navigation stars in the ceiling.

As Ike began navigating his own way through the press conference that day, all seemed well. He was enormously popular with most reporters, who appreciated his willingness to meet with them so often and so candidly. In fact, he was the first president to allow press conferences to be filmed by television cameras.

This was his fourth press conference since taking office. In his first one, Ike discussed the rumor that he might not want to meet with the press. "I wouldn't know why" people doubted his willingness to work with the press, Ike said, harkening back to his World War II days. "That is the kind of relationship I hope we can continue."

At 10:30 on the morning of the 19th, Ike's press conference began when he strolled into the Indian Treaty Room. He opened by briefly discussing the death of Stalin. Eisenhower had personally known the Soviet leader during the war. But he harbored no apparent sadness over his death, merely warning Americans not to expect much of a change out of the Kremlin. So far, he didn't see "anything different than has been the attitude in the past." The Cold War would go on.

The eighth question of the press conference came from Alice Dunnigan of the *Associated Negro Press*. "Mr. President," she asked, "the Department of the Army is now operating several schools on military posts in Virginia, Oklahoma, and Texas, which eliminate colored children." Eisenhower's eyes fixed on Dunnigan as she reminded him of the campaign pledge to remove segregation from the military. "I wonder if anything has been done to correct that situation?"

After admitting that he "hadn't heard" about it, Ike turned to Press Secretary Jim Hagerty, seated behind him. "Will you make a point of it?" Then, Ike gave a general description of his policy: "Wherever federal funds are expended for anything, I do not see how any American can justify—legally, or logically, or morally—a discrimination in the expenditure of those funds as among our citizens. All are taxed to provide those funds. If there is any benefit to be derived from them, I think they must all share, regardless of such inconsequential factors as race and religion."[13]

It was the first time Eisenhower had been challenged by a black reporter on his civil rights policy. But it would not be the last. Alice Dunnigan and Ethel Payne, of the *Chicago Defender*, would continue to raise tough questions during Eisenhower's presidency. To his credit, the president would continue to call on them and seek answers to their questions.

Indeed, Eisenhower told Hagerty, he would make a point of not ignoring the black press, although even here, his ambivalence was evident. "I suppose nobody knows how they feel or how many pressures or insults they have to take. I guess the only way you can realize exactly how they feel is to have a black skin for several weeks."

Since Ike couldn't change into black skin, he would do the next best thing and try to answer the questions of black reporters. "I'm going to continue to give them a break at the press conferences despite the questions they ask."[14] Revealingly, Ike would call on black reporters, but he often found their questions to be irritating.

Washington is an echo chamber, where a whisper at the White House can scream in the next day's headlines. The day after the press conference, the *Washington Post* story was titled "Ike Orders Probe of Segregated Schools At Fort Belvoir and Other Posts in South." Eisenhower had not intended to announce any such policy. But confronted by the question, he gave his honest opinion.

On March 25th, the president issued a memorandum to Secretary of Defense Charles Wilson, urging him to help "bring about the agreement with local authorities for integrating the schools." But still hedging a bit, he added: "If such integration is not achieved, other arrangements in these instances will be considered."[15]

Even more revealing about Eisenhower's mind on the matter was an appearance later that spring at the United Negro College Fund. The group was in town holding a meeting at the National Press Club. As it happened, the chairman of the 1953 UNCF Campaign was C.D. Jackson. Speechwriters are often the most idealistic members of a president's staff. People who love words usually love ideas. Speechwriters often use their words to paint a picture of not just the way it is, but the way it ought to be. It was no surprise, then, that C.D. Jackson was a believer in the cause of racial justice. And it was no challenge to secure his boss, the president, to speak to the UNCF.

Ike's brief talk was a continuation of the broad themes he had outlined in his Inaugural and State of the Union Addresses. "I believe the only way to protect my own rights," he told the assembly, "is to protect the rights of others." Eisenhower recounted a recent visit to the Naval Academy, where he had inspected the midshipmen. He was pleased to see that there were several African-Americans in the ranks. He was especially pleased to see one who was in a leadership role. Ike recalled that, years earlier, when he had been "working for the cause of eliminating segregation in the armed services, it was said that white men would not willingly serve under a Negro superior." He was glad to see that at the Naval Academy "it was evidently not true."

Ike next described his conversation with an official at the Naval Academy about that particular black midshipman. He had praised the young man, and the official had responded: "I must tell you that this man, when it came to the making of non-commissioned officers, could not pass the rigid mental examination we gave. But his personality was so fine, his qualities of leadership so evident, his character and reputation in the company so great that we had to make special arrangements so that it was unnecessary for him to pass completely the mental examination."

Unintentionally, Eisenhower's story probably offended more than a few in the audience. In those days, it was not uncommon for white people of goodwill to condescend unknowingly when discussing race. Eisenhower intended to say that this young man was a leader and was succeeding in the military. But some probably only heard the president refer to the man's intellectual inabilities.

Later in the same speech, Ike spoke of how this young midshipman had had "less opportunity than has his brothers for the mental training that would have given him exactly the same opportunities."[16] Years earlier, Ike had learned an important lesson about blacks in the military: They typically didn't have the same training and the same opportunities as others. Now, he saw evidence that the military academies were addressing this issue. His intention in telling the story may have been to suggest progress, even if his execution suggested patronization.

◇

In the House, the distinguished gentleman from Harlem wasn't feeling too distinguished in the spring of 1953. After nearly eight years of neglect from the Truman White House, Congressman Adam Clayton Powell had looked forward to a change at 1600 Pennsylvania Avenue. As the most famous black politician in the country, Powell was a key player on race matters. And he thought that he and Ike could work together on the issue.

Not that he agreed with the new president on most issues. He didn't. And not that he was committed to working with the new president in good faith. He wasn't. But Powell was, first and foremost, a politician. He understood issues, and he appreciated timing. He had the foresight to sense an opportunity. And he had the wherewithal to seize it. In Dwight David Eisenhower, Powell saw a chance to be included, to be heard, and above all, to be seen.

Powell decided early on he would try to nudge the Eisenhower White House forward on civil rights. He would do this with a specific, calculated strategy. Powell knew that Ike was widely popular. He could not attack segregation by attacking Eisenhower. But he also knew that if he only praised Ike, he might encourage complacency. So, the strategy Powell settled upon was simple: Praise Ike, bash his staff.

Powell first implemented his strategy on June 3rd, 1953, releasing to the media a telegram that he had sent to the White House. "The hour has arrived for you to decisively assert your integrity," the congressman told the president in decidedly melodramatic tones. He then quoted Ike's words to Alice Dunnigan in the press conference: "'I find no moral or legal justification for the use of federal funds in support of segregation.'" Powell saluted Eisenhower for this pledge but blamed his staff for not carrying it out. "Your official family in the past 5 days has completely undermined your stated position on segregation."[17]

Powell was referring to HEW Secretary Oveta Culp Hobby and Navy Secretary Robert Anderson, Texans both. Powell accused them of subverting Ike's policy and preserving segregation on military installations.

If Powell wanted to get the White House's attention, his telegram was a smashing success. "Hobby Flouts Seg Order, Powell Charges," screamed the headline in the *Washington Evening Star*. No president likes to read his personal mail in the newspaper. And Ike was no different.

Sensing that civil rights needed a designated staffer to keep track of it all, Eisenhower turned to an able hand to handle Powell. Max Rabb was a New York lawyer who was serving as secretary to the Cabinet. Talented and tough, he was a seasoned man whose intense face was accented by a thick shock of black hair. Almost by default, he took on the unofficial civil rights portfolio. For Rabb, it was an account that would produce mixed returns for the next few years.

His first assignment was to talk sense into Powell. Rabb showed up in Powell's congressional office in early June. The congressman, knowing he was about to hear a lecture about protocol, tried to lighten the mood: "You're a little late. I expected you a bit sooner than this." Rabb wasn't laughing.

"Adam, I'm ashamed of you. You've done irreparable harm to the United States," Rabb scolded. "You have gone to the press rather to the president with your problems."

Powell wasn't really sorry. This was all playing out precisely as he had hoped. He was the center of attention. Still, he had to put on a convincing show of concern. "Okay, Max, you win," he sighed. "What do we do?"

"The first thing you do is you write President Eisenhower and tell him how sorry you are that you went to the press without giving him the courtesy of seeing the letter first." Rabb's anger was subsiding a bit now that Powell was seemingly cooperating. "I can assure you he will remedy all this because it deserves to be remedied. And we'll get to work on it immediately."[18]

Rabb left thinking he had won. But it was Powell who had gotten what he wanted. He now had a commitment from the White House to follow through on the pledge to desegregate the military. It was the first triumph produced by his strategy.

Upon his return to the White House, Rabb wasted no time. He went straight to Ike. Candidly, the president feared that Powell might be right about his staff, particularly Navy Secretary Anderson. He told Rabb to go to Anderson. And he gave him a specific message. Eisenhower knew exactly what he wanted said to the Texan. And Rabb promised to deliver it.

When he met with Anderson, Rabb got to the point. After acknowledging the difficulties of integrating naval facilities in the South, he gave Secretary Anderson the president's personal message: "President Eisenhower says he wants segregation at the bases to be terminated. This is the solution he wants, unless there really is some reason that truly makes this impossible."

A quiet pause in the conversation ensued. Then Anderson slowly reached across his desk. He placed his hand on a button and rang his secretary. He told her to immediately send in Undersecretary Charles Thomas, as well as Admiral George Holderness, the head of the Office of Industrial Relations. Rabb wasn't sure what was about to happen.

When the two men arrived in the office, Rabb watched as Anderson gave them their orders. "Mr. Thomas," he began, "go to Norfolk, Virginia....I want you to see if we can't desegregate that place from top to bottom. If we can't do it, let me know, but I want you to know that I want it done, that the only way I'm really going to be happy is if it's done."

Anderson then turned to the admiral. "You, Admiral Holderness, go down to Charleston. Desegregate the place in all aspects."[19] As the men prepared to leave the office, Anderson told them that he would expect a report back in three days.

Less than two days later, Anderson called Rabb to report that progress was being made. "I want you to know that we are now proceeding to desegregate both installations, and we will do it every place else."[20] Anderson's team had already begun a silent campaign to remove segregation at Southern naval bases.

Rabb, meanwhile, continued his efforts to keep Powell happy and, more important, keep him quiet. He had Eisenhower write the Harlem congressman a letter. In it, the president pledged his commitment to the "purpose of eliminating segregation in federally supported institutions." Eisenhower also wrote that his administration had "not taken and we shall not take a single backward step. There must be no second class in this country."

The letter was magic to Powell. He was now officially engaged in a correspondence with the leader of the free world. His personal stock, which he was constantly and carefully monitoring, was on the rise. To keep it soaring, he kept the conversation going. Powell had many gifts. Understatement was not one of them. He wrote back to Eisenhower in glowing, hyperbolic terms. He told the president that his pledge to fight against second-class citizenship was a "Magna Carta for minorities and a second Emancipation Proclamation."

Powell then returned to his original strategy—separating Ike from his staff. "Whenever and wherever I find any instance which seems to indicate that any of your official family is not cooperating with your program, I shall communicate immediately with the proper persons on your White House staff."

Critics are friends, Ben Franklin wrote, because they point out faults. By that standard, Powell was proving to be a fairly good critic, if not friend. But he was more interested in advancing himself than in rewarding Eisenhower. Whatever his motive, the mercurial Powell had forced the White House to confront the race issue head-on. The administration likely would not have been quite as aggressive in pursuing military desegregation but for Alice Dunnigan and Adam Clayton Powell. But pursue it they did. In a roundabout way, Ike was making good on his pledge to finish the work of Truman and integrate the military.

◇

The president, according to Georgia congressman James Davis, was attempting to "outdeal the New Deal." He referred to the Eisenhower Department of Justice's involvement in a case called *District of Columbia v. John R. Thompson Co.* The case tested whether the "Lost Laws" that banned segregation in D.C. were still valid. An earlier court ruling said no. The nation's capital continued its segregated ways.

Attorney General Brownell briefed Eisenhower on the case. Sitting together in the Oval Office, the two men played two different roles. Ike was the judge, listening intently, asking questions, weighing the options. Brownell was the attorney, the advocate who made impassioned, rigorous pleas. On the *Thompson* case, Ike could hardly sit out, because he had repeatedly pledged to make the nation's capital a bright, shining example of freedom. Brownell told him that "Lost Laws" were valid and that the appeals court had gotten it wrong. The president agreed and asked Brownell to take charge of the case. He did. The Eisenhower Department of Justice filed a brief on March 10th in support of the "Lost Laws."

And so it was that Southern Democrats came to see Eisenhower as standing to the left of the New Deal. Still, Congressman Davis could not have been surprised by Ike's position on the District. But he probably was surprised by the ruling of the Supreme Court. On June 8th, 1953, the Court rendered the "Lost Laws" valid. Segregation was again illegal in Washington.

As a young officer, Ike (seen here as a West Point cadet in 1915) was often skeptical of his black soldiers' abilities.

The 99th Fighting Squadron—the famed Tuskegee Airmen—earned Ike's admiration and respect with their stunning successes in combat.

Eisenhower visited the 101st Airborne on June 5, 1944, the eve of the D-Day invasion. Years later, Ike would call on this same unit during the Little Rock crisis.

Sir Winston Churchill, who was uniquely qualified to speak to Ike's military achievements, predicted Ike would continue to influence world

On June 19, 1945, New York welcomed Ike (waving in car in foreground) home from the war with a ticker tape parade.

Ike made foreign policy—especially the Cold War—the centerpiece of his presidential campaign, but America's greatest war leader would soon be forced to confront America's greatest national sin.

Eisenhower found the right vice president in Richard Nixon of California (seen here on November 7, 1956 celebrating a Republican landslide). Nixon possessed an intense and gifted political mind and was quite progressive on civil rights.

When Rosa Parks refused to give up her bus seat, the entire nation realized the issue of civil rights could no longer be ignored.

Jackie Robinson, probably the most respected African-American in the country in the 1950s, liked Ike, but became concerned the president wasn't doing enough on civil rights.

In September of 1957, nine black students faced mob violence and the Arkansas National Guard when they attempted to enter Little Rock Central High School. The event, televised across the nation, put a new face on racism.

President Eisenhower and Arkansas governor Orval Faubus met at Newport. Ike thought they had a deal to end the standoff and let the Little Rock Nine enter the school. He later decided Faubus had double-crossed him.

The 101st standing guard in Little Rock—the first time since Reconstruction federal troops governed Southern territory.

The Little Rock Nine, seen here in undated photos collected by the Associated Press.

In 1958, Eisenhower met with civil rights leaders in the Oval Office. Pictured (l-r) are National Urban League executive secretary Lester B. Granger, Dr. Martin Luther King, Jr., White House admin. officer E. Frederic Morrow, Pres. Eisenhower, AFL-CIO vice president A. Philip Randolph, Attny. Gen. William Rogers, and NAACP executive secretary Roy Wilkins.

Ike greets President-elect Kennedy as Kennedy arrives at the White House on December 6, 1960. Ike didn't think much of his successor, but the two men did work together behind the scenes on civil rights.

Despite the outrage of Southerners in Congress, the ruling nicely fit with Eisenhower's policy and strategy. Now, with the majesty of the Court to strengthen his hand, Ike soon met with local leaders. Max Rabb coordinated all of this. When Rabb first asked Ike how he intended to go about civil rights, Ike told him: "We are not going to send a bill up to Congress. We are not going to have it subjected to debate, well-knowing that it's a useless gesture, even though it might make some of our people happy in that those who are for it would have a chance to sound off and those who are against it would have their day at bat, yet knowing within our heart of hearts that it had no chance of passage."[21]

Instead, Rabb helped to arrange a series of meetings where Ike could turn on his charm and encourage local D.C. leaders to do the right thing and desegregate. Rabb organized a presidential session with Spiro Spyros Skouras of 20th Century-Fox and Barney Balaban of Paramount. He urged the Hollywood moguls to pressure movie theaters in D.C. to desegregate. At first, they resisted. They told Ike that they didn't actually own any theaters, they just supplied the movies. They wondered whether it was improper for them to pressure the theater owners. "I'll wink at that one," Ike re-assured them. Soon, the two men were busy urging D.C. theater owners to desegregate. Few people can resist the pressure of Hollywood glamour and celebrity. It wasn't long before the movie moguls had succeeded in opening the doors of integrated theaters.[22]

Within months, the District as a whole was desegregating. In the meantime, Thurgood Marshall and the NAACP were trying to change the rest of the nation.

◇

The same day that the Supreme Court handed down a decision in the *Thompson* case, it also addressed some questions on the *Brown* case. Rather than rule on the integration of public schools, the Supreme Court asked the lawyers on both sides to research the histories of the 14th Amendment and segregation. The Court announced that it would rehear arguments in October that year.

What was the Supreme Court doing? The justices had undoubtedly noticed the Eisenhower administration's involvement in the *Thompson* case. Since school segregation was such an explosive issue, the Court appeared to be hoping for executive involvement again. "They wanted to get them [the administration] in the act," remembered Warren Burger, who was then an assistant attorney general.

In fact, even before the Court rescheduled arguments for the fall of 1953, Attorney General Brownell had been informed of the Court's desire. Chief Justice Fred Vinson let it be known that the Court was interested in what the White House thought about the *Brown* case.

Brownell was eager to get involved in the case. He wasn't sure his boss would share that enthusiasm. "I knew that the matter posed a dilemma for Eisenhower," he recalled, "and because I very much wanted the Justice Department to support desegregation I knew I had my work cut out for me."[23]

Brownell and others knew that Eisenhower wished to move slowly, incrementally on the issue. He did not want radical change. And *Brown* certainly held out the possibility of creating a radically different America.

According to one aide, Eisenhower personally was "humane whenever he ran up against the problem [segregation], which is a quite different thing from having any kind of a substratum of personal knowledge and philosophy about the problem that would have caused him to reach out to do something about it." Indeed, the same staffer suggested that had Eisenhower understood how the Supreme Court might rule on *Brown*—effectively restructuring the public-education system all around the nation—he would have been "flabbergasted."[24]

Yet, Brownell was determined that the commander in chief take a more active role. Brownell began to consider how best to enlist the president. He knew that Ike "did not intend to be a crusader" on civil rights. But he believed he could move Eisenhower "toward the position I favored."

Brownell visited with Eisenhower that summer. He told him that the Supreme Court hoped the administration would take part in the *Brown* case. Eisenhower demurred. Reflecting his Whig-like view of the three branches of government, Ike thought he should stay out of it. Having mulled it over further, Ike called Brownell on August 19th. "As I understand it," he said, "the courts were established by the Constitution to interpret the laws; the responsibility of the Executive Department is to execute them." Eisenhower was also suspicious. He wondered whether the court was pursuing a "motive that is not strictly functional." He told his attorney general that the Court should not "delegate its responsibility." Instead, Brownell should merely present the Court with "a resume of fact and historical record."[25]

In fact, Brownell had not been the first to appeal to the president on *Brown.* On July 16th, Texas governor Allan Shivers had written to the president. Shivers, a Democrat, had played a crucial role in Ike's electoral victory when he endorsed the Republican over Adlai Stevenson. "There is nothing more local than the public school system," Shivers wrote in words carefully chosen to match Ike's philosophy of limited federal government.[26] Then, on July 20th, Governor Byrnes strode into the Oval Office. Byrnes had briefly mentioned the case to Ike earlier that year. Eisenhower, always following procedure, urged him to talk to the Department of Justice. But Byrnes was determined to talk to the president, too.

Eisenhower was genuinely fond of Byrnes, and not just because of his support during the campaign. In his diary, Ike wrote that the South Carolina governor was a "great friend, a man in whose company I always find a great deal of enjoyment."[27]

Most white adults in the South had no problem dealing with black adults, Byrnes told Ike. The issue, he said, was the children. Southerners simply didn't like the idea of their white kids sitting next to black kids in classrooms. In his diary entry about the meeting, Ike noted that the governor was afraid that the president would be "carried away by the hope of capturing the Negro vote in this country." Eisenhower answered that he did not take positions on court cases that he had not studied. But he assured Byrnes that politics would play no role whatsoever in his views on the issue. Indeed, Eisenhower noted in his diary his long-standing doubt that prejudice would ever "succumb to compulsion":

> ...I believe that federal law imposed upon our states in such a way as to bring about a conflict of the police powers of the states and of the nation, would set back the cause of progress in race relations for a long, long time.

That summer, Eisenhower announced the formation of the President's Committee on Government Contracts. The group, to be chaired by Vice President Nixon, would devote itself to implementing Eisenhower's wishes that the federal government no longer discriminate based on race. Serving alongside Nixon was an eclectic group that, among others, included an African-American, J. Ernest Wilkins; a Democrat, FDR's youngest son, John; and, at Ike's personal request, a Southerner, John Minor Wisdom. The most interesting choice was Nixon.

By placing his vice president in charge of the committee, Ike was giving it prestige while still keeping some distance from it himself. Nixon was, if anything, to the left of Ike on race. Perhaps due to his Quaker roots, he had no problems with minorities and had little sympathy with those who did. Eisenhower thanked Nixon for taking on the job and reminded him that freedom must be "honestly exemplified by the Federal establishment. I know that you and your Committee share this resolute purpose. I know that you will succeed in achieving it."[28]

At this point, Eisenhower still hoped that goodwill and gradualism could alleviate the problem. He didn't know it, but he was sitting on a volcano that was only beginning to grumble.

<>

On August 6th, Eisenhower offered the nation a progress report. Speaking over the radio, he gave a summary of the administration's highlights, including a recently completed truce in Korea. On domestic policy, he touched briefly on civil rights and said he had "used the power of the federal government...to combat and erase racial discrimination."[29] The next morning, the *Washington Post* mocked this claim, editorializing that "relatively little has been done."[30]

Max Rabb was furious. He alone knew the success that Eisenhower was having, particularly in desegregating the military and the District of Columbia. "Mr. President, someday they will eat their words," he fumed to his boss.

"We'll see," said Eisenhower, who was eager to leave Washington for a few days and begin his Colorado vacation. Perhaps he understood a contradiction in his civil rights efforts. He was pleased with the work of Rabb and Secretary Anderson, not only because it was effective, but also because it was quiet. At one naval base, for example, Anderson ordered that the signs marking separate "colored" and "white" facilities be taken down during the weekend when no one was around. When the sailors arrived back on Monday, they were too busy to notice. This suited Ike just fine. He was trying to make as much progress as possible with as little noise as possible. Yet, he couldn't then expect the media to praise him for achievements they knew little about.

Once he arrived in Denver, Eisenhower renewed his conversation with Jimmy Byrnes on the subject of segregation. Eisenhower knew that he would have to prepare his friend for the modest changes that were coming. He was also mindful of his meeting with Brownell, which forced him to revisit the issues involved in the *Brown* case.

In writing to Byrnes, Eisenhower reiterated his commitment to "eliminate discrimination within the definite areas of Federal responsibility." This included the Charleston Navy Yard. He went on to say that in order to help with the execution of his policy of equal treatment in federal areas he was establishing a Committee on Government Contracts.

Eisenhower's goal in pursuing this incremental approach was to "prove to be mistaken those who insist that true reforms can come only through overriding Federal law and Federal police methods."[31]

But Byrnes was becoming worried. This did not sound like the same man who had stood at attention when "Dixie" was played in Columbia during the campaign. This was a man moving forward on equal rights, albeit at a slow pace.

Byrnes wrote back. Though he acknowledged the president's authority over the Navy Yard at Charleston, he wondered why Ike was taking action when there was "no claim of discrimination." Byrnes even went so far as to point out that "not even President Truman deemed necessary" the desegregation of naval installations. Still, having stated his concern, Byrnes pledged his support of the policy.

"But," he continued, "your other proposal is entirely different." He compared Ike's Committee on Government Contracts to the Federal Employment Practices Committee. "In your recent political campaign you steadfastly adhered to your position that you were opposed to Congress enacting a Federal FEPC," Byrnes reminded him, "believing that question should be left to the States."

Byrnes feared that Eisenhower's panel might have too much muscle. "The Federal Government purchases about one-fourth of our national product," he wrote. If Ike's committee was to encourage equal rights, then "I respectfully submit the executive would be usurping the powers of the Congress."

Byrnes vowed that it pained him to write such a letter, which spanned four pages. But he felt that because of his relationship with Ike, he was entitled to "unburden myself freely."[32]

On September 3rd, while still vacationing in Denver, Eisenhower called Byrnes on the phone. He stressed again that the federal government has a "duty to ensure equality in all areas in which it has complete and unquestioned jurisdiction."[33] But he then went out of his way to assure Byrnes that he did not support an FEPC and that he did not believe that the Nixon committee would become an FEPC. As he later repeated to Nixon, Ike saw the Nixon committee as "an agency that will not only find out whether existing laws are being enforced...but will also point out all those paths in which people in official and private activities can be helpful in assisting progress toward economic and political equality, regardless of race." Here, in one sentence, was the entire Eisenhower philosophy on civil rights in 1953. By bringing people together, he hoped to end discrimination in the federal government and to discourage it elsewhere.

By the end of the year, many of Ike's modest goals had been achieved. The dream of a desegregated military—first articulated by Truman in 1948—was largely a reality. On November 11th, Hagerty released a statement from the president, highlighting the achievements in desegregating naval facilities. Ike claimed that "of 60 Southern installations on Federal-owned property only one reported partial segregation. That is a record of accomplishment of which we all can be proud...." And the District of Columbia was also busy opening the doors of its theaters, restaurants, and hotels to blacks on an equal basis with whites. Perhaps the only truly segregated part of the nation's capital by the end of the year was its school system, which was still operating under the *Plessy* doctrine of "separate but equal."

Eisenhower's initial policies on race reflected his innate caution: He was still a commander, worried about overextending his lines of battle. Better to fight battles on friendly terrain.

Revealingly, his policies reflected his own limited definition of civil rights. At this point, Eisenhower saw racism as a problem to be managed, not a passion from which to lead. The federal government should stop discriminating, he believed. But beyond that, there wasn't much he thought he could do. He still believed what he had told Congress in 1948: Congress couldn't, and shouldn't, pass laws to make people "like" each other. That was beyond his power.

As a general, he had tried to seek a balance between utilizing black troops and overturning War Department policy. On race relations, he wanted an evolution, not a revolution.

Perhaps visitors to the White House noticed a visual display of Ike's ambivalence. Inside the Oval Office, the president hung portraits of four of his heroes. The first two were George Washington and Benjamin Franklin. But the other two spoke volumes about the president and the nation: Abraham Lincoln and Robert E. Lee.

◇

Early on Tuesday morning, September 8th, a doctor was summoned to the Wardman-Park Hotel in Washington, D.C. Inside one of the apartments, a man had suffered a heart attack. When the doctor arrived at 1:30 a.m., he found that the man was in critical condition. For several minutes he struggled mightily to save the man. He breathed into his lungs...searched in vain for a pulse...breathed again into his lungs.

He couldn't save him. A lifetime of cigarettes and stress had doomed the man. Fred Vinson, the chief justice of the United States, was pronounced dead at the age of sixty-three.

With less than a month before the opening of the new term of the Supreme Court, the Eisenhower administration had to find a replacement. They also had a very difficult political problem on their hands.

Eisenhower had promised California governor Earl Warren that he would be named to fill the "first vacancy" on the court. In fact, Ike was so fond of Warren that he and Brownell were already in the process of grooming him by naming him solicitor general. The announcement had not yet been made when Vinson succumbed on September 8th. But Warren had accepted.

Now all bets were off. Warren didn't want to be on the junior varsity team when he could be on the varsity. He played hardball, telling the White House that Ike had promised him the "first vacancy," and that this was it. He wanted to be chief justice.

Eisenhower disagreed. He denied that he was ever "thinking of the special post of chief justice...." To help resolve the issue, Ike sent Brownell to meet with Warren. In the meantime, Ike thought over a wide range of names, including everyone from John Foster Dulles to John W. Davis, who was at that moment preparing for the new arguments scheduled in the *Brown* case.

When Brownell arrived at McClellan Air Force Base in California, he found the governor of California in a foul mood. Fresh off a hunting trip, Warren was angry and fearful that he was about to be double-crossed. Brownell told him that the president had intended for Warren to receive an "associate justiceship," not "the post of Chief Justice."[34] Warren wouldn't budge. He did, however, acknowledge that Ike could promote an associate justice to chief justice, thereby creating an opening for Warren. In this way, the president could keep his word. Of course, Warren knew full well that after twenty years of Democratic nominees, there was almost no one on the Court whom the president would want to promote.

The California governor's tactics paid off, but at a price. On September 30th, 1953, Eisenhower nominated Earl Warren as the fourteenth chief justice of the United States. But relations between the two men would never recover.

<>

As the shadow that was 1953 began to fall softly, Eisenhower was awarded the America's Democratic Legacy Award at the Annual B'nai B'rith Dinner. Held in the ballroom of the Mayflower Hotel in Washington, the event was a star-studded event that was televised nationally.

Eschewing a formal text, the president spoke off the cuff. He praised the group for its devotion to "the great human rights." He talked about why Americans should be proud of their country. Not because of its resources or land, but because of its values. "We are proud, first of all, because from the beginning of this Nation, a man can walk upright, no matter who he is, or who she is," Ike told the crowd. Then he issued a challenge: "[I]f we are going to continue to be proud that we are Americans, there must be no weakening of the code by which we have lived...."

"Ladies and gentlemen," he concluded, "the things that make us proud to be Americans are of the soul and of the spirit." America was special because "here the individual is dignified because he is created in the image of his God. Let us not forget it."[35]

As he ended his speech, the celebrity-laden crowd erupted in applause. Lucille Ball, Desi Arnaz, Ethel Merman, Helen Hayes, and Eddie Fisher were all on hand, and several of them made their way up to the dais to congratulate the president on his remarks. One who didn't go was baseball legend Jackie Robinson. Perhaps the former Army officer was in awe of his commander in chief. But by the time the other celebrities had congratulated the president, Robinson was just getting out of his chair. It looked like he was too late.

Then, to Robinson's astonishment, Eisenhower spotted him. Ike, the sports fan, was eager to meet the baseball legend. The president left the dais and went out into the audience. He navigated the ballroom until he reached Robinson. The two men shook hands and exchanged words.

Robinson was overwhelmed by the gesture. "To think the President of the United States would come halfway across a room just to shake my hand!" he later told the press.[36] A couple of days later, still aglow, he wrote a letter to Ike. Like most people who meet the president, Robinson found that it was "great for me to experience the warmth and sincerity of your handshake in the midst of such an illustrious group of Americans." It was proof to the baseball icon that "our faith in democracy is indeed justified."

Though his views on politics and civil rights were still developing, Robinson's faith in Eisenhower was at an all-time high. He was thrilled to meet the hero of World War II.

It would not be the last time the two men's paths would cross.

Eisenhower enjoyed a final achievement in the waning days of 1953. On December 8th, he gave one of the most celebrated addresses of his career. Speaking in the ornate general assembly room at the United Nations headquarters in New York, the American president proposed using atomic technology for peaceful purposes. He wanted to "take this weapon out of the hands of soldiers" and give it to those who would "adapt it to the arts of peace."[37]

Eisenhower won huge credit in the press, but his initiative sparked little reaction from the Soviets. With his "Atoms for Peace" proposal, he had hoped to restrain, even reverse, the spiraling arms race. But the Cold War had its own momentum that no words, however eloquent or heartfelt, could halt.

Closer to home, another moral struggle gathered force. Yet, here, Ike was strangely mute. It didn't matter, in a sense; history was about to be made. Ike, and the entire nation, would soon be talking about it.

CHAPTER SEVEN

THE RULING

*"I think ... that the best interests of the United States demand an
answer in keeping with past decisions."*

—Dwight D. Eisenhower

A S THE YEAR OF 1954 began, the country was gripped by
one pressing, vital issue. Dominating the headlines, it was
discussed at the office and in the home. It was considered one of
the greatest constitutional crises to confront America in years. It
involved the government at its highest levels, and it concerned
the ways in which all Americans viewed and treated each other.
The issue? McCarthyism.

Since his famous speech at Wheeling, West Virginia, in 1950,
Senator Joseph McCarthy of Wisconsin had made a name for
himself by hurling accusations of Communism at everyone in his
path. McCarthy's rumpled looks and perpetual five o'clock
shadow gave him the appearance of a hard-working vigilante or
a sinister child playing with constitutional matches.

But he was more than that. He was an opportunist who gave
conservatism a bad name. Never willing to let the facts interfere
with his fame, McCarthy saw Communists around every corner
and in every office. One of the vilest demagogues in history, he
exaggerated, misled, and ultimately did more damage to the anti-
Communist cause than to his sworn enemies.

In 1952, McCarthy officially crossed the line from the cynical to
the absurd. He took on Ike's friend and mentor, General George
Marshall. Eisenhower defended Marshall from charges of Com-

munism and denounced McCarthy on the campaign trail. But when the campaign train stopped for an event in Wisconsin, Ike refrained from taking on McCarthy in his own backyard. Privately, in his car on the train, Eisenhower gave McCarthy a profane dressing down that the senator would not soon forget.

By 1954, Eisenhower had changed his mind. He no longer disliked McCarthy; he hated him. He despised him with a passion reserved for few men this side of Adolf Hitler. "President Eisenhower had a sense of loathing and contempt that had to be seen to be believed," is how presidential aide Art Larson described Ike's view of McCarthy. At a staff meeting to consider a "sudden-death insurance policy" for government employees, Ike interjected: "I know one fellow I'd like to take that policy out for."[1]

During the first year of his presidency, Eisenhower ignored McCarthy. "I'm not going to get into a gutter with that guy," Ike told his staff. Believing that McCarthy's engine was fueled by the high octane of publicity, he felt, not unreasonably, that a presidential confrontation would be welcomed by McCarthy. It was also, yet again, a reaction against the Truman precedent. Truman had denounced McCarthy from the Oval Office. In Ike's view, that was exactly what McCarthy wanted and needed in order to stay in the news. Eisenhower refused to play McCarthy's game.

Not that McCarthy didn't have plenty of warnings that Ike's silence did not equal an endorsement. Earlier, when the Wisconsin Republican tried to block the nomination of Ike's friend, Harvard president James Conant, as high commissioner in Germany, the president called the senator personally and told him to knock it off. He did, and Conant was confirmed.

Such episodes not withstanding, Eisenhower was content to let McCarthy discredit himself. By 1954, he had shown every sign of doing just that. Not content to take on obscure figures in the federal government, McCarthy decided to attack the singular American institution closest to the heart of Eisenhower: the U.S. Army.

At this point, Ike had had enough. Enraged at McCarthy's tactics as well his target—the Army—Eisenhower became much more engaged. The "full force of Eisenhower's disgust led to a concerted effort from the administration to do the senator in," according to Attorney General Brownell.[2]

As the White House staff began to prepare for more direct combat, they learned that McCarthy himself had some flanks to protect. As it happened, McCarthy had sought favors for one of his staffers who had been drafted into the Army. When Attorney General Brownell informed the president of this, Ike decided it was time to put an end to McCarthy.

First, he cut off the flow of information. McCarthy had subpoenaed the Army for its records. The Army, acting on Eisenhower's order, refused. Eisenhower then went further and denied McCarthy access to all executive agency records. Without documents, McCarthy had nothing.

Eisenhower had also been talking off the record with key senators about McCarthy. Thanks to this cultivation, most of them supported Ike's aggressive assertion of executive privilege even though it ran counter to their own congressional prerogative.

Not only did administration officials refuse to cooperate with McCarthy's investigation and cut him off from key documents, they even suggested the attorney who would confront the Wisconsin Republican on national television. Sherman Adams, acting on a tip from Tom Dewey, suggested that the Army hire Joseph Welch—a bow-tied exemplar of Yankee rectitude. Welch was an inspired choice who memorably chastised McCarthy to his face during the televised hearings: "Have you no sense of decency?"

When the Senate, finally fed up with his antics, censured McCarthy, Eisenhower celebrated it as a victory. He invited one of McCarthy's leading critics, Senator Arthur Watkins, to the Oval Office.[3] The next morning, newspapers carried the photo of Eisenhower with Watkins, reveling in the demise of McCarthy.

Ike's voice may have been largely silent during the decline and fall of McCarthy, but his fingerprints were everywhere. With his eloquent pleas on television, Edward R. Morrow was largely credited with breaking McCarthy's momentum. But it was Eisenhower who broke his back. It was a case study in how Eisenhower would choose to handle difficult domestic issues. He would seek a low profile, he would give the players space to operate, in the hope of finding the solution, and in the end, if necessary, after all options had been explored, he would act decisively, even ruthlessly.

Few knew it at the time, but Ike's handling of McCarthy was a harbinger of how he would act in future struggles.

◇

"I am reminded," intoned the silver-haired man, "of Aesop's fable of the god and the meat." It was December 7th, 1953. As new Chief Justice Earl Warren presided over the Supreme Court, John W. Davis and Thurgood Marshall resumed their duel during the reconsideration of the *Brown* case.[4]

To Davis, the case was as simple as the famous child's tale: "The dog, with a fine piece of meat in his mouth, crossed a bridge and saw the shadow in the stream and plunged for it and lost both substance and shadow." Tears filled his eyes as he urged the justices not to be fooled by Marshall's persuasive words. "Here is equal education, not promised, not prophesied, but present. Shall it be thrown away on some fancied question of racial prestige?" he asked.

Marshall was more than ready to shred this argument. In his rebuttal, he mocked Davis's claim that the NAACP sought "prestige" of any sort. The only prestige that African-Americans desired was to have "the same status as anybody else, regardless of race."

Marshall had numerous weapons in his arsenal, first among them his own keen mind and powerful rhetoric. But he also had something else: a supporting brief from the Eisenhower Department of Justice.

After Brownell's first meeting with the president on whether to submit an amicus brief, he duly followed Ike's orders, putting together a presentation based on the facts and history of the case. The two men had different perspectives, but the same goal. Ike wanted to tread more cautiously, but both believed that segregation was wrong.

Like a geometric formulation, their different shapes came together to create a more powerful whole. Thanks to Brownell, Ike was going to weigh in on the emotional issue of civil rights.

Thanks to Ike, the brief was carefully worded and deeply grounded in history and law.

Still, Brownell made sure that the Eisenhower brief was issued as a supplement to the Truman brief that had been filed during earlier rounds of the *Brown* case. That document explicitly opposed segregation in schools. Brownell hoped that "our brief, by association as a supplement, might be interpreted to share" this view.[5]

Nevertheless, Brownell was still out in front of his boss on civil rights. When the question was raised of coordinating the writing of the Department of Justice brief with the NAACP lawyers, Eisenhower forbade it.

Like any conscientious staffer, Brownell continued to raise the issue with Ike. As he later wrote, he conducted a campaign aimed at "easing Eisenhower toward the position I favored."[6]

Once the brief was ready to submit to the Supreme Court, Brownell again visited with Eisenhower. It wouldn't be enough to submit the brief, Brownell said. Surely, the justices would ask questions about the brief. And Brownell would have to answer them.

What Brownell didn't tell Ike is that he *wanted* to answer questions before the court. He welcomed the opportunity to give his opinion to the High Court. But he knew that Ike would be nervous about that. Indeed, the president told his attorney general that he didn't know why any questions would be asked when the administration had fulfilled its duties in submitting the brief.

Like a college professor, Brownell explained how the hearings would work. Assistant Attorney General Lee Rankin would be required to stand make an oral presentation of the administration's brief. An any point, any justice could ask him any question. It was inevitable, Brownell told him, that the question would be posed: "Is school segregation constitutional?" The administrative representative must be prepared to give a response.

Eisenhower pondered the civics lesson, then posed the question Brownell had wanted him to ask. What did the attorney general think about school segregation? "I answered that in my professional opinion public school segregation was unconstitutional and that the old *Plessy* case had been wrongly decided," Brownell later wrote. Ike responded that if that was his opinion, and the court asked the question, Brownell—or Rankin—should say so.[7]

As it happened, the question was asked of Assistant Attorney General Rankin. Acting on orders from the attorney general, and with the grudging blessing of the president, Rankin, speaking as a representative of the administration, told the nine justices that he believed school segregation was unconstitutional.

Even now, Eisenhower wanted to have it both ways. He told his friend Jimmy Byrnes that Rankin spoke from "his own conviction and understanding" and that he did not speak for the entire administration.[8]

Brownell reported back to the president to tell him that the hearings had gone very well. The chief justice had personally praised the attorney general, classifying "my brief on the segregation cases as outstanding."[9] It was one thing for Eisenhower to officially support desegregation in schools. But it was another to revel in it. Ike chose his course of action because Brownell had convinced him that he had to do it. But he didn't have to act as though he liked it.

Brownell liked where the case was heading. So did the other side. After the Supreme Court concluded the arguments on *Brown*, John W. Davis and his patron were certain of victory. Davis wrote to Governor Byrnes, triumphantly predicting that his arguments were "unanswerable": "Let us hope the Olympian Nine will take the same point of view—*and I really think they will and must.*" (italics original)[10]

Not everyone on Davis's team was so certain. Paul Wilson, a lawyer who represented Kansas, was impressed not by Davis but by Marshall. If last impressions are the most lasting, then Byrnes and Davis might be in for a shock. Wilson wrote that in the last day of arguments, Marshall was powerful and persuasive and that he "came on like a locomotive."[11]

◇

The White House sits like an ivory island in a sea of bronzed steel and gray concrete. All around it, a vibrant, urban downtown looms. Yet, the White House itself is peacefully surrounded by eighteen acres of lush emerald lawn. The symbolism is perfect: The president's home and office are located in the middle of the city, yet they are apart from the city. Likewise, every president must have the proximity to hear the people and the space to think for himself.

On a typical morning, President Eisenhower would rise early. His military aide and valet from World War II, Sgt. John Moaney, was still with him. Moaney would lay out his clothes for him, even tie his neckwear. The president now weighed 175 pounds and still seemed full of energy and life.

His easy command was on display every morning. Heading downstairs from the Executive Mansion, he would enter the Rose Garden and stride alongside Jefferson's colonnade, sometimes carrying a golf club that he used to loosen up his wrists. As he walked, he could see the putting green built for his use that spring by the American Public Golf Association.[12] He might already be anticipating the afternoon when he might do some chipping. If he saw squirrels tearing up his precious putting green, he became irate. "The next time you see one of those squirrels go near my putting green, take a gun and shoot it!" he ordered Moaney.

He would step through the French doors and enter the Oval Office. Setting down the golf club against the credenza, Ike sat down behind the HMS *Resolute* desk. The desk had been made from the timbers of a British ship and given to President Rutherford B. Hayes by Queen Victoria in 1880. The top of the desk was typically clean, save for a small block of wood. It was a gift from Gabriel Hauge, a staffer. A simple inscription in Latin read: "Gentle in manner, strong in deed."[13]

A small room connected the Oval Office with the Cabinet Room next door. Across the hall was the Fish Room, where Ike could greet larger groups of people. Still, the West Wing is notable for its size—it's small. Theodore Roosevelt, in search of office space away from the family quarters in the mansion, hired the New York architecture firm McKim, Mead and White to build it in 1902. It was intended to be a temporary solution. But it soon became the president's permanent office in spite of its size. By the 1950s, as the size of the presidential staff continued to outgrow the West Wing, more and more staffers were finding a home next door in the Old Executive Building, where Major Eisenhower had served MacArthur in the 1930s. To reach its French Second Empire Splendor, staffers would leave the West Wing, cross West Executive Street inside the White House compound, march up the granite steps of the OEB, and enter a nineteenth century environment, complete with marble floors, cast iron pilasters, and bronze balusters.

But the primary business of the nation was conducted by the man inside the Oval Office. Once he was at his battle station, Ike would begin work. As in his military days, his schedule included a seemingly endless array of meetings, briefings, speeches, and appearances. His friend, the poet Robert Frost, joked that Ike was a "very, very fine man, even if he doesn't read too many books." No, Ike wasn't reading much poetry those days, but he was poring over mounds of intelligence documents, staff briefings, and even a good deal of his mail.

In the spring of 1954, having dispensed with McCarthy, Eisenhower began to wonder, like millions of his countrymen, about the ruling the Supreme Court might hand down in *Brown.*

Perhaps nowhere was Ike's ambivalence more evident than it was in the lead-up to the *Brown* ruling. He was, quite literally, a torn man. On the one hand, the man who was perhaps his most respected cabinet officer, Herbert Brownell, had filed a brief supporting the NAACP position, with Ike's approval. On the other hand, another man who was one of Ike's most respected friends, Governor Jimmy Byrnes, had handpicked the lawyer and helped to write the brief arguing against the NAACP position. Like millions of other Americans, Ike appeared to be squarely on both sides of the issue. He repeatedly said that he believed that racial discrimination was "criminally stupid." But he wasn't sure he was ready to se?e a revolution in the way countless public schools all across the country conducted their affairs.

This split personality was on full display in the spring of 1954, when Eisenhower hosted a stag dinner at the White House.

Ike loved these gatherings. He would typically bring in a variety of people from politics and business to have dinner and cocktails and talk things over. The affairs were off the record. Participants were allowed—even encouraged—to speak freely.

This particular night, Eisenhower invited the chief justice to attend. Warren later wrote that he had had a bad feeling about the event even before he arrived. "I wondered why I should be invited because the dinners were political in nature," he complained, "and there was no place for me in such discussions."

Warren's concern likely turned to dismay when he arrived and saw that among the other guests was the man arguing before his court—John W. Davis. Here was Eisenhower again sending mixed signals. As Warren was shown to his seat, he learned that he would be placed at the same table as Eisenhower and Davis. Warren later wrote that during the meal Ike "went to great lengths to tell me what a great man Mr. Davis was."

After dinner, Eisenhower invited the guests to join him for drinks. The president made his way over to Warren. Grabbing Warren's arm, Ike pleaded with him: "These are not bad people. All they are concerned about is to see that their sweet little girls are not required to sit in school alongside some big, overgrown Negroes."[14]

There it was. Almost word for word, Eisenhower was repeating to Warren the argument that Byrnes had first made to him the previous July. In his memoirs, Warren wrote that he didn't respond to Eisenhower because others had walked up, and the conversation had quickly ended. But he was clearly offended. He viewed it as interference by the Executive Branch in the affairs of the Judicial Branch. Eisenhower's conversation with Warren was effective, though perhaps not in the way it was intended. Warren would never again believe that the president was serious about civil rights.

Word of the story eventually seeped out of the confines of the White House. When it made its way to Thurgood Marshall, he was outraged. He later called it the "most despicable job that any president has done."

For his part, Eisenhower was convinced that he was doing the right thing. Like the nine justices of the court, he was trying to navigate a maze of issues and challenges.

Eisenhower's open mind on the issue was further evidenced by his willingness to talk about it with his staff. Ann Whitman, who had served him so well in the campaign, was now his secretary in the White House. She was more than that. In many ways, she was a precursor to the executive assistant role that so dominates government offices today. She didn't just type for her boss, she also talked to him. She gave him her opinions, especially when she thought he was wrong.

Whitman spent more time with Eisenhower than almost anyone did, a fact not lost on Mamie, who didn't much care for her. Whitman knew her boss and his views. On civil rights, she basically shared Brownell's assessment that Ike's heart was in the right place but that he would rather manage the problem than lead a crusade. Whitman often challenged Ike on the matter. "The president always argued with me," she remembered. When she persisted and urged Ike to do more on race issues, Ike responded that she "would feel differently" if she had lived in the South, as he had.[15]

One concern that was especially heavy on his mind that spring was that public schools might simply shut down, rather than desegregate.

The seed for this thought was planted by Louisiana governor Robert F. Kennon. In a November 20, 1953, letter to the president, Kennon warned that a "federal edict contrary to the established order and customs could well disrupt many local systems, particularly in the rural areas." He feared that this could "interrupt the present orderly improvement and do great damage to the fine racial relationships that have existed."[16]

When Eisenhower raised this concern with Brownell, the attorney general reassured him. Brownell believed that the Supreme Court would give the South enough time to adjust, should it strike down separate schools. He envisioned a "period of years" while Southern school districts acclimated to the new law.

He did not envision a wholesale series of school closings throughout the South.

But he couldn't be certain of what would happen, because he wasn't certain how the Supreme Court would rule. Neither was Ike. As he thought about the tangle of issues being considered by Warren and his brethren, he staked out in his own mind what was right and what was best for the country. "I don't know where I stand," he concluded that spring, "but I think … that the best interests of the United States demand an answer in keeping with past decisions."[17]

◇

Just after noon on May 17th, 1954, the nine men clothed in black robes entered the courtroom. Justice Robert Jackson, still recuperating from a heart attack, had left his hospital room that morning so that he could be on hand for the court's business that day. He knew that the Supreme Court was about to make a decision that would make history. He wanted to be part of it.

Sitting in the gallery were many of the players whose lives were entwined with the *Brown* case. Of course, Thurgood Marshall was there, nervously waiting on the decision. So was Herbert Brownell, sitting in the chair assigned to the attorney general. The session started when Chief Justice Warren began reading through the decisions in several other cases in a businesslike manner.

At last he reached the most important case: *Brown v. Board of Education of Topeka, Kansas.* "We come then to the question presented," he said. "Does segregation of children in public schools solely on the basis of race, even though the physical facilities and other tangible factors may be equal, deprive the children of the minority group of equal educational opportunities?"

Tension filled the air. People leaned forward in their seats, not wanting to miss a word.

"We unanimously believe that it does," Warren announced. The chief justice later recalled sensing a "wave of emotion" throughout the courtroom as his words were uttered.

Marshall was ecstatic. "We hit the jackpot," he announced outside the courtroom. He then spotted young Bill Greenhill, the son of the Texas attorney general whom Marshall had befriended even though they were on opposite sides of the issue. He picked the little boy up on his shoulders and carried him "down the corridor of the Supreme Court," recalled the Texas attorney general. In his own inimitable way, Marshall was ushering in the new era of desegregation.[18]

If Marshall was satisfied, Brownell was shocked. Not that he disagreed with the decision. Not at all. This was precisely the outcome he had hoped and worked for. Instead, Brownell was surprised at the unanimous verdict. He never guessed that all nine justices would be of one accord.

The man most responsible for the unanimous ruling was the chief justice. Warren believed that any dissent would give the South an excuse to resist implementing the decision. He had worked tirelessly to build a consensus. And he had gotten it.

But not everyone was so impressed. In South Carolina, Governor Byrnes displayed a mixture of outrage and bitterness. Relying on the now dubious precedent of *Plessy*, Byrnes said that he was "shocked to learn that the Court has reversed itself."[19]

The ruling was even harder on John W. Davis. He returned to South Carolina a broken, beaten man. The strain of preparing and arguing the case left him exhausted. The exasperation of losing finished him off. He died less than a year later.

Byrnes, however, would carry on. Like the skillful political general he was, he would shift his strategy. No longer would he deny desegregation; now he would delay it.

The Court's own ruling almost seemed to invite such tactics. In an effort to reach a consensus and ease the shock of the revolution that its ruling proposed, the nine justices had promised to revisit the issue of implementation in a second case. This one, to become known as *Brown II*, would not be argued until the spring of 1955.

The movement to desegregate America's public schools had won an impressive battle, but the war for integration would rage on.

◇

At the White House, Eisenhower wasn't surprised so much as he was worried. The president was "considerably concerned," one day after the ruling, according to Jim Hagerty. Ike didn't dispute

the basic principle on which the court had ruled—that segregation was wrong. He had publicly and repeatedly said the same
thing regarding federal installations. But typically, he fretted over
the practical effect of the decision. Halting segregation within the
limited confines of the federal government was one matter. But
desegregating every public school in America? No wonder an
aide said that his boss had been"flabbergasted" at the size and
scope of the ruling. Nothing in Ike's life experience had prepared
him for such a sweeping revolution in social policy.[20]

When he discussed it with Brownell, Ike used a historical
analogy. "Well, isn't it true that Andrew Jackson said when a Supreme Court decision was handed down that resulted in an awful
headache for the executive branch in the area of enforcement,
'The Supreme Court has made its decision, let them enforce it?'"[21]
Interestingly, Eisenhower saw the decision as not necessarily
wrong, but rather as a "headache." And, typical of his views of
the separation of powers, he was already worried about the "enforcement" of such a sweeping reform.

"I never heard him say yes or no" as to whether he agreed
with the ruling, Brownell later recalled. Instead, his boss was focused on the aftermath. "I think he was realistic where a lot of
other people weren't seeing the difficulties."[22]

Was Eisenhower surprised by Warren's role in crafting the
ruling? It seems likely that he was. According to Brownell, Eisenhower "never asked Warren how he was going to vote on any
particular subject."[23] In the lead-up to Warren's nomination, Ike
was generally aware of the Californian's "progressive" views on
race. But to be a progressive on race as governor of California
meant supporting equal employment actions at the state level.
This was something that Ike explicitly supported, though he opposed a federal version of the FEPC. To Eisenhower, a state law
on discrimination made perfect sense and was the perfect place to
fight racism. But an "edict" from the federal government that ordered local schools to desegregate? The thought that Warren
would have orchestrated such a ruling almost certainly never
crossed Ike's mind in late 1953.

In the Eisenhower White House, justice, like charity, began at home. Ike's first substantive response to the *Brown* ruling came in the District of Columbia. The day after the ruling, he brought the commissioners of the District to the White House and urged them to take the lead in desegregating Washington's schools.

On May 19th, Eisenhower's weekly press conference provided the occasion for his first public comments on the *Brown* decision. A reporter asked whether he had any advice for the South as it responded to the ruling. "Not in the slightest," he said. "The Supreme Court has spoken, and I am sworn to uphold the constitutional processes in this country; and I will obey."[24]

Eisenhower was in a perfectly difficult political environment. Two days after his press conference, Gallup went into the field with a new poll. Americans were asked whether they approved of the *Brown* decision. While a healthy majority agreed—fifty-five percent—a sizable minority disapproved—forty percent.[25] The country was split. Whatever he did, Ike would have to tread carefully to avoid upsetting the majority or angering the minority.

And so began Eisenhower's public positioning on the new law of the land. In various forms, and to different degrees, he would continue to argue that it didn't matter what he thought of any court rulings. What mattered was that what the court decreed was the law. His role was to enforce the law. And he intended to do just that.

<>

The *Brown* decision was a bombshell, with the fallout yet to be assessed. Southern leaders weren't ready to surrender. They were ready to fight. "There will never be mixed schools while I am governor," Georgia's Herman Talmadge announced, speaking for millions of other Southerners.

Ironically, perhaps the one person other than Eisenhower who fully appreciated the challenge of implementing the court decision in the South was Thurgood Marshall. One day, in his NAACP office, he told some staffers a story that gave them pause. Marshall had heard about three white Southerners discussing the *Brown* ruling. Two of them said that they opposed desegregation. The third man disagreed. "I'm not for integration," the man said, "I'm for slavery." As the full impact of the story settled on the room, Marshall concluded: "There's a whole lot to that story."[26]

Here, Marshall and the president, though singing different parts, were on the same sheet of music. Eisenhower wondered how this revolution could come to pass peacefully in the South. He had always tried to lead by example. He hoped Southerners would follow his lead.

Still, Eisenhower made a conscious decision to speak softly on the subject. This was true on any number of domestic issues. It flowed from his policy of keeping an open mind on domestic matters. And it was evidenced by his handling of McCarthy, when he showed that pulling wires backstage was more effective than pounding the bully pulpit.

Part of the reason for this rhetorical strategy—or lack thereof—was Eisenhower's relatively narrow view of the role of rhetorical leadership. He once told a staffer that if the American people wanted a wordsmith as president, then "we ought to elect Ernest Hemingway."[27] To Ike, speeches had not won World War II; heroism, courage, and action had. He took the same philosophy with him to the White House.

Not that he didn't have good speechwriters or that he couldn't deliver some memorable speeches. Emmet John Hughes, in particular, was one of the greatest presidential speechwriters ever. And Ike's first inaugural, no less than his "Atoms for Peace" trumpet blast, still reads well decades later.

No, Eisenhower's complaint about speeches was that they were just words. He wanted action. More than most presidents, he had given considerable thought to the nature of executive leadership. He once told an aide: "Leadership is the ability to decide what is to be done, and then to get others to want to do it." Now, in the wake of the *Brown* ruling, Eisenhower faced one of the greatest leadership riddles of his lifetime: how to make the people of the South accept and implement a radically different system of operating their schools. Ike didn't know exactly how to do this. But he did know how *not* to do it—with a lot of speeches. He feared that moralizing from the bully pulpit would raise not only awareness, but also the collective blood pressure of the South. He saw no point in riling an already angry population.

Another important part of Eisenhower's thinking, in the aftermath of *Brown*, was his desire to speak for, not at, the American people. Ike was the very symbol of the American Dream. He had come from so little, yet achieved so much. Millions of Americans saw in Ike a man very much like them, and they were right.

To put it bluntly, Eisenhower had little interest in trying to change the minds of millions of Southerners. He was an executive, charged with navigating the ship of state through the high seas of the 1950s. He implicitly rejected the imperial presidencies of his predecessors. He was a throwback to the stewardship presidential model of Taft and McKinley.

Eisenhower's thinking on presidential leadership may have been unique in the New Deal era, but it was not without merit. The Founding Fathers had created the presidency by combining two British models into one. In England, the monarch serves as the head of state, and the prime minister serves as the chief political leader. In America, the president does both. He must simultaneously symbolize the country and deal with the difficult issues confronting the country. He must both unite and divide.

This paradoxical job description has doomed many presidents. Some are able to succeed as political leaders, but they fail miserably at uniting the country. Others reverse this order, but they are equally unsuccessful. Eisenhower accepted both features of his job and tried to do them both well. He wanted to be a unifying figure. The grandfatherly demeanor, the smile, and the focus on foreign policy were all part of his effort to be a successful head of state. But he also was serious about political leadership. By relying on behind-the-scenes actions rather than public speeches, Ike hoped to address tough political issues in a nondivisive way. This was the Hidden Hand that Fred Greenstein's pioneering Eisenhower research uncovered.

Eisenhower also understood the checks and balances inherent in the American system of government. Perhaps the most powerful, and least appreciated, check on presidential power is the will of the people. More than congressional oversight committees and judicial review, presidents are limited in what they can do by what the people want. Public opinion is the lifeblood of any White House. Perhaps no president has proved this better than FDR. Many historians credit FDR with bold and courageous leadership in pushing for the New Deal. While it was leadership, and while it was unique, it was hardly bold or courageous. The country was in crisis. The people demanded action. They wanted something bold and courageous. FDR, always with his finger on the pulse of the people, sensed this and acted accordingly. Had a majority of the American people opposed the New Deal, FDR likely would have tacked to a different course.

Here was the heart of the dilemma facing Ike in 1954. In confronting segregation, the Supreme Court may have been unanimous, but the American people were not.

Eisenhower would have to find a way both to enforce the decision and bring the nation closer together. It was an almost impossible challenge.

◇

Where President Eisenhower saw problems with the new ruling, Congressman Powell saw opportunities. In the lead-up to the *Brown* decision, Powell had continued his strategy of praising Ike publicly while nudging his administration forward behind the scenes. In October 1953, the *Atlanta Daily World*, an African-American paper, quoted Powell praising the president at length. "I can bear witness to the fact that there has not been a single problem of a moral or ethical nature which I have presented to the White House that he has not done his best to solve, and when he has given his word he has kept it."[28]

The White House loved reading this kind of press. Max Rabb sent a copy to the Republican National Committee and predicted that Powell could be used to "develop a strong pro-Eisenhower sentiment among Negroes."[29] To chief of staff Sherman Adams, Rabb said the clippings proved that Powell had transformed from a "difficult Democrat," thanks to the "friendly treatment" he was getting from the White House.

That friendly treatment continued into the spring of 1954. Powell learned that the emperor of Ethiopia would soon visit

America. He wanted the emperor to include a stop in Harlem on his itinerary. This would require involving the State Department officials who were handling the details of the trip. Powell asked Rabb to intercede. He did, telling the State Department that Powell had been "most friendly and has made speeches in favor of the president." The trip to Harlem was approved. Powell's strategy of co-opting the White House was working.

Rabb thought it was working for the White House, too. He was growing more comfortable in his relationship with Powell. He was pleased with a speech that Powell had made that spring in Chicago, where he had spoken favorably of the Republican in the White House. So pleased, in fact, that he asked the editors at *Reader's Digest* to consider having Powell write an article about Eisenhower and civil rights. Stanley High, the magazine's senior editor, told Rabb that it was a "grand suggestion."[30] The piece, entitled, "The President and the Negro," ran in the October 1954 issue. It was classic Powell. With breathless excitement in his words, he described the "silent revolution" on race relations being ushered in by Ike. He approvingly quoted a black paper, the *Chicago Defender*, which had praised the president for acting "not so much from a political motive, but more from the deep-seated moral and spiritual convictions" he possessed. And Powell concluded by observing that Eisenhower was proving to be "president of all the people."

Rabb was ecstatic. In a cover note he sent to Ann Whitman, he called the piece "wonderful." Then, knowing of her constant, daily conversations with Eisenhower, he planted a thought in her mind. "Ann," he wrote, "we have underplayed what the president has done from a publicity sense far too much." Whitman agreed. In a response, she wrote that the president had read it but that she "wasn't there, no comment to report." But if she was uncertain about his reaction, her own feelings mirrored Rabb's enthusiasm. The Powell piece was "wonderful."[31]

In some ways, Rabb was operating on a parallel track with Brownell. They were on different paths but both headed toward the same destination. Both were broadly supportive of civil rights. And both wanted Eisenhower to play a bigger role in the unfolding drama of race relations. But knowing their boss's cautious view on the subject, they both engaged in attempts to create some momentum in the hope that Ike would eventually join in. Brownell did it when he nudged Ike forward on the amicus brief in the *Brown* case. Rabb did it by getting Powell to say and write words of approval about the president. Brownell with the legal track, and Rabb with the political track, hoped to galvanize the administration.

And yet, as president, Eisenhower still had not held a meeting with Powell. In a way, both men needed and used each other. It was a relationship of necessity. And it would be sorely tested as the nation grappled with the consequences of *Brown*.

◇

Like all successful armies, the civil rights community sought to exploit its victory with another advance. If segregation was illegal in schools, wasn't it also illegal in interstate commerce? After all, interstate commerce is a federal issue. The Eisenhower Department of Justice agreed. A letter that had been written by Deputy Attorney General William Rogers and sent to the House Interstate and Foreign Commerce Committee seemed to support legislation that would ban such segregation. When Ethel Payne, of the *Chicago Defender,* brought the matter to Ike's attention at his July 7th press conference, Eisenhower responded that "these opinions were sent down…as part of the administration belief, because we think it just and right." Yet he didn't personally say what he thought of the opinion, and his tone was more one of irritation than of sympathy.[32]

Ike had always warned that change could only happen over time. Now, he feared that too much was happening too quickly. Indeed, in the days and weeks that followed the *Brown* decision, Chief Justice Warren listened in vain to hear an endorsement from the White House. It never came. He and his staff concluded that Ike's silence spoke quite eloquently about his views. "Dwight Eisenhower was just completely opposed to the segregation decision and the chief justice knew that," was how Warren's secretary, Margaret McHugh, remembered it.[33]

Warren's relationship with Eisenhower had already deteriorated beyond repair. This likely clouded the chief justice's judgment of presidential motives and methods. Warren, perhaps
quite impressed with the opinion that he had written and with
the unanimous vote that he had orchestrated, could not imagine
how anyone could disagree. In his mind it must have seemed that
only one reason could be behind Eisenhower's muted public
voice: He must have opposed desegregation of schools.

But in politics, as in life, the truth is always more complicated
and more interesting than that. Black and white issues often fade
into shades of gray. In many ways, Eisenhower was exactly what
his critics on the right said he was not: a conservative. Not in the
conventional, 1950s sense of the term. He did not oppose NATO.
And he did not seem eager to repeal New Deal legislation such as
Social Security or the FDIC. But personally, culturally, and temperamentally, he was conservative.

Ironically, in the first year of Ike's presidency, scholar Russell
Kirk exhumed Edmund Burke from his grave and brought him to
life in a book called *The Conservative Mind*. In it, Kirk told American
conservatives that they should look to the eighteenth-century British statesman for inspiration. One of the interesting attributes of
Burke's legacy is that he espoused a set of broad principles, but
refrained from endorsing a specific ideology. That is, Burke didn't
have a conservative philosophy so much as he had a conservative
mindset. He saw conservatism not as an agenda of issues but as an
approach with which to deal with issues as they developed.

Perhaps the most illuminating example of this contrast was
Burke's open mind on the American Revolution, as compared to
his hardened anger with the French Revolution. Burke believed
that the Americans had a specific complaint—taxation without
representation. He also believed that their complaint had merit.
In contrast, he viewed French revolutionaries as dangerous radi-
cals with a broader, metaphysical goal—equality of all men—
that could never be satisfied. The Americans fought for political
freedom. The French fought for a philosophical equality. Thus,
Burke was considerate of the former and unalterably opposed to
the latter.

Eisenhower, though he might not have been a political conservative, was certainly a personal one. Like Burke, he believed in "organic evolution," the idea that change happens over time, step by step. When Burke spoke of the "wisdom of the ancients," he cautioned that decades and centuries of tradition and reverence for institutions should not be disregarded overnight. Like a coral reef, society is built up over centuries, eventually becoming a wave-resistant sanctuary for life.

The leaders of the civil rights movement were not Burkeans. As the pace of their legal victories accelerated, they grew in confidence and were disinclined to slow the pace. Here is the heart of the historical debate between liberalism and conservatism—revolution or evolution? Freedom or equality? And it was the very essence of the civil rights debate in the 1950s.

In confronting the challenge of civil rights, Eisenhower hoped to promote freedom. In desegregating the military and the District of Columbia, he wanted to give all Americans the freedom to compete in a free society. In the *Brown* decision, the Supreme Court sought to promote equality. Having the freedom to attend a well-funded public school was not good enough, the Court had ruled. Separate was still unequal.

As 1954 began to wind down, the fault lines on civil rights politics were growing clearer. Ike was more concerned with opportunity, while the courts—and the civil rights community—were increasingly concerned with outcomes.

Eisenhower was the last twentieth-century president born in the nineteenth century. He had spent a career in the military, where planning and organization were stressed more than creativity and imagination. He was learning to adjust, to grow. Conservative by nature, he hoped that the advance of the civil rights movement would be gradual, allowing time for the South to change.

To that end, he hoped the second *Brown* ruling would help ease the way. "The segregation issue will, I think, become acute or tend to die out according to the character of the procedure orders that the Court will probably issue this winter," he wrote to his life-long friend, Swede Hazlett. "My own guess is that they will be very moderate and accord a maximum of initiative to local courts."[34]

Like all warriors, his fervent hope was that victory could be achieved with the fewest casualties possible.

CHAPTER EIGHT

THE RUMBLING

"We could have another civil war on our hands...."

—Dwight D. Eisenhower

INITIALLY, IT LOOKED like the South might gracefully accept its fate and begin the hard work of divorcing its public schools from Jim Crow. Within a week of the *Brown v. Board of Education* ruling in May 1954, several school districts, including that of Little Rock, Arkansas, indicated they indeed would accept the verdict.

But soon, an ominous rumbling could be heard gathering in the distance. In Mississippi, a new group organized, calling itself the White Citizens' Council. A similar group with a different name set up shop in Virginia. These white Southerners were not about to watch their schools desegregate. In Delaware, the resistance scored a complete victory. After two schools shut down in defiance of the *Brown* ruling, desegregation in Delaware public schools was rescinded.

Watching all of this was Thurgood Marshall. He was worried. He was upset that the Court had eschewed its typical practice of banning the procedure once it was outlawed. Instead, the Court outlawed desegregated schools but gave some time and flexibility in carrying out that order. To Marshall, the Court was asking for trouble. If segregation was wrong, it should be stopped. Why give the wily Southerners a chance to stall and regroup?

But a young lawyer named Bill Coleman helped Marshall change his mind. He told Marshall to urge the Court to "permit the gradual effective transition" into integrated schools. Marshall, having already won the big one, decided that he could be flexible. In the fall of 1954, the NAACP sent their brief to the Supreme Court. In it, Marshall and his team urged the Court to require that local integration plans be effective as of 1955. By the next year, the NAACP urged, full integration should be reached.

For their part, the Southerners submitted briefs that asked the Court to give them a maximum amount of time.

Attorney General Herbert Brownell again wanted President Eisenhower to submit a friend-of-the-court brief. He knew from previous experience that this wouldn't be easy. He challenged his staff to work up some draft language. At the same time, he warned them that no decision would be made until he had a "conference with the president, at which time we will present to him the arguments pro and con as to the filing of a brief and participation in the oral argument."

The first tip about Eisenhower's thinking on the implementation of the ruling came in a telegram that he sent to the NAACP's forty-fifth annual meeting in the summer of 1954. "We must have patience without compromise of principle. We must have understanding without disregard for differences of opinion which actually exist." To these temporizing phrases, Ike added less-ambiguous prose: "We must have continued social progress…so that we may prove without doubt to all the world that our nation and our people are truly dedicated to liberty and justice for all."

On November 20, 1954, Eisenhower met at the White House with representatives of the Department of Justice to discuss filing a brief with the court on the implementation case. Deputy Attorney General William Rogers represented Brownell, and he was joined by Max Rabb and Simon Sobeloff, the solicitor general. Eisenhower reviewed the draft brief and personally wrote his own edits in the margins. On page 8, he expressed his concern over the implementation of the *Brown* ruling. He wanted the brief to stress that segregation, though wrong, had "existed a long time in many areas throughout the country." Eisenhower then added his own unique twist on the NAACP argument that segregation stunted the emotional development of black children. "In similar fashion emotions are involved in the alterations that must now take place" throughout the South, he suggested. On page 19, the Department of Justice recommended the phrase "Racial segregation in public schools is unconstitutional and will have to be terminated as quickly as possible." Eisenhower instead recommended the word "feasible" rather than "possible." With these suggested changes, Eisenhower gave his blessing for the brief to be submitted.[1]

The day before it was filed, Eisenhower hosted his weekly press conference. Harry Dent, of the *Columbia State and Record,* asked the president whether he had any personal preferences on the way the case should be decided. "Not particularly," Eisenhower responded. He also was vague about the amicus brief that he had authorized, saying that the "attorney general is required to file his brief." He then reiterated his concern as the case went forward. "I am sure America wants to obey the Constitution, but there is a very great practical problem involved, and there are certainly deep-seated emotions." He urged the Court to "take into consideration these great emotional strains and the practical problems."[2]

Eisenhower was in a bind. He was sworn to enforce the law. But he wanted to do so in a way that didn't antagonize millions of Southerners. It is estimated that, after the first *Brown* ruling, eighty percent of his mail came from Southern and border states and that most of it expressed opposition to the ruling. For a man who prided himself on being the typical American, this was a leadership challenge unlike any he had ever faced. The law was in one place. The people were in another. How could Ike be in two places at once?

He would emphasize the principles of a lifetime: cooperation, consensus, and gradual change. Above all, by focusing on the Cold War, he hoped to remind Americans that they were all playing on the same team. The Soviets, not the Southerners, were the enemy.

On November 24th, 1954, the Eisenhower administration submitted its brief, which urged that each school district be required to submit an integration plan to a local federal court. It also proposed that these plans be submitted within ninety days. At the conclusion of the ninety-day period, once plans were approved by the local courts, the Executive Branch would assume enforcement responsibilities.

Here was the latest triumph of Brownell's subtle diplomacy with Ike. In August, Eisenhower had been asked at a press conference whether he would support legislation giving him the authority to enforce the *Brown* ruling. Perhaps reflecting his innately conservative view of the role of the federal government, Ike responded that the "subject has not even been mentioned to me." But if he didn't support legislation to put his administration in charge of enforcement, he had now filed a court briefing that would have the same effect.

Not everyone was impressed with the briefing. Though he publicly said nice things about the Eisenhower proposal, Thurgood Marshall was not pleased. "Between you and me," he said to publisher Carl Murphy, "it stinks."[3]

<><

The oral arguments on what would become known as *Brown II* began on April 11th, 1955. The distant rumbling in the South in the months after the first *Brown* ruling was now growing into a tremor that was about to shake the Supreme Court itself.

The Southern states now abandoned the soft, grandfatherly tones of John W. Davis for the heated rhetoric that more closely resembled John C. Calhoun. Lawyers for the South made threats poorly disguised as speeches. Having lost the first case, they were reduced to fighting a guerrilla battle to protect their way of life by warning of dire consequences should integration be forced on them. Once again, nullification—the Calhounian belief that an individual state could disregard a federal law—became the dagger aimed at the Court's jurisprudence.

When Chief Justice Warren asked one lawyer whether the people of the South would "immediately undertake to conform to the opinion of this Court," he was startled by the response.

"Mr. Chief Justice," replied Clarendon County, South Carolina attorney S. Emory Rogers, "to say we will conform depends on the decree handed down." When Warren challenged him on this, Rogers cautioned, "I would have to tell you right now we would not conform." Nothing in his long career had prepared

Warren for so brazen a moment of insurrection in the nation's highest court. He was stunned to hear a lawyer come before the bench and tell the Court that the South would probably just ignore the law. Warren was so speechless he could only end the exchange with Rogers by saying, "Thank you."[4]

But the approach of the Southern lawyers may have worked. When the justices met later to consider their ruling, Warren announced that he opposed imposing a fixed deadline for the Southern states to implement desegregated schools. The Court's resident Southern expert, Hugo Black, agreed: "The less we say, the better off we all are."[5]

A few days later, Warren wrote out the ruling in his own hand. After it was typed up and edited by the other justices, it was ready to be delivered. On May 31st, 1955, Warren read the opinion, which called for district courts to "enter such orders and decrees consistent with this opinion as are necessary and proper to admit to public schools on a racially nondiscriminatory basis with all deliberate speed the parties to these cases."

Proponents of desegregation were upset; specifically, with the phrase "with all deliberate speed." It was Justice Felix Frankfurter who suggested the phrase, which he had borrowed from an Oliver Wendell Holmes ruling decades earlier. It proved to be an unfortunate word choice that would exacerbate, rather than help solve, the dilemma.

Had Warren blinked? Having heard the words of nullification from the Southern lawyers, had he backed down? It does seem that the chief justice carefully considered the threats and realized that any real change on segregation would take time. Ironically, this was exactly the view of the man in the White House. Even more ironic, the Warren Court's ruling in *Brown II* was much softer and less definite than the Eisenhower brief orchestrated by Attorney General Brownell.

To be sure, the ruling tracked closely to the Eisenhower proposal, up to a point. The Court called for giving the power of enforcement to the federal district courts. But where the Eisenhower brief had called for a period of "ninety days" for the school districts to respond with a plan for integration, the Warren Court merely suggested "all deliberate speed." No explicit role was carved out for the Executive Branch in enforcement. In essence, the Court told the people of the South to desegregate their schools and to take their time. How this would be achieved and enforced was unclear.

Warren may have thought that he had struck the right tone. Almost no one else agreed. Marshall vowed in a press conference that any school district that didn't get about the business of desegregating might face an NAACP lawsuit. This was the new frontier in the landscape of desegregation. Having won in the Supreme Court, the NAACP would push individual school districts throughout the South to get moving on desegregation.

For his part, Ike didn't think much of the ruling, either. "Eisenhower was annoyed at *Brown II*," Brownell recalled, "as I was, which left 'all deliberate speed' without limitations. Ike felt he had been left out on a limb."[6]

It was, in many ways, the worst of all worlds for Ike. The Court had taken a fundamentally local issue and federalized it, thus violating his innate sense of limited powers for the national government. Then, rather than providing a specific set of orders for carrying out their ruling, the Court seemed to invite chaos and confusion by merely suggesting "all deliberate speed." Yes, Eisenhower had told friends that he hoped the Court would provide time to implement the decision. But his orderly mind was likely confused by the implementation ruling of the Court. His military sense of events, timing, and battlefield strategy likely heightened his fears that his overriding domestic goal—national unity—would soon be undone. *Brown II* seemed a perfect predicate for more trouble in the South.

◇

He was a bright, handsome youth, just fourteen years old. Brash and sure of himself, he loved to tease and wasn't easily intimidated. Hailing from the south side of Chicago, he traveled to visit some relatives near the town of Money, Mississippi, in August of 1955. His name was Emmett Till.

Emmett wasn't afraid to head southward, but his mother was scared enough for both of them. Unlike her son, Mamie Bradley had lived in Mississippi. She knew the toxic air that black Mississippians were forced to breathe every day. Before her son left, she gave him some advice: "If you have to get on your knees and bow when a white person goes past, do it willingly."

On August 24th, Emmett and his cousin, Curtis Jones, drove into town to Bryant's Grocery and Meat Market. To several other black kids at the front of the store, Emmett bragged that he had a white girlfriend back home in Chicago. When one of the other black kids spotted a white girl inside, he issued a challenge to young Emmett: "Hey, there's a [white] girl in that store there. I bet you won't go in there and talk to her."

Emmett accepted the challenge. He entered the store. As he left, he looked back at Carolyn Bryant: "Bye, Baby." An older black gentleman, perched behind a checkerboard on the front porch of the store, was horrified. He warned Emmett to leave immediately before he was killed. As the boys drove off in their car, Bryant came out of the store to get a good look at them.

For the next few days, nothing happened, and the boys assumed that the storm had passed. But in the early morning hours of August 28th, a knock was heard on the door of Mose Wright's cabin. Mose was Emmett's uncle and was hosting his nephew from up North.

The visitors told Mose that they were looking for the "boy who done the talking." As they dragged the terrified boy out of his bed, the men threatened his uncle.

"How old are you, preacher?" they asked Mose.

"Sixty-four."

"If you cause any trouble, you'll never live to be sixty-five." Mose duly acceded to their requests. He didn't call the police that night. Instead, he waited until the next day to call for help. Three days later, a bludgeoned body was found in the Tallahatchie River. It was Emmett Till, or what remained of him. His head held a bullet, an eye had been poked out, and his forehead had been smashed. For added effect, barbed wire was wrapped around the boy's neck, tying him to a cotton-gin fan. So badly decomposed was the body that Mose Wright could only identify it by noticing the initials "ET" on a ring still circling the boy's finger.

The body was shipped back to Chicago, where Emmett's grieving mother bravely declared that there would be an open-casket funeral. She wanted America to see what unchecked racism could do. "Have you ever sent a loved son on vacation and had him returned to you in a pine box," Mamie Bradley asked, "so horribly battered and water-logged that someone needs to tell you this sickening sight is your son—lynched?"[7]

Thousands waited in line to view Emmett Till. Thousands more returned for the funeral on September 3rd. The picture of the beaten body ran in black publications, outraging those who saw it. The civil rights movement had a martyr.

The blood of the innocent boy only fueled more momentum for the movement nationwide. But back in Mississippi, two men, Roy Bryant, the husband of the woman at the store, and J.W. Milam, were arrested and charged with murder. The state's pretense of justice fooled no one. The only righteous moment of the trial came when Mose Wright courageously took the stand to confront the two murderers. When asked by the prosecutor whether he could identify the murderers, the old man raised his finger and pointed it at Milam. "Thar he," he told the court, and then went on to identify Bryant as well.[8]

After a one-hour deliberation, the all-white jury returned a verdict of "not guilty." "We wouldn't have taken so long if we hadn't stopped to drink pop," a jury member said later. The trial was a huge media event. Millions followed the proceedings. All across America, people were talking about the judicial outrage that had just occurred in Mississippi.

Nor were the defendants content to fade away with their court exonerations. They were ready for a victory lap. With many white Southerners cheering them on, Bryant and Milam agreed to tell the real story to a reporter for $4,000. "What else could we do?" Milam asked the reporter, William Bradford Huie. "I never hurt a nigger in my life," he said in an attempt to paint himself as a sympathetic murderer. Still, he had to act because "I like niggers in their place." A society that was beginning to desegregate, especially its schools, was too much for men like Bryant and Milam. To them, if blacks refused to stay "in their place," then perhaps a little violence was necessary. And by targeting a black child, a stern message was sent to any black family who was eager to have their children enter white establishments.

The article, published months after the trial, showed the two men unrepentant to the point of boastfulness. Segregation was going to die hard in the South.

In Washington, political leaders were shocked by the events in Mississippi. But the White House was mysteriously silent. On September 2nd, before the trial began, Mrs. Bradley sent a telegram to the president. She asked him to "personally see that justice is meted out to all persons involved in the beastly lynching of my son." She added that she was "awaiting a direct reply from you."[9]

The Chicago Defender sent its own telegram to the White House, asking the president to "let us know if your office has plans to take any action with reference to this shocking act of lawlessness."

Curiously, Ike responded to the *Defender* but not to Mrs. Bradley. William Barba, a presidential aide, wrote back to the *Defender*, explaining the limits on what the Department of Justice could do. "We are advised that the Department of Justice has been in close contact with the development of this case, but that so far their inquiry has failed to reveal any facts which provide a basis for Federal jurisdiction."[10] In 1955, there were no federal civil rights laws that allowed Washington to be involved in local court cases. On this point, the White House was correct—there wasn't much that could be done legally.

But there was something that could be done morally. For starters, Ike could respond to Mrs. Bradley's telegram. He didn't.

How could Eisenhower have failed to sympathize, at least, with a grieving mother whose son had been the victim of a monstrous crime? The answer lies in the geopolitical environment in which Ike lived and governed. These were the days of the Cold War. Having beaten back the extremes of McCarthyism, Eisenhower still feared the influence of Communists in America. His vice president, Richard Nixon, first came to national prominence exposing the Communist affiliation of State Department official Alger Hiss.

Though Ike deplored McCarthy's tactics, he did not doubt that Communists posed a threat inside America. With this in mind, he had sponsored his own program to purge Communists from the State Department. And when Senator Hubert Humphrey proposed outlawing the Communist Party, Ike countered by signing the Communist Control Act of 1954, which revoked the citizenship of anyone who espoused violence as a means to overthrow the U.S. government.

Part of Ike's concern about domestic Communism came from information given to him by his advisors. One man in particular made sure that the president was aware of how serious a threat Communism was in America.

In 1955, J. Edgar Hoover was more powerful than ever. The first and only director of the Federal Bureau of Investigation, Hoover was renowned for his intelligence operations. A bulky figure with a pugnacious personality, he was a natural-born hater. He especially hated Communists.

The tentacles of his FBI operation reached far and wide. Such was his reputation that few challenged Hoover on his information, much less his conclusions. If Hoover said there was a problem with a certain organization or person, then it must be so.

And Hoover was convinced there was a problem with Emmett Till's mother. Within days of the murder, the FBI began sending ominous warnings to the White House. On September 6th, an FBI memo warned that the "Communist Party, USA...will launch a huge campaign protesting the killing of the 14-year-old Chicago Negro boy, Emmett Louis Till...."[11] One week later, Hoover followed up with another communiqué, this time notifying the president that the "Communist Party, USA, has instituted agitational activity in connection with the murder in Mississippi...."[12]

To learn more, Max Rabb conferred with representatives of both the Department of Justice and the FBI. The latter's Lou Nichols told Rabb that Mrs. Bradley was a "phoney." He and Warren Olney, from Justice, informed Rabb that Mrs. Bradley had fallen under the influence of Communist agents. Rabb later told Jim Hagerty that Nichols and Olney believed that Mrs. Bradley was being used by the Communists as a "prize exhibit."[13] Nichols and Olney made the "direct suggestion" that the president refrain from responding to Mrs. Bradley's telegram. Instead, the Department of Justice issued a response to a letter from William Henry Huff, an NAACP lawyer working with Mrs. Bradley.

Whether Hoover's concerns were warranted or not, it didn't change the fact that Eisenhower did not reach out to a grieving mother. To many blacks, the president's silent voice was seen as, at worst, an endorsement of the crime and, at best, complete indifference. Both of these conclusions were wrong. But only those inside the White House knew of the advice that Ike was receiving from the FBI. Even still, the president might simply have expressed his sympathy for the grieving mother. Years before, Eisenhower and Mamie had themselves lost a young child to death. He knew the heartache and could have empathized with Mrs. Bradley. That he said nothing was a mistake that would haunt him for years.

<>

On September 23rd, 1955, the president, vacationing in Denver, sent a note to the Senate Majority Leader, Lyndon Baines Johnson. LBJ had recently suffered a heart attack, and Ike urged him not to "try to do too much too quickly."[14]

Early the next morning, Ike was awakened by a sharp pain in his chest. His groaning woke Mamie. "Are you having a nightmare?" she asked.

"No dear," he responded. "But thank you." Yet, the pain wouldn't end. It then got worse. Mamie called for help. At 3:00 a.m., the president's doctor, Howard Snyder, arrived in their bedroom. Snyder incorrectly diagnosed acute indigestion. To comfort the patient, the doctor ordered Ike's longtime valet, Sergeant Moaney, to massage the president using a warm rubbing alcohol. The next morning, Dr. Snyder insisted on performing an EKG test and taking the president to the Fitzsimons Army Hospital. The results of the test changed the doctor's mind. The president had suffered a heart attack.

As Eisenhower got the news, he was typically upbeat and in control. His mind, still fully functioning, thought back to President Wilson. When Wilson had been stricken by a stroke in 1919, his wife had taken charge, and the public had not been fully informed about the president's illness. Eisenhower instructed his press secretary to take the opposite approach: "Tell the truth, the whole truth; don't try to conceal anything." He also gave orders that regular Cabinet meetings continue as scheduled, with Vice President Nixon presiding.

Soon, Eisenhower's health began to improve. His smoking habit had been abandoned years before, on the orders of doctors. And he was still a relatively healthy, active man. The day before his heart attack, he had played golf. His vigor and stamina served him well as he fought to recover from the heart attack.

Still, for the next several weeks, Eisenhower would have to slow down his routine. Meanwhile, events paused for no one.

◇

The seams of the established order in the South were beginning to grow weak from years of resistance. The civil rights revolution continued to grow in the South. But white Southerners were increasing their opposition, too.

One particularly disturbing case took place in Hoxie, Arkansas. Considered a more enlightened Southern state than Mississippi or Alabama, Arkansas was a bellwether for ways in which reasonable people of the South would respond to desegregation.

Hoxie appeared to be moving along smoothly. There, the school board, in compliance with the *Brown* rulings, had begun allowing both white and black students to attend the same school in the summer of 1955. (This being a cotton area, school was offered in the summer so that kids could harvest in the fall.) All went well until *Life* magazine ran a feature on the desegregated education that Hoxie was now offering.

White supremacists in Arkansas erupted. White parents, made nervous, began withdrawing their children from school. Finally, the school board itself surrendered and closed all schools before the term was up. Curiously, the governor of Arkansas was largely silent. Orval Faubus was known to be sympathetic to civil rights, while his likely opponent in the next Democratic primary, Jim Johnson, was plenty hot about the mess in Hoxie.

But Faubus refused to take the bait. Sounding a little like the president, he deemed the events in Hoxie a local matter beyond his control. As it happened, the president was on the governor's mind in those days. He was proud to have served in the Thirty-Fifth Infantry in Europe during World War II. Like millions of other Americans, he worried about Ike's health in the wake of the heart attack. In September, Orval Faubus wrote to Ike to express his concern.

<>

On December 1st, 1955, a small, attractive woman, her dark hair pulled back and glasses resting on her nose, left her shift at the Montgomery Fair department store. Arriving at her bus stop soon afterward, she boarded the bus and took a seat in the section reserved for black passengers. When the white section filled up, the bus driver asked her to move. She refused. The police came and arrested her. It became an instant news story. Thus the nation was introduced to the quiet courage of Rosa Parks.

Centuries of frustration had long simmered just beneath the surface in the black community. Righteous anger at the indignities that Jim Crow imposed could no longer be contained. In Rosa Parks, millions of black Americans found a soulmate of resistance.

In Montgomery, mass meetings were held to decide how best to oppose the segregated bus policies. A strategy was chosen. Battle lines were drawn. The Montgomery Bus Boycott was born.

More important, a leader was chosen—his name was Martin Luther King, Jr. The young preacher who had studied the philosophy of Thoreau and the tactics of Ghandi in graduate school was now ready to lead his own movement of civil disobedience. The man and the mission had found their moment.

In Washington, politicians of all stripes were closely watching this dynamic, new force that King was leading in Montgomery. No one had ever seen anything like it—mass meetings, organized carpools, direct negotiations with city leaders. Before the eyes of the nation, the civil rights movement took shape.

Polls showed that strong majorities of Northerners and Westerners supported desegregation but didn't have to deal with it, while strong majorities of Southerners opposed it and confronted it every day. Since Southerners were a small part of the overall population, the result was that most national polls showed a majority in favor of desegregation, while the intensity level on the topic was largely confined to the South. A Gallup Poll released in the summer of 1955 showed that while the president was still enormously popular, one of the complaints about him was that he "encourages segregation."[15]

The poll outraged Max Rabb. In large part, he blamed the White House. "We have been more than tender in soft-pedaling our accomplishments," he wrote. "Perhaps it is time to give some serious thought to this whole problem."[16]

The Montgomery Bus Boycott was custom-made for the White House. By merely sympathizing with the boycotters, Ike could have shown the country that Brownell had been right all along—his heart was in the right place.

But by doing so, Ike would have alienated the millions of Southerners who were already quite worked up about the issue. And since Eisenhower saw himself as almost a Roman-style tribune, his ultimate desire was to bring people together, to be one of them, to be one with them. The more he said, the more likely he was to inflame passions on both sides.

And so the president was quiet as 1956 began, and the Montgomery Bus Boycott gained momentum. Around the same time, a black student named Autherine Lucy tried to enroll at the University of Alabama in Tuscaloosa, north of Montgomery. The school suspended her from attending classes "for her safety." On February 8th, Ike was asked about Lucy in a press conference. "I would certainly hope that we could avoid any interference with anybody else as long as that state, from its governor on down, will do its best to straighten it out," he responded.[17]

Privately, Ike's words were much more sympathetic. The subject of the Montgomery Bus Boycott came up during a Cabinet meeting. The president announced that he was "much impressed with the moderation of the Negroes in Alabama."[18] He later talked about what he called the "two big mistakes" that white Southerners had made.[19] They should have admitted Autherine Lucy to the

University of Alabama, and they should have tried to reasonably meet the demands of the Montgomery protestors.

Though he clearly saw what was transpiring in the South and correctly guessed that the South had misplayed its hand, he still could not bring himself to comment publicly. "Well, you are asking me, I think, to be more of a lawyer than I certainly am," he said to Robert Spivack of the *New York Post* during a press conference that spring. "But, as I understand it, there is a state law about boycotts, and it is under that kind of thing that these people are being brought to trial." When Rowland Evans of the *New York Herald Tribune* asked about rumors that blacks might actually vote for a Republican in the upcoming election, Ike offered a philosophical view. He claimed that categories mattered not at all to him, not "geographically or racially or religiously." Instead, he simply said, "I am for America."[20]

◇

Despite the rulings of the Supreme Court, Eisenhower still viewed education as a local concern. But the ripples of the Court's ruling were about to impact even the small federal jurisdiction over education.

Early in 1956, Eisenhower confronted the need for more schools. Thanks to the post war baby-boom, the population of America's cities was burgeoning. Millions of kids were approaching school age. There weren't nearly enough schools for them. Eisenhower's plan was to spend more than a billion dollars in poor areas to build new schools. The money, which the states would match, was a major federal investment in a local issue. Though Eisenhower supported local control of schools, he did see a national-security reason to help build more schools. Eisenhower saw the classroom as an important front in the Cold War.

Sensing a new opportunity to be seen, Congressman Adam Clayton Powell soon reappeared. He wanted to amend the administration's legislation so that it would deny school-construction funds to states that refused to implement the *Brown* ruling. Eisenhower was sympathetic but not committed. In a meeting with Republican leaders, he admitted that the Powell amendment would mean the end of his education initiative because Southern Democrats would "filibuster it to death." Yet, he didn't see how anyone could object, on principle, to the amendment because "in view of the Supreme Court decision, a vote against Powell would seem to be a vote against the Constitution."[21]

Eisenhower was still trying to find a balance on race issues. Around the same time he sent to Congress his newest plans for school construction, Ike suggested that a bipartisan commission be established to examine race relations and make recommendations. What better way to bring people together than to create a forum where grievances were aired, differences resolved, and a consensus reached?

His plans were idealistic and somewhat naïve. Attorney General Brownell realized this. He saw the insurrection brewing in the South. "In the wake of the *Brown* decision, I turned my attention to the enforcement of civil rights," Brownell wrote. "I soon concluded that federal laws and appropriations were completely inadequate for effecting the civil rights promises of equal protection under the Fourteenth Amendment."[22]

Brownell later wrote that his desire to pursue new civil rights legislation stemmed from the "strategy of the Southern segregationist forces," which became clear in early 1956. In March, the "Southern Manifesto" was issued by more than a hundred members of Congress: "We pledge ourselves to use all lawful means to bring about a reversal of this decision [*Brown*] which is contrary to the Constitution and to prevent the use of force in its implementation." At his weekly press conference, the president reminded reporters that "the people who have this deep emotional reaction on the other side were not acting over these past three generations in defiance of law. They were acting in compliance with the law as interpreted by the Supreme Court."

In other words, *Brown* was a lot different from *Plessy,* and the South would need time to adjust. Ike praised the authors of the Southern Manifesto for vowing to "use every legal means" and said that "no one in any responsible position anywhere has talked nullification."[23] On another occasion, Ike reiterated his favorite themes of patience and evolution: "As far as I am concerned, I am for moderation, but I am for progress."[24]

That March, J. Edgar Hoover delivered to the Cabinet a presentation on the volatile climate in the South. Dark clouds were gathering on the horizon, Hoover suggested. And they came from both directions. He criticized both the White Citizens Council and the NAACP. Indeed, he appeared to see a moral equivalence between the two organizations. When the FBI Director finished, Ike voiced concern that Communists were attempting to "drive a wedge between the Administration and its friends in the South...."[25]

After the melodrama of Hoover, Brownell supplied a heavy dose of reality. The attorney general told the president and his Cabinet that no civil rights laws had been passed since Reconstruction. It was time to change that. He outlined his bill that, among other things, would: fulfill Ike's wish for a bipartisan commission with the power to subpoena and investigate civil rights crimes; create a new assistant attorney general in the Department of Justice to deal exclusively with civil rights; empower the attorney general to sue individuals suspected of obstructing civil rights; and establish new protections on voting rights.

Eisenhower expressed support for the plan. His Cabinet was less convinced. George Humphrey sounded an ominous note. Noting that the whole conversation had centered on the Southern region, the Treasury Secretary worried that "your worst problems can come in Detroit, Chicago, et al."

"I'm at sea on all this," Ike responded. "I want to put something forward that I can show as an advance." Still, though he liked Brownell's proposal, he was mindful of Hoover's presentation. "We could have another civil war on our hands" if the White House were to move too quickly or do too much to promote civil rights. "They come in and say I should force the university to accept Miss Lucy," he moaned.[26] Though Ike was sympathetic, he had refused to intervene on her behalf. That was a decision for the people of Alabama.

After the Cabinet meeting, Brownell learned from Max Rabb that the president would support all but section three of the Brownell proposal. This was the piece providing the attorney general with broad, new powers to pursue injunctive relief against individuals who obstructed civil rights. The most radical piece of the plan, it tripped the wire of Eisenhower's caution. One of Ike's primary goals was to calm passions on both sides. He feared that the South would not take kindly to the Department of Justice suing people for discrimination. And revealingly, in a replay of the *Brown* briefs and the writing of the GOP platform, Ike insisted that Brownell present the bill to Congress as a Department of Justice proposal, not a White House proposal.

Brownell, as always, followed orders but also his conscience. When he went to Capitol Hill to testify in support of the three proposals that Ike had approved, he did so on behalf of the Department of Justice. He also knew that questions about whether the bill should include a provision authorizing the Department of Justice to sue were likely to be raised. And so, he took with him to the hearing proposed legislation on the attorney general's enforcement powers. When Congressman Kenneth Keating of New York asked whether he had any recommendations on strengthening the attorney general's enforcement powers, Brownell handed him the draft legislation. By the time the Judiciary Committee had voted on the entire package, all four sections of the plan that Brownell had first proposed before the Cabinet were included. The attorney general had done what the president had asked him to do; he had also done what he thought was right.

It didn't matter. Like every civil rights proposal since Reconstruction, the bill was buried in the Senate wasteland of committee hearings and threats of filibusters. Yet Eisenhower would campaign in 1956 as a supporter of the bill, including the enforcement section he had earlier worried about.

He did a lot of worrying that spring. He was still sensitive to the concerns of white Southerners. He retold to Republican leaders a joke that his Augusta golfing buddy, Bobby Jones, had shared with him. Jones claimed that a black man had told him: "If someone doesn't shut up around here, particularly these Negroes from the North, they're going to get a lot of us niggers killed!"[27] Still, in the same conversation, Ike complained bitterly about Southern Democrats opposing his civil rights bill even though they had never even read it. At this stage, Ike was guilty not of being on the side of the segregationists, but rather of thinking that segregationists and civil rights advocates were cut from the same cloth. He saw both sides as too emotional, too unreasonable, and too unwilling to sit down and work something out.

Eisenhower, like the cottonwood trees in his hometown of Abilene, could sway from the gusts on both sides. But he was still deeply rooted in the ground and determined not to bend too far either way.

As the spring wore on, Eisenhower continued to say little about the events in the South. But the hidden hand of his presidency could be felt in Montgomery. There, the grassroots organization formed in the aftermath of the Rosa Parks arrest called itself the Montgomery Improvement Association. One of the key figures in the movement was a bright, young lawyer named Fred Gray. Most important, his legal analysis and strategy served to keep Dr. King out of jail.

To cripple the MIA, the local Montgomery draft board decided to induct Gray into the Army. But the Eisenhower administration intervened. The director of the National Selective Service System, General Lewis B. Hershey, overruled various attempts to draft Gray. Furious, members of the draft board in Montgomery blamed the White House for "political interference."[28] One local judge was so angry at the administration that he resigned in protest. His name was George Corley Wallace.

◇

A familiar, if distinct, face could be seen around the White House in 1956. Fred Morrow, the young, African-American lawyer who had challenged Ike on the campaign train about his civil rights views, was now the first black to ever serve on a president's executive staff. He had started the summer before. And he immediately ran into problems. None of the white secretaries wanted to type for him. But Morrow was a problem-solver. He found some willing staff and got about the job of helping the president on civil rights.

And it was a big job. One of his first tasks was to encourage the White House to sympathize publicly with the family of Emmett Till. In a memo, Morrow fretted that failure to speak out would reinforce the average black person's view that the "Republican Party deserts him in crisis." Unbeknownst to Morrow, while he was recommending sympathy for the family, J. Edgar Hoover was recommending silence. Morrow lost that debate.

But he labored on. And so did Ike, in his own way. Since the president believed that laws were not enough to change people's minds, he began to think about people who could change people's minds. On March 20, 1956, Eisenhower hosted his old friend Billy Graham at the White House. The president told Graham that civil rights represented a great ministry opportunity. Ministers could use their pulpits to promote "both tolerance and progress in our race relations problems." Graham agreed. Two days later, the president, with the topic still very much on his mind, wrote a letter to Graham. In his effort to enlist Graham's involvement, Ike revealed a good deal about his fears as the country came to terms with equal rights. He wrote that ministers were well aware that the "most effective peacemaker is one who prevents a quarrel from developing, rather than one who has to pick up the pieces remaining after an unfortunate fight."[29]

Throughout his presidency, Ike had the nagging suspicion that an explosion might erupt if he didn't tread carefully. Almost alone among his advisors, he sensed that a real battle, one that might actually involve troops, could develop in the South. He had seen the protests of the 101 Southern political leaders, he had watched the violence in Montgomery, and he had read about the resistance to school segregation in places across the South.

He also believed that too much of the desegregation fight was focused on the very young. Why not start desegregation with adults? In education, this would mean starting with graduate schools and colleges and working his way down. He told Graham that he often thought of the "ease with which effective steps might be taken in the adult as compared to the juvenile field." He also wrote that he thought it would be wise to "elect a few qualified Negroes to school boards," as well as "City Commissioners" and "County Commissioners."

If Ike was convinced that graduate schools and universities should lead the way on desegregation, he had the perfect event with which to make that case—Autherine Lucy at the University of Alabama. Instead, Ike wrote that "things like that [desegregation of colleges] could properly be mentioned in a pulpit." He remained privately sympathetic, but publicly silent, about Autherine Lucy and the University of Alabama.

◇

By the summer of 1956, the eyes of the nation turned to politics. The major issue was Ike's health. After the heart attack, was he up to another four years in office? An ilcitis attack that summer only added to the public's concern. But Eisenhower was a quick recoverer. He was soon carrying on an aggressive schedule. And he seemed fit for duty.

While Republicans worried over the health of their candidate, Democrats had their own problems. By the summer, Adlai Stevenson appeared likely to get another chance as the Democrats' standard bearer.

Stevenson again would try to piece together the old New Deal coalition. But it would be even more difficult this time. With the temperature of the South rising over civil rights, Stevenson sought to cool it down a bit and reassure his base. Historian and part-time presidential advisor Arthur Schlesinger met with Stevenson in April to feel him out. Stevenson told Schlesinger that if he were to become president, his "role [would be] that of the conciliator," on racial issues. It was a "role requiring far more courage than pro-civil rights demagoguery." And, "making remarks which provoked the South would only delay the eventual achievement of the objective." Stevenson even suggested to Schlesinger the "idea of a year moratorium on all further agitation, legal action, etc., in the civil rights field."

Schlesinger tried to dissuade Stevenson. He said that civil rights was a matter of principle and that he should not let party unity come before principle. Stevenson disagreed. According to Schlesinger, Stevenson said that if principle and unity were to collide, "he was bound to stand by unity." He further shocked Schlesinger by saying he hoped the 1956 Democratic Platform could avoid mentioning the *Brown* rulings.[30]

Schlesinger was "deeply disheartened" by the meeting. "It seems evident that he does not feel any strong moral issue in the civil rights fight," Schlesinger concluded. Stevenson saw the success that Eisenhower had had in the South in 1952. He was determined not to let that happen again. He didn't want to antagonize Southern Democrats over civil rights.

As it happened, Eisenhower had problems with his own platform. On August 1st, 1956, Eisenhower met with the chairman of the Republican Platform Committee, Senator Prescott Bush of Connecticut. Bush was a tall, handsome man with a shock of flowing, brown hair and an easy, aristocratic manner. He was the quintessential East Coast Republican. He and Ike were allies and friends.

Bush told the president that the party should make a strong stand on civil rights in the platform. Eisenhower encouraged caution. The country itself would have to change before there was real equality. The platform should not promise more than he or the party could deliver, he felt.

Evidently, Bush didn't get the message. Working with input from the Department of Justice, the Platform Committee circulated draft language on civil rights. When Ike read it, he was not pleased. "What are you going to do," the president asked Deputy Attorney General William Rogers on the phone, "get an injunction against the governor of Georgia, for instance?"[31]

The next day, still worried about the civil rights plank, Ike called Herbert Brownell, who was already in San Francisco, the city hosting the party's convention. He wanted the words "Eisenhower administration" taken out of the sentence in the platform that expressed support for the *Brown* rulings. He told Brownell that he had been authorized to testify in the *Brown* case as a lawyer, not as a representative of the administration. This undoubtedly surprised Brownell, who had explicitly testified as the attorney general of the United States. Ike told Brownell that if the platform language did not change, he would not "go to San Francisco."[32]

Ike's secretary, Ann Whitman, wrote in her notes of the call that Ike felt he was "between compulsion of duty on one side, and his firm conviction, on the other, that because of the Supreme Court's ruling, the whole issue had been set back badly."[33] Later in the day, General Wilton Persons, a top White House aide and an Alabamian, told Whitman that Eisenhower objected also to the platform's use of the word "concur." Instead, Ike suggested "the Republican Party accepts" the *Brown* ruling.

Whitman also noted another conversation that she had had with her boss on the subject, in which he had said that the "troubles brought about by the Supreme Court decision were the most important problem facing the government, domestically, today."

Whitman was not one to back down. "I asked the president what alternative course the Supreme Court could have adopted." Ike responded by repeating the ideas he had discussed with Billy Graham: Desegregation should start with graduate schools, then colleges, then secondary schools.[34]

The civil rights plank in the platform was rewritten largely along the lines that Eisenhower had suggested. Two years after *Brown,* the party of Lincoln publicly "accepted" the Court's ruling even though the president privately worried about its impact.

◇

As the re-election campaign began in earnest, staff couldn't help but notice Eisenhower's mixture of sympathy for blacks and caution over how best to proceed. Emmet John Hughes was again pressed into duty writing speeches. He was still a bit gunshy. At one of their first meetings, the president vented his frustrations. "I am convinced that the Supreme Court decision set back progress in the South at least fifteen years," he told the wordsmith. "It's all very well to talk about school integration—if you remember you may be also talking about social disintegration," he added in a play on words that Hughes might have appreciated had he not so vehemently disagreed with his boss on the issue. "Feelings are deep on this, especially where children are involved," he continued, his voice and tone increasing as he talked through the issue. "You take the attitude of a fellow like Jimmy Byrnes. We used to be pretty good friends, and now I've not heard from him...all because of bitterness on this thing."

So far, Ike had given his speechwriter a pretty good summary of his practical concerns on civil rights: Desegregating schools would rile up the South, creating disunity; the courts should have started with older people rather than kids; and change would only happen gradually over time.

But he didn't stop there. Having covered his concerns over the practical impact of the ruling, he then addressed the philosophical underpinnings of it. "We can't demand perfection in these moral questions," he said, as lines of frustration creased his forehead. "All we can do is keep working toward a goal and keep it high." And then, with a trace of ominous foreshadowing in his voice, the president added: "And the fellow who tries to tell me that you can do these things by force is just plain nuts."[35]

Hughes was stunned, not so much by the words themselves, but by the "vigor and certitude" with which the president spoke.

Meanwhile, Adlai Stevenson had decided that even though he needed party unity in the South, he still needed black votes in the North. In October, the Democratic presidential candidate traveled to Harlem, where, four years earlier, Ike had laid down a blistering attack on the weakness of the Truman civil rights agenda. Now, Stevenson attacked the Republican president for his civil rights agenda. The speech was highlighted by Stevenson's adamant declaration on the *Brown* ruling: "I support this decision." But he provided precious little detail about what he would do to enforce it.

Around the same time, Eisenhower decided to take in a baseball game. On October 10th, he went to Ebbetts Field, site of Jackie Robinson's barrier-breaking game nearly ten years earlier. Ike sat in the presidential box. As his invited guest, Fred Morrow sat proudly in the box with him. The Negro press was quick to publicize stories and photos of the president sitting in the VIP box with his African-American aide. And those stories observed that Stevenson could not afford to be seen in public with a black aide without infuriating Democrats in the South.

But Eisenhower wasn't done with his outreach campaign. The very next day, he at last met with the estimable gentleman from Harlem, Congressman Adam Clayton Powell. This was a seminal, sublime moment in the congressman's career. All of his efforts to praise the president, while nudging him forward, seemed to have paid off.

Powell wasted little time in telling the president that he had no choice but to endorse him for president due to the "vacillating" that his own party was doing. Ike responded that he was "greatly honored" to be endorsed by a man "who is elected by the people." After a brief, inconclusive discussion about the Powell amendment on school construction, the congressman pledged to "lead an independent movement for the president" throughout the country during the remainder of the campaign.[36]

If Powell had hoped that Ike would be overcome with emotion and gratitude that a black Democratic congressman was endorsing him, he was wrong. Eisenhower recited his philosophy on integration: He would enforce the ruling, but it would take more than that to change hearts and minds.

Having returned home to New York, Powell astonished reporters by saying that Ike had made specific commitments to him, presumably in exchange for the endorsement. The president, according to Powell, had pledged to support a voting rights bill. He also thought that school officials who resisted integration should be arrested. And finally, reported Powell, he completely supported the Powell amendment to withhold school-construction funds from school districts that refused to desegregate. Besides, Powell added, how could he not support a president who had hired 316 blacks to administration jobs "as compared to twenty-five under the Democrats"? He couldn't help but add that on no fewer than seven occasions he had been denied a meeting with Stevenson.

The White House was outraged by Powell's recollections of the meeting. This discrepancy was astonishing, even by Powell's standards. Press Secretary Hagerty, who had been in the meeting in the Oval Office, wrote a clarification for Powell to issue publicly. In it, Powell apologized for being "inadvertently confused" about the meeting.[37]

Powell would be dogged for years by those who were angered at his endorsement of Ike. Rumors of a backroom deal to assist him with a tax investigation soon could be heard throughout the Capitol. (That Powell was later indicted by the Eisenhower Department of Justice should have rebutted those claims.)

But Powell never looked back. As promised, he hit the campaign trail, urging African-Americans to vote for the Republican president because of his civil rights record.

While Powell spoke for Ike on civil rights, the president himself said little publicly. Indeed, to some aides, he seemed concerned that perhaps his black outreach had gone too far. The night before the election, Ike sat watching a telecast of a Detroit rally in which a black speaker endorsed the president. "*That* will sure win us a lot of votes in Houston!" the president was heard to say.[38]

The next day, he won a lot of votes everywhere, including the most black votes of any Republican since before the New Deal.

◇

The fall campaign had been the backdrop for much drama that fall. Just before the election, an Anglo-French force took control of the Suez Canal, precipitating an international crisis. Ike was outraged, sensing that the lingering impulses of colonialism had motivated the actions of his World War II allies. Virtually single-handedly, he stared down the British and the French. He demanded that they withdraw their troops. It was no small measure of his power that they did.

Closer to home, another crisis with equally profound repercussions got lost in the shuffle of campaign and international news. As the school year of 1956 opened, the school district in Mansfield, Texas, prepared to allow black students to enter the local high school for the first time. Democratic governor Allan Shivers had other plans. With his finger on the pulse of the white voters of his state, Shivers sent Texas Rangers to keep the black kids out of the white school. "I defy the federal government," Shivers announced, speaking for millions across the South. "Tell the federal courts if they want to come after anyone, to come after me and cite me in this matter."

Southern resisters rejoiced in this act of defiance by Shivers, who was again supporting Ike for president. At his next press conference, the president was asked to weigh in on the matter. Eisenhower said that it was a matter for the courts to clear up. If the courts were to decide that "anyone is in contempt," Ike pondered, "I assume that it is the job of the U.S. Marshal to serve the warrants...."

He again displayed his premonition that violence could lay on the horizon if careful steps were not taken. "No one can deplore violence in this more than I do," he added. He proudly cited the example of the Louisville school system, which had, so far, dealt successfully and quietly with integration. "I read about...the Superintendent of Schools there, who, I understand, campaigned for two years in an educational program before they integrated the schools this fall. He had, so far at least, not the slightest trouble." Ike said that he hoped "to get some advice" from those in Louisville as to how they had pulled it off so well.[39]

These words were little comfort to the black families of Mansfield, Texas. They remained at a segregated and unequal school, while Allan Shivers rode a crest of praise having defied the federal government.

Eisenhower probably did not relish a political fight with a key Democratic supporter two months from the election. He was guided in this, as on all legal matters, by the advice of his attorney general. Herbert Brownell, though sympathetic to the black students in Mansfield, saw no grounds for federal intervention. "President Eisenhower or the Justice Department could not simply order a local school district to desegregate 'or else,'" he later wrote.

Rather, the president had to await the unfolding of a specific process: "the submission of a plan for desegregation to the district court, the approval of the plan, the defiance of the court-approved plan, and a request from the district court to the executive branch of the federal government to enter the proceedings and exercise its vast resources for enforcement."

In the attorney general's view, Mansfield did not meet these standards. "We were powerless to intervene," he later explained. "The local school board did not initiate an effort in the federal court that might have led...the Justice Department...to enforce the federal court's decision."

Indeed, around the same time as the Mansfield crisis, the school board in Clinton, Tennessee, followed all the steps outlined by Brownell, with the result that the Department of Justice intervened and jailed an agitator named John Kasper.

But Mansfield was different. Brownell reflected that if the Department of Justice were to step in, "We might have lost the case at the federal appeals court level (the court might have reasoned that we were exceeding our authority under *Brown II* or that we had abridged the judicial process of remedy)." Brownell essentially urged the president to pick his battles carefully. "We could not under any circumstances lose in court in any of these early cases." A legal defeat on enforcement "would have meant a grave setback to our civil rights efforts and encouraged greater resistance."[40]

As Southern resisters celebrated their victory in Texas, they might have been forgiven for misreading the cautious response in Washington. Brownell was not afraid to fight. He wanted to make sure to fight on favorable terrain.

That battle would come soon enough. But it would not be in Mansfield.

CHAPTER NINE

THE INSURRECTION

"The United States government and the governor of Arkansas were now heading toward a collision."

—Dwight Eisenhower

OUR ENEMIES ABROAD have profited greatly from the efforts of these Americans who would deny their own Constitution. No man has ever waged the battle for equality under our law in a more lawful and *Christian* way than you have."[1]

So read the letter that Dr. Martin Luther King, Jr. opened in Montgomery in January of 1957. He received countless messages; not all were so laudatory. Some included death threats. What provoked this postal cascade was his victory in the Montgomery Bus Boycott.

To the end, the city elders failed to do what the president had privately hoped they would—be reasonable. Instead, reeling from the economic losses brought about by the boycott, they sought legal relief. A specious argument was made in court—that the boycott was an unlicensed system of municipal transportation and should be declared illegal.

Eventually, the Supreme Court made it all moot. A previous lower court ruling had decreed bus segregation unconstitutional. On November 13th, one week after the Eisenhower landslide, King got his own win. He was in an Alabama courtroom for a hearing on the legality of the bus boycott when he received word of a Supreme Court ruling on the legality of segregation. The nation's highest court had upheld the lower court's ruling and essentially declared bus segregation illegal.

It was over. The seed planted by Rosa Parks a year before had blossomed into a glorious victory. It was the perfect bookend to the *Brown* ruling of two years before. Thurgood Marshall, pursuing a legal strategy, had struck a mighty blow against segregation in schools. Now, Martin Luther King, pursuing a political and even public-relations strategy, had landed a blow against segregation in public transportation.

The civil rights movement was a force to be reckoned with. In Marshall, it had a great lawyer who could persuade courts of law. In King, it had a great communicator, organizer, and leader who could persuade the court of public opinion. It was a powerful one-two combination that had segregationists on the ropes.

Almost overnight, King became a national celebrity. People had paid attention to him before, mainly as a novelty. Few dreamed that he could actually take on the city of Montgomery and win. Now, he was a national figure who appeared on the cover of *Time* and on *Meet the Press*.

It was this newfound celebrity that brought about the gracious letter praising him for pursuing civil rights "in a more lawful and *Christian* way." It came from Clare Boothe Luce (the wife of *Time* founder Henry Luce), who was both the first woman to serve as a U.S. ambassador and an Eisenhower appointee. Her letter went on to speak to her experience as ambassador to Italy: "No day passed but the Italian Communists pointed to events in our South to prove that American democracy was a 'capitalistic myth.'…"

King shared her concern that segregation exposed America to charges of hypocrisy overseas. But he also harbored the hope that his native land was changing, albeit too slowly for him. The signs were unmistakable: The country was waking from its moral hibernation and beginning to grapple with race in important, if subtle, ways.

◇

Around the same time that King arrived in Montgomery in 1954 to serve as the minister at Dexter Avenue, a young man walked into Sam Phillips's office in Memphis. Phillips operated a small, regional record company that bore the label *Sun Records*. With a shrewd sense of trends and timing, he looked out over the landscape of the music scene in the early 1950s and was instinctively attracted to black sounds. The rhythms of the Mississippi Delta, combined with the mournful soul and gospel music heard on Sunday mornings, had created a hybrid of blues and rock music that was more exciting than anything heard on white radio stations.

Phillips saw the commercial potential of the music. He undoubtedly had heard the sounds of artists like Big Mama Thornton in Memphis. But artists like Thornton were to be heard, not seen. She was six feet tall and weighed 350 pounds. More important, she was black. Although they might listen, middle-class Americans did not want to watch Big Mama sing her big hit, "Hound Dog."

Then, one day in 1954, lightening struck for Phillips when a young truck driver appeared in the *Sun Records* studios. He said he wanted to record a song for his mother. When he was asked whom he sounded like, he responded: "I don't sound like nobody." As he began performing, Phillips decided that the boy was partially right: He didn't sound like anybody *white*. But he had a remarkably black sound and groove. He was also handsome, charismatic, talented, and white.

Phillips couldn't believe his luck. Here was the solution to his problem—a white face who could sing black music. For the next two years, *Sun Records* produced and promoted young Elvis Presley all across the South. He was a sensation. Soon, the whole nation was talking about him. By 1956, Presley had signed a lucrative contract with RCA and had gone to number one on the *Billboard* charts with his version of Big Mama's "Hound Dog."

Sam Phillips's intuition had been right: White people would respond to black music as long as it was correctly packaged. Perhaps American law wasn't ready for integration, but American culture seemed to be. Jackie Robinson had been a national celebrity for more than ten years. American theatergoers saw Sidney Poitier in *Edge of the City*. At bookstores, readers bought *Invisible*

Man, black novelist Ralph Ellison's portrait of a nameless black man's journey.

Culture is often a leading indicator for politics. By the spring of 1957, it was clear that black culture was entering the popular mainstream on the radio, in the theater, and even on the bookshelves. But it was still far from clear how willing America was to embrace the change. For many white Americans, listening to an Elvis record was one matter. Having their children sit next to black kids in school was another.

School desegregation remained a volatile issue in the South. By 1957, eight Southern legislatures had passed resolutions that were tantamount to nullification. James Kilpatrick, who had succeeded Ike's friend Douglas Southall Freeman as editor of the *Richmond News Leader*, spoke for millions across the South when he wrote of nullification: "This right rests in the incontrovertible theory that ours is a union of sovereign states, that the Federal government exists only by reason of a solemn compact among the states...." Evidently, Kilpatrick was unaware that a civil war had been fought to settle that very issue.

But the fierce cry of protest masked an emerging reality: The resisters were losing. They were losing in the courts as Marshall and King continued to beat them back. And they were losing in the public square as their kids listened to rock and roll and cheered black athletes.

Like their Confederate ancestors of a century earlier, the defiant Southerners realized that victory was slipping away. But even a beaten army can still wage a potent counterattack.

Ominous, dark clouds could now be seen gathering on the horizon. It would only be a matter of time before the storm would break.

<>

As Eisenhower began his second term, an unlikely visitor provided a glimpse of life backstage, behind the curtain. The outsider was a young, promising novelist who had been called upon to help write a speech for the president. "[T]he White House was as serene as a resort hotel out of season," Gore Vidal later wrote. "The corridors were empty. In the various offices of the Executive (wings contiguous to the White House proper) quiet gray men in waistcoats talked to one another in low-pitched tones." The writer, always looking for great drama, sadly decided that the "only color, or choler, curiously enough, was provided by President Eisenhower himself." The president, Vidal remembered, "scowled when he stalked the corridors...."[2]

In 1957, there was much to scowl about, particularly on the domestic front. Ike's attorney general, Herbert Brownell, was extremely concerned about what was brewing in the South. He urged the president to resubmit his civil rights legislation of the year before. Ike agreed and identified the voting rights section of the bill as its most important feature.

Eisenhower seemed genuinely interested in the bill. He might still have been "at sea" on the issue, but he was sailing with a clearer sense of direction. He had witnessed with admiration the tactics and tone of the successful Montgomery Bus Boycott. He had seen the positive results of his efforts to finish desegregating the military and to end Jim Crow in the nation's capital.

Though Ike feared that the *Brown* rulings had fueled Southern discontent, he believed that segregation was wrong and that it should end. The question was how to get there. The issue was the means, not the end. Like millions of other Americans, Eisenhower was wrestling with a seemingly intractable issue, one that had confounded even the genius of America's Founding Fathers—how to reconcile centuries of racism with the promise of freedom for all.

Ike felt that the civil rights bill sent to Congress was an important, and yet reasonable, step in the right direction. "I have said as emphatically as I know how," he told reporters in February, "that I want a civil rights bill of the character that we recommended to the Congress." In using the pronoun "we" Ike was no longer relegating the bill to the auspices of the Department of Justice. It was his bill now. "In it is nothing that is inimical to the interests of anyone. It is intended to preserve rights without arousing passions and without disturbing the rights of anybody else," he added, again striking a balance by improving the lot of minorities without enraging white Southerners. "I think it is a very decent and very needful piece of legislation."[3]

But he knew it would be an uphill struggle. He lobbied his friend Arthur Sulzberger, asking for an endorsement from *The New York Times*. Sulzberger "shamefacedly admitted, for private use only, that even he would not want his granddaughter to go to school with Negro boys."[4]

As the bill began making its way through Congress, Ike received a telegram from Dr. King. The hero of the Montgomery Bus Boycott asked the president to come to the South and use the bully pulpit to encourage racial reconciliation. He also suggested that the president convene a White House conference to discuss ways of enforcing integration. "In the absence of some early and effective remedial action we will have no moral choice but to lead a Pilgrimage of Prayer to Washington."[5]

But the bully pulpit was the last thing Ike wanted to use. "You can't legislate morality," he said to a minister after a sermon on the need for civil rights legislation.[6] Yet his civil rights bill, in a way, did just that. Better a moderate law than moralizing speeches. On civil rights, Ike relied less on the hidden hand than on a quiet voice. He wanted to turn the volume down, not up.

That summer, as Congress debated the bill, Ike monitored its prospects against a backdrop of rising tensions in the South. Privately, the president was "shocked" by the plight of blacks in the South. In particular, he was outraged that only 7,000 black Mississippians, out of 900,000, were registered to vote. Part of the reason for this, he was told, was that voting registrars were acting as gatekeepers, asking potential black voters questions like "How many bubbles are there in a bar of soap?"

Like Lincoln, Ike often used humor to make a serious point. He told Republican leaders that a young, white law student in the South had failed the bar exam on two occasions. His father, knowing how smart the boy was, was mystified. He visited the bar and demanded to know what was amiss. They showed him the test his son had failed. Then it dawned on him: "For goodness' sake you have given him the Negro examination!"[7]

The real battleground over the administration's civil rights bill, as everyone knew, would come in the Senate. The first round was won by Vice President Nixon. Sympathetic to civil rights, Nixon viewed the GOP as the party of Lincoln.

Previous civil rights bills had languished in the Senate Judiciary Committee, where Senator James Eastland of Mississippi had effectively killed them. But the youthful Nixon outmaneuvered the veteran Eastland. Acting as president of the Senate, Nixon referred the bill immediately to the full Senate, rather than to the Judiciary Committee.

It was a brilliant move, but it enraged many Democrats, not all of them Southerners. Nixon's action was a "highly questionable legislative course," Massachusetts Senator John F. Kennedy said in explaining his vote against it.[8] Kennedy, a serious contender for the Democratic vice presidential nomination in 1956, was thought to be considering a run for the presidency in 1960. To do so, he needed to appease both Southern Democrats and Northern liberals.

For now, he took cover behind procedure and Senate rules. But Kennedy could not easily hide. At just over six feet tall, his shock of brown hair and immaculate suits made him one of the most recognizable members of the Senate. His Massachusetts accent and natural grace and charm drew people to him. It also helped that he was a genuinely handsome man. People noticed him. Ironically, Kennedy was good friends with Nixon, dating back to their days in the House of Representatives.

The vice president was the point man in the fight in the Senate over the bill. Having grown up poor in California, he had no racial baggage of his own. One day at the White House, he asked Fred Morrow whether he played golf. When Morrow complained that he couldn't get on most Washington courses because of his skin, Nixon was genuinely outraged.

On June 13th, Nixon met with Martin Luther King, Jr. at the Capitol. King and Nixon had first crossed paths during independence ceremonies for the African country of Ghana. They had gotten along quite well, and Nixon had invited King to visit him in Washington. After King had finished his Prayer Pilgrimage in May, he had decided that it was time to take the vice president up on his offer. He didn't know it at the time, but King's rivals were already busy trying to discredit him with the White House. Thurgood Marshall, unwilling to yield the spotlight to the young preacher, called him a "first-rate rabble-rouser."[9] Roy Wilkins and Clarence Mitchell of the NAACP assured Max Rabb that the "entire character" of the Prayer Pilgrimage had been changed after the NAACP demanded that King refrain from attacking the president.

Nixon was either unaware of these back-channel conversations or, more likely, unconvinced by them. He had been impressed by King's measured tones in Ghana. He thought this was a man he could do business with. At their meeting in the Formal Room of the Capitol, King was joined by his aide Ralph Abernathy, while Nixon brought Labor Secretary James P. Mitchell. After photographers finished taking pictures of the four, the meeting commenced.

As was his custom, King began with a short, effective speech detailing the sad plight of blacks in the South. Gifted with the magical ability to say harsh words in soft tones, King could deliver a monologue and yet somehow convince the listener that it was a dialogue. Nixon appeared quite sympathetic. In lieu of King's longstanding request for Ike to deliver a speech to the South, the vice president suggested that King testify before the president's Committee on Government Contracts.

Ever the political strategist, Nixon also wasted no time in pointing out to King and Abernathy that they shared a common enemy—Southern Democrats. Nixon complained about the tactics of these Democrats as they sought to emasculate the president's civil rights bill. King was impressed by Nixon, yet somewhat suspicious. He later wrote that if "Richard Nixon is not sincere, he is the most dangerous man in America."[10]

◇

Later that summer, Ike began personally lobbying senators, beginning with the Senate Majority Leader. He had a cordial relationship with Texan Lyndon Baines Johnson. LBJ, a great flatterer, loved to spend time with the president and express his admiration. Ike, for his part, respected LBJ's ability and, more important, his position as the most important member of the Senate. Theirs was an alliance of convenience and necessity. They needed each other.

Johnson, a master political strategist, had arrived at one of the supreme moments of his career. His six-foot-three frame could be seen darting around the Senate floor, going to meetings, gathering votes, slapping backs. His hair was swept back tightly, exposing his cauliflower ears. His bulging nose and sad eyes were offset by his thick accent and easy charm. When talking to a senator, he would often put his hands on him, literally buttonholing him.

He also had a way of convincing whomever he was with that he was in complete agreement. When Virginia Durr, a champion of civil rights, complained to LBJ that he hadn't done enough for racial justice, the senator put his arm around her: "Honey, you're dead right! I'm all for you, but we ain't got the votes. Let's wait till we get the votes."[11]

But Johnson's real views on the matter were more complicated than that.

His earliest experiences with race had come with Hispanics in Texas. He often talked about how he had learned compassion when teaching school to Hispanic kids as a young man in Texas. Yet, he didn't always paint such an idyllic picture of his former students and neighbors. "I grew up with Mexicans," he later told a journalist. "They'll come right into your back yard and take it over if you let them. And the next day they'll be right up on your porch, barefoot and weighing one hundred and thirty pounds, and they'll take that, too. But if you say to 'em right at the start, 'Hold on, just wait a minute,' they'll know they're dealing with somebody who'll stand up. And after that, you can get along just fine."[12]

Johnson's views on blacks were also negative. Robert Parker served as bartender and waiter at LBJ's parties. He also often filled in as Johnson's chauffeur. Often, Johnson would bring other senators with him for rides in his limousine. "He especially liked to call me 'nigger' in front of Southerners and racists like Richard Russell," recalled Parker. Yet, even when he didn't have an audience, Johnson could be less than sympathetic. One day, as the senator read the paper in the back seat, he asked Parker whether he liked to be called by his name. When Parker answered that he did, Johnson exploded. "Let me tell you one thing, nigger. As long as you are black, and you're gonna be black till the day you die, no one's gonna call you by your goddamn name....Just pretend you're a goddamn piece of furniture."[13]

Johnson's philosophy was to do whatever it took to win. To liberal crowds, he spoke and acted like a liberal. In front of Southern Democrats, he made free use of racial epithets. Winning was what mattered.

His energy and talent had led him to the seat of power in the Senate. His ambitions did not end there. He was not content to be the most powerful man in the Senate. Johnson also wanted to be president.

That meant overcoming his main handicap—he was a Southerner. No Southerner, save Wilson, had been elected president since before the Civil War (and Wilson had long since relocated to New Jersey). Johnson saw opportunity in every obstacle. There was a specific way he could make himself acceptable to Northern voters—he could help pass the first civil rights legislation since Reconstruction.

But he would have to do so in a way that didn't offend his Southern base. This tightrope act required the skills of a consummate professional. And that's exactly what Johnson was. As the Senate began consideration on Ike's bill, Johnson formulated a compromise solution. He would support the bill, but he would amend the enforcement provisions to require a "trial by jury" for anyone accused of a civil rights violation. Since a "trial by jury" meant a trial by other white Southerners, there was little chance that any Southerner would be convicted.

It was a brilliant tactical move. Johnson could claim that he supported the first civil rights law of the twentieth century. He could also wink at Southerners who knew that the trial-by-jury provision rendered the bill impotent.

Still, many Southern Democrats opposed the bill in any form. Georgia's Richard Russell predicted that it would lead to "the whole might of the federal government, including the armed forces if necessary, to force a commingling of white and Negro children." When Eisenhower was asked about these comments at a July 3rd press conference, he hesitated. He admitted that there were "certain phrases I didn't completely understand" in the bill.[14] He added he would "want to talk to the attorney general and see exactly what they do mean."

This equivocation likely broke the momentum for a bill that bore the stamp of the Eisenhower administration, if not of Eisenhower. Johnson and other Senate Democrats began pushing hard for the "trial by jury" amendment. Ike had given opponents an opening with his less than full-throated endorsement. If the president doesn't understand his own bill, Southern Democrats asked, why should we vote for it?

Realizing that he had made a mistake, Ike began lobbying hard against the "trial by jury" amendment. On July 10th, he met with Senator Russell. Eisenhower later recounted his conversation with a "violent exponent of the segregation doctrine," most likely referring to the Georgia senator. According to Ike, the man told him that the *Plessy* precedent was holy because it had been handed down by the Supreme Court. "Then why is the 1954 decision not equally sacrosanct?" the president shot back. The response was that back in the good old days there had been "wise men on the court," whereas now there were "politicians," a clear dig at Earl Warren.

But Ike didn't take the bait. Instead, he asked his friend to name one justice who had served at the time of the *Plessy* ruling. "He just looked at me in consternation and the subject was dropped," the president later wrote in a letter to his friend, Swede Hazlett.[15]

Still, Eisenhower's powers of persuasion did not appear to be changing the minds of any Southern Democrats. It was a troubling beginning to his lobbying efforts.

<>

On July 17th, Eisenhower held another press conference. A reporter asked whether he was willing to use the military to enforce desegregation. "I can't imagine any set of circumstances that would ever induce me to send federal troops...," he said.[16]

There it was. Ike had unintentionally given a green light to the Southern resistance in the South. In fairness, his whole philosophy demanded such an answer. He believed that gradual change was taking place and that while the people of the South might be misguided, they weren't evil. To admit that he might have to use troops would be to acknowledge Southerners as malevolent, unreasonable people. Eisenhower didn't believe this. In many ways, he was an American exceptionalist who regarded his countrymen as unique in the world. Above all, they were basically good, he felt.

Even now, it's hard to imagine any other answer that Eisenhower could have given. The president of the United States threatening the use of force against his own countrymen, when, as yet, no crisis had emerged? Presidents don't like hypotheticals. Probably any president would have answered the question in a similar fashion as Eisenhower.

When Jimmy Byrnes wrote to him that summer urging him to demonstrate his "confidence in the people of the South," Eisenhower was insulted. "I am compelled to wonder why you have to express such a thought as nothing more than a hope," he indignantly responded.[17] "I do not feel that I need yield to anyone in my respect for the sentiments, convictions, and character of the average American, no matter where he may happen to dwell."

Though he often worried aloud to his staff about "another civil war," the conversation was always about the federal government provoking a violent reaction. He likely didn't believe that Southerners, on their own, would react violently if moderate policies and gradual change were pursued. And to talk openly in a press conference about possibly using troops was exactly the type of language he wanted to avoid. He was trying to turn the thermostat down, not up.

Still, what he said did have an impact. Despite all of his protestations about the bully pulpit not being crucial to presidential leadership, the television age was changing that. Though he complained about the public personae of the presidencies of FDR and Truman, he didn't seem to realize that those men had transformed the modern presidency. Words mattered. If Ike were to choose not to speak, or not to speak clearly, then that, too, would send a message that would be heard and pondered throughout the country.

He had admitted that there were parts of his civil rights bill that he didn't understand. Now, he admitted that he couldn't imagine using troops to enforce integration. Now, in his candor, or carelessness, he was unknowingly, unintentionally encouraging even more resistance.

In that same press conference, Ike was asked whether "it would be a wise extension of federal power at this stage to permit the attorney general to bring suits on his own motion, to enforce school integration in the South?"

"I personally believe if you try to go too far too fast in laws in this delicate field that has involved the emotions of so many millions of Americans, you are making a mistake," Ike responded.[18] He had now come full-circle on Brownell's injunction proposal. He had started out against the injunction provision, then endorsed it during the 1956 campaign, and now appeared to be against it again.

As a result, Eisenhower's civil rights bill was mortally wounded. In politics, hesitation is interpreted as weakness, not strength. The Senate responded accordingly. LBJ remained adamant on the jury-trial amendment. "The people will never accept a concept that a man can be publicly branded a criminal without a jury trial," he piously declared. In a private Oval Office meeting, Johnson insisted that Ike drop the section of the bill giving the attorney general injunction powers. Ike agreed. He later told a heartsick Brownell that he felt this concession was necessary to get the rest of the bill passed.

He remained hopeful that the jury-trial amendment would not make it into the final bill. On August 2nd, the Senate disappointed him. Senator Kennedy justified his vote in favor of the amendment as having been necessary to avoid a filibuster.

Still, JFK's maneuvering left him open to criticism and even ridicule. Roy Wilkins of the NAACP accused him of "rubbing political elbows" with Dixiecrats. And one senator was heard to joke that Kennedy needed to "show a little less profile and a little more courage."[19]

Eisenhower was outraged by the vote. He told his Cabinet that it was "one of the most serious political defeats of the past four years...."[20] Ann Whitman called it the "blackest of black days." Nixon was no less angry: "It was a vote against the right to vote," he said as he left the Senate that day. But he wasn't particularly surprised. He realized that Southern Democrats could not afford to have the entire package passed into law.

Now that the bill had been fundamentally changed on the legislative chessboard, it was Ike's move. Publicly, in order to pressure Congressional negotiators, he urged rejection of the jury-trial amendment because it would effectively leave many black Americans "disenfranchised." Privately, he worried that it might be worse to veto the first civil rights law since the late 19th century.

As he thought about his options, no shortage of advice came his way. The leadership of the black community was divided. Jackie Robinson, who was beginning to have doubts about his hero in the White House, urged a veto: "Have waited this long...can wait a little longer." But Martin Luther King, Jr. saw it as an important step forward. He urged a signature.

In the end, the bill that reached Ike's desk was a classic compromise. The jury-trial amendment remained, but it had been re-written so that a federal judge would decide whether a jury trial would be held in a particular case. The same legislation provided for a new Civil Rights Commission, a Civil Rights Division at the Department of Justice, and injunction powers for the attorney general (but only on voting rights cases).

As Ike weighed his options, a new school year was about to begin.

<>

While Eisenhower was fighting Senate Democrats that summer, Deputy Attorney General William Rogers received a phone call from the governor of Arkansas, Orval Faubus. What was the federal government planning to do to prevent violence once school began, the governor asked. Rogers was speechless. Until now, Arkansas had been considered a moderate Southern state where, Hoxie notwithstanding, reasonable people were expected to prevail. Indeed, Superintendent of Schools Virgil Blossom, with the blessing of Mayor Woodrow Mann, had crafted a desegregation plan in accordance with the two Supreme Court rulings. Blossom's plan was to drag out desegregation as long as possible. It would take seven years to integrate fully. But this year, 1957, it would start with a handful of carefully chosen black students entering the doors of Central High School.

Faubus's phone call to the deputy attorney general ended with a pledge from Rogers: A representative from the Department of Justice would fly to Little Rock to visit with the governor. But he wouldn't be the first visitor. On August 22nd, the Citizens Council hosted Georgia governor Marvin Griffin. The Georgian complained bitterly in his speech about the "ruthless decisions of the Supreme Court."[21] Urging defiance of the court order, Griffin asserted that the only federal role in local education was the school lunch program. "If they try and tell us then to integrate the races," he said, working the crowd into a rage, "I will be compelled to tell them to get their black-eyed peas and soup pots out of Georgia." If the subtlety of his remarks was lost on the crowd, another speaker made it clear that if "this happened in Georgia, we'd call out the National Guard."

If Griffin's goal had been to stir up passions, he succeeded. That night, Daisy Bates, the local NAACP official who had been most personally involved with integrating the schools, was at her home in Little Rock. Suddenly, a rock smashed through her window and landed in her living room. Attached to the projectile was a helpful note of explanation: "Stone this time. Dynamite next."[22]

On August 28th, Arthur Caldwell, the Department of Justice emissary, arrived and met with Governor Faubus for more than an hour. Caldwell explained that the new civil rights law making its way through Congress would not give the feds any more power over school desegregation. However, he reminded the governor that the Department of Justice could intervene to restore order, as it had done in Hoxie, Arkansas.

During the meeting, Caldwell later reported back to Washington, Faubus seemed less "interested in the application of the law as he was in explaining to the Department what he planned to do."[23] Perhaps because Caldwell was an Arkansas native, Faubus spoke candidly. He said he had reason to believe there would be violence if the school-desegregation plan were to go forward. When Caldwell challenged him on this, Faubus said that his information, though reliable, was "too vague and indefinite to be of any use to a law enforcement agency." Caldwell suspected, and told Washington, that Faubus was up to no good.

Indeed, he was. Faubus had helped to encourage a lawsuit by the Mothers' League of Little Rock Central High. The group sought a temporary injunction from a local court to stop the desegregation plan set to commence on the first day of school. During a court hearing, Faubus took the stand to testify. He said he feared there would be violence on the first day of school. And he blamed the governor of Georgia for stirring up passions: "People are coming to me and saying, 'If Georgia doesn't have to integrate, why does Arkansas have to?'"[24]

The local court agreed and temporarily postponed desegregation. This signaled the reappearance of the civil rights community's legal lion, Thurgood Marshall, who went to federal court to have the local ruling overturned. The judge, Ronald N. Davies, quickly agreed. Little Rock Central High would start integration on September 3rd, the first day of school.

At last, the moment had arrived. The culmination of the civil rights community's drive for equality was about to clash with ancient hatreds and impassioned anger. The insurrection was about to come out into the open. The struggle for equality would face its biggest, most important challenge yet at a place called Central High School in Little Rock, Arkansas.

◇

"The mission of the state militia," Governor Faubus told the people of Arkansas on September 3rd, "is to maintain or restore order and to protect the lives and property of citizens. They will not act as segregationists or integrationists but as soldiers," he promised, trying to strike the right tone as a law-and-order man.[25] Few people were fooled.

Winthrop Rockefeller certainly wasn't. The head of Arkansas's Industrial Development Commission went to see the governor to try and walk him down from the ledge. "I'm sorry, but I'm committed," Faubus told him. "I'm going to run for a third term, and if I don't do this, Jim Johnson and Bruce Bennett will tear me to shreds."[26] Rockefeller had hoped to talk some sense into Faubus. Instead, Faubus talked raw politics: In order to survive in the 1958 gubernatorial primary, he would pander to white voters.

And so it was that 250 Arkansas National Guardsmen surrounded the school the next day. Soon, large crowds, galvanized by the governor's televised words of defiance, also ringed the building.

But there were no black students to repel. The school board had met with NAACP officials and agreed to postpone integration until the federal courts could sort out the mess. That took only a day. Judge Ronald Davis ordered integration to move forward and warned that he viewed this as an "obligation from which I shall not shrink."

On September 4th, 1957, Faubus crossed his Rubicon. In their morning paper, Arkansans read an eloquent editorial entitled "The Crisis Mr. Faubus Made." The author, a transplanted South Carolinian named Harry Ashmore, was starting to make a name as a fine writer and an honest man. His words that day in the *Arkansas Gazette* communicated outrage at Faubus's maneuverings. "Thus the issue is no longer segregation versus integration," he wrote. "The question has now become the supremacy of the government of the United States in all matters of law." With a touch of prophecy, he predicted: "And clearly the federal government cannot let this issue remain unsolved, no matter what the cost to this community."[27]

Nine brave black students arrived at Central High School that morning. Most were repelled by the crowd. Faubus had counted on that. But he hadn't counted on Elizabeth Eckerd. The little girl in the white dress was shown on television screens around the country, engulfed by a vicious mob yelling, "Lynch her! Lynch her!"[28]

After she was rebuffed at the front door of the school, Elizabeth waited for the school bus to take her home. Benjamin Fine, a reporter with the *New York Times*, was moved by the little girl's courage. He walked over to her, lifted her chin with his hand, and said: "Don't let them see you cry."

If Faubus thought he had solved the problem, he thought wrong. It was the classic battlefield mistake of securing a tactical win at the expense of a strategic setback. No longer could Faubus hide behind the measured tones of his official speeches. He was now publicly and irrevocably on the side of the segregationists. The news media made sure that the whole nation, indeed the whole world, saw what had happened that day and who had been responsible for it. Faubus's only hope was that Harry Ashmore had been wrong and that perhaps the federal government would leave the issue alone.

The very next day, the governor received an indication that the federal government would not sit idly by. Making good on his pledge, Judge Davies invited the Department of Justice to investigate the fracas at Central High. On September 9th, the Department of Justice, having researched the events of the previous few days, concluded that Faubus had had no evidence to suggest violence and that he had merely used the Guard to appease white voters. Judge Davies then requested that the Department of Justice file a petition demanding the governor's cooperation with the federal court.

Faubus, seeing the battle lines closing in on him, looked for a way around the court. His last hope was a direct appeal to the leader of the nation.

<><>

The town of Newport, Rhode Island hugs descending cliffs that overlook the deep and salty waters of the Atlantic. Thirty-two miles to the North is Providence, the capital of the smallest state in the Union. Nearby, on Coaster's Harbor Island, a U.S. naval facility can be found. It offered a perfect reprieve for a tired president worn down by a long, hot summer of legislative battles. The facility's isolation added to its attraction.

Dwight and Mamie Eisenhower arrived in Newport for a vacation the same day that the Little Rock Nine were turned away from the doors of Central High. He attended a welcoming reception that was hosted at the Old Colony House. And he hoped to get on the golf course as soon as possible. "Never did I feel so good on the first two hours of getting away from Washington," he told his hosts, "and I assure you it is not just because I am getting away from Washington." He added: "I assure you, we look forward to the time of our lives...." It was a Wednesday, September 4th. Eisenhower was looking forward to some rounds at the Newport Country Club, a course he enjoyed playing.[29]

Eisenhower stayed in the stone-and-brick quarters that housed the base commander. Twelve rooms in the building gave him plenty of room to both work and relax.

One hundred and sixty-seven years before, Newport had been on the mind of another president grappling with equal rights. The Bill of Rights had not yet been ratified, and George Washington found himself responding to an appeal from the Hebrew Congregation of Newport:

> It is now no more that toleration is spoken of, as if it was by the indulgence of one class of people that another enjoyed the exercise of their inherent natural rights. For happily the Government of the United States, which gives to bigotry no sanction, to persecution no assistance, requires only that they who live under its protection, should demean themselves as good citizens.

Eisenhower could not have known that Newport would again be the backdrop for a dramatic moment in the long arc of equal rights. Or that his actions in the coming days would be as memorable as Washington's words.

Though he hoped to relax, business soon beckoned. For the first couple of days in Newport, with his eye on the drama in Little Rock, Eisenhower tried to decide whether to sign or veto the civil rights legislation. He had grave reservations about it. His deputy attorney general, Bill Rogers, compared it to a policeman having a gun without any bullets.

On September 9th, Ike decided he would sign the bill anyway. But he didn't have time to ponder the new law. Events in Little Rock were exploding.

That first week of September, he had received a telegram from the governor of Arkansas, who sounded like a besieged battlefield commander in need of urgent reinforcements. "I am reliably informed that federal authorities in Little Rock have this day been discussing plans to take into custody, by force, the head of a sovereign state," Faubus wired. Saying that he must have the right to command the National Guard troops without federal interference, the governor claimed Eisenhower himself as his inspiration. "I must follow the precedent set by you as a chief executive when you declined to have your administrative aides summoned to testify before a Congressional committee," he wrote in a bizarre reference to Ike's tactics in dealing with Senator McCarthy.

Eisenhower might be forgiven for believing that the governor of Arkansas was delusional, hysterical, or both. "I have strong reasons to believe that the telephone lines to the Arkansas Executive Mansion have been tapped," Faubus added.

If the governor thought his conspiracy theories—or his invocation of his service as "one of the soldiers of your command" during the war—would impress the president, he was profoundly mistaken.

From the outset, Eisenhower sensed that Faubus was an odd man and up to no good. His response to Faubus, issued the next day, was direct and stern. "The only assurance I can give you is that the Federal Constitution will be upheld by me by every legal means at my command." Ike then mocked the governor's paranoid claims: "There is no basis of fact to the statements you make in your telegram that Federal authorities have been considering taking you into custody or that telephone lines to your Executive Mansion have been tapped by any agency of the Federal Government."[30]

The president then concluded with a tough warning: He fully expected the governor to cooperate with the Department of Justice's investigation of the "failure to comply with the District Court's order. You and other state officials—as well as the National Guard which, of course, is uniformed, armed and partially sustained by the [Federal] Government—will, I am sure, give full cooperation to the United States District Court."

Thus it began. Perhaps the two men didn't realize it, but they were both preparing the battlefield for a great clash. This was the first set of maneuvers between the two. Faubus had hoped he could co-opt Ike by appealing to his sympathy for law and order and states' rights. Ike had hoped to slap some sense into Faubus by reminding him of how clear the law was on this matter. Faubus's tone was conciliatory. Ike's response was blunt. So far, neither seemed impressed with the arguments of the other.

Yet, early on, Eisenhower had made two issues perfectly clear. First, he did not see this as a states' rights or law-and-order issue. In his mind, the ruling of a federal court had been usurped by a state official. Even his conservative views on federalism did not allow for this type of disobedience. Second, Eisenhower reminded Faubus in this his first communiqué with, him that the National Guard units were not exclusively state troops. Faubus could not have missed the hint—at any moment, Eisenhower might federalize the troops and take them away from the governor.

Faubus may well have been surprised by Eisenhower's relatively strong rebuke. After all, this was the same president who just a few weeks before had assured reporters that he could not imagine ever sending troops in to enforce desegregation. And wasn't this the same president who had declined to intervene after Governor Allan Shivers sent Texas Rangers into Mansfield, Texas to stop integration?

It was. But there was a difference. At Mansfield, Ike's attorney general advised him to stay out of it because there was no federal court case and no request from the school board for intervention. Now, at Little Rock, both of these criteria had been met.

As Eisenhower tried to work on his golf handicap that September in Newport, he seemed genuinely shocked by the unfolding events in Little Rock. Again, he turned to Brownell for advice. "I asked Attorney General Brownell's opinion on whether the United States courts had the power to review the action of the governor in preventing the execution of the orders of the federal court by the use of military force," Ike wrote later. "He said that federal courts could rule on the legality of the action of a state governor which contravenes a federal court order, even though the governor seeks to justify his action by claiming it is necessary to keep the peace." This conversation had likely influenced Ike's strong response to Faubus's initial telegram.[31]

On September 9th, the federal court asked the Department of Justice to file an amicus curiae brief and to petition for an injunction against Faubus. A hearing was set for September 20th, 1957.

In Eisenhower's own words: "The United States government and the governor of Arkansas were now heading toward a collision."[32] Nothing could stop it now.

CHAPTER TEN

THE RECKONING

"...I did not want to see any governor humiliated."

—Dwight D. Eisenhower

A COUPLE OF DAYS into his vacation, Eisenhower flew back to Washington to confer with his attorney general. To get from Newport to the Naval Air Station at Quonset, Ike unknowingly started a trend. When he had first arrived in Rhode Island on September 4th, the presidential yacht named for his granddaughter, *Barbara Anne*, had carried him from the naval base to his lodging on the other side of Narragansett Bay. The trip took twenty-five minutes; too long for a man in a hurry.

Eager to confer with his staff in person about the events in Little Rock, Ike decided he needed to get back to Washington as soon as possible. Now, he boarded a khaki-colored Marine helicopter. The four-minute flight allowed him to reach the air base much more quickly and to get on the plane and back to Washington much sooner. Ike was impressed by how much time he had saved. The Air Force had previously given him a test ride in a Bell H-13J Helicopter. But Ike was convinced that the Marine UH-34 was a better fit. The Marine One helicopter service for presidents was born.

Once he arrived in Washington, Ike turned to the battle ahead. Like a war council, he met with his top staff to chart a course of action. His chief of staff, Sherman Adams, said that Eisenhower's mindset in the early days of the standoff was very much a military one. "Eisenhower," Adams observed, "as he did when a soldier, wanted to give Faubus every opportunity to make an orderly retreat by no longer defying the order of the Court.[1] But, the president insisted, even though he would explore every alternative to the use of force, there could be "no compromise or capitulation by the administration on this issue."

Ike had always been able to see clearly the flag in the midst of the smoke and sounds of the battlefield. Now, looking at Little Rock, Eisenhower quietly assessed what was at stake and what might have to be done. Still, he hoped that Faubus would have the sense to back down.

He didn't. And he wouldn't. Faubus had too much to gain from his defiance. But others shared Ike's hope that a standoff could be avoided. On Monday, September 9th, Chief of Staff Adams received a phone call from an old friend of his, Brooks Hays. As a congressman from Arkansas, Hays had served with Adams in the House. A mild-mannered and measured man, he was, in many ways, the antithesis of Faubus, who had stirred up the boiling pot and was now watching it overflow. Hays was also guided by spiritual convictions. He was currently serving as the president of the Southern Baptist Convention. He was a decent man who wanted to do what was right.

His views on civil rights, though progressive by Arkansas standards, were fairly close to Ike's. In 1956, Hays had helped to write the Democratic Party National Platform that generally endorsed civil rights without specifically endorsing the *Brown* ruling.

Most of all, Hays was a practical man who now offered a practical solution to Adams. Would Eisenhower consider meeting personally with Faubus to resolve the crisis? Hays claimed that the idea had first been put to him by Faubus. Adams was receptive. He thought Ike might do it, he told Hays. But there was a condition: The governor must agree to enforce the law as defined by the federal courts. Eisenhower would not discuss whether desegregation was the law, but merely how best to enforce it.

Hays agreed and promised to get back to Adams after he talked to the governor. In the meantime, Adams mentioned the call to Ike. "Without a moment of hesitation, Eisenhower said that he would be in favor of it, under the proviso I had expected him to mention—that the governor not come to the meeting in his present mood of defiance."[2]

When Hays called back, he reported that the governor wanted to meet with the president. "What would be a convenient time for the president?"[3] Adams reminded him of the conditions they had previously discussed.

Hays and Adams discussed a request letter from Faubus. In it, the governor would express his "intention of observing the federal law." Hays said that he understood this, but that it would be difficult to arrange given the governor's current position. Though he was being castigated in the national press and in the federal courts, Faubus was being celebrating by white Arkansans. He was not ready to change course.

Hays now set about a thankless task—to get Faubus to request a meeting with the president on the terms laid down by the White House. A series of discussions ensued. Faubus would appear to agree to the conditions, only to change his mind just as Hays was about to call the White House. Finally, Hays called with good news. A deal had been reached. Faubus would wire the president, promising to cooperate and enforce the law. Hays read the proposed language to Adams on the phone: "[I]t is certainly my intention to comply with the order that has been issued by the District Court. May I confer with you on this matter at your earliest convenience?"[4] Adams thought this sounded fine. Hays hung up and promised that the governor's letter would follow shortly.

It did, and it was different. Instead of the language that Hays and Adams had agreed to, Faubus wrote that he would "comply with the order that has been issued by the District Court in this case, consistent with my responsibilities under the Constitution of the United States and that of Arkansas."[5] The meeting was already off to a bad start. Adams was outraged at the double-crossing. On the telephone, he complained to Hays. The congressman, embarrassed, told Adams that Faubus's advisors had insisted on the change.

It would not be the last time Faubus disappointed the White House.

◇

By now Ike had resumed his vacation in Rhode Island. On September 11th, Ike was playing golf at the Newport Country Club when Faubus's telegram arrived. Earlier that day, the president had called Brownell in Washington to discuss matters. He complained that "the whole U.S. thinks the president has a right to walk in and say 'disperse—we are going to have Negroes in the high schools and so on.' That is not so."[6] Sitting in his golf cart after finishing the first hole, he wrote a response with his press secretary, Jim Hagerty. Faubus would arrive in Providence on the 13th. He would then fly over to Newport by helicopter for a meeting on the 14th.

It was a risky strategy for Ike. His attorney general believed that the governor had "soiled" himself, and he was pessimistic. "Perhaps the time is now ripe," Ike responded on the phone that day.[7] He had always believed that people of different views could reason together. He had also publicly talked about how the people of the South were good people who just needed time to change. He could hardly refuse to meet with one of their leaders now. He had also spoken of how laws alone were not enough to bring about racial justice. If reason and persuasion were needed—and he believed that they were—he was dutybound to talk some sense into Faubus.

Yet, as the date of the meeting approached, Eisenhower could not help but notice that Faubus was already negotiating in bad faith. The governor had been told what his request should say. And Ike had seen the change that Faubus had inserted into it. "This significant change made by Faubus supported the attorney general's skepticism that any good could come out of a meeting with him," Ike later observed.[8]

Orval Faubus was now an international celebrity. The *New York Times'* front page carried a story on the showdown at Little Rock virtually every day that September. Foreign media were captivated by the story as well. Hypocrisy makes a great story. People undoubtedly enjoyed the irony of democratic America keeping black kids oppressed by the use of force. Radio Moscow had a particularly good time embellishing the story by informing listeners that Elizabeth Eckford had been "brutally murdered."

Like many politicians, Faubus seemed to believe that all press was good press. His standing with white voters in Arkansas had seldom been any higher. And now, he was about to receive the greatest prize of all for the governor of a small state—face time with the president. Sure, he was worried about the firm hand that Judge Davies was exercising in the courtroom. But hadn't Ike said he couldn't imagine a scenario where he would have to intervene with troops? This was a man the governor could do business with.

Eisenhower was less optimistic. To him, a man's word was his bond. And Faubus had already been caught lying once. Still, Eisenhower had long believed in his own powers of personal persuasion. He had first-hand experience dealing with the likes of Montgomery, Patton, and Churchill. Certainly he could handle the governor of Arkansas.

And so, as the summit date approached, the two principal players tried to judge the situation. Faubus essentially hoped that Eisenhower would be sympathetic and, as Ike had done at Mansfield, refuse to intervene. Eisenhower hoped that Faubus was looking for a way to save face.

Both men were wrong.

⟡

A glorious Rhode Island morning dawned on Saturday, September 14th. Governor Faubus and Congressman Hays had arrived in Providence the night before. They were ready for the meeting.

Eisenhower also had reinforcements for the day's confrontation. Chief of Staff Adams, Attorney General Brownell, and Gerald Morgan, the president's special counsel, all flew up from Washington early that morning. When they arrived at Quonset, they were taken by helicopter to Ike's summer headquarters on Coaster's Harbor Island. The chopper landed on the front lawn, and the men exited. They entered the building and went up a flight of stairs to the president's office.

Ike was already there. He greeted his staff members "in a bright and good-humored mood," Adams recalled.[9] This was perhaps the biggest tip-off of what was going on inside the president's mind. Ever since he had sat in that dank, Gibraltar cave during the war, Ike made every effort to bring a positive attitude to his work. His mood was an inverse measure of how grave he believed the crisis to be. The more strenuous the moment, the more upbeat he seemed to become. And that morning, Ike was in an exceptionally upbeat mood "as he usually was before tackling an important and difficult job," Adams said. The president knew what was at stake. The newspapers were already calling this the most serious constitutional crisis since the Civil War.

Ike's team discussed the tactics for the upcoming meeting. Ike wanted to be alone with Faubus first. Undoubtedly, he wanted to remove the tension that inevitably increases with the presence of additional people. It was agreed that Ike would take Faubus into his private office—a small room with a desk and only two or three chairs. Like Grant at Appomattox, Ike was determined to give Faubus the consideration and dignity necessary for a complete surrender. After his private visit, the president would take Faubus into the bigger conference room, where the staff would join and finalize the capitulation.

A few minutes before 9:00 a.m., Adams, joined by Jim Hagerty, walked out to the front lawn to await the arrival of Governor Faubus and Congressman Hays. Adams had arranged for a helicopter to transport them from Providence to the front lawn. The helicopter soon appeared over the horizon, shuddering the ground below as it got closer. It sat down easily on the lawn. As the blades relaxed, Adams walked over to greet the visitors. Hays emerged and shook the hand of his old colleague. He then introduced Adams to Governor Faubus. Nearby reporters snapped photos of the men, who soon disappeared into the building. Faubus carried a briefcase and wore a dark suit.

To Adams, the governor of Arkansas possessed a "quiet-mannered but forceful and determined" personality.[10] His first impression led him to believe that Faubus would "not be unreasonable or difficult to deal with."

After the four men made their way up the stairs, they entered the office, where the president greeted them, accompanied by Brownell and Morgan. Ike was wearing a light-colored, three-button summer suit. His skin was a bit bronzed from his golf outings. He was relaxed, warm, and gracious. Ike talked to the governor about his trip from Little Rock. He also talked a little history, discussing the naval base and the surrounding area. But the velvet exterior only served to mask the steel inside of the president. He meant business.

With the greetings out of the way and the tension seemingly eased, Ike carefully choreographed his visitor into the smaller, private office. After Faubus entered, the door shut, leaving the others behind. For the next twenty minutes, the two men talked alone about Little Rock.

◇

As the meeting began in earnest, the Arkansas governor talked at some length of his admiration for the commander in chief. Eisenhower later recalled that Faubus had "protested again and again that he was a law abiding citizen, that he was a veteran, fought in the war, and that everybody recognizes that the Federal law is supreme to State law." Faubus later said he had asked Ike for "breathing room," by which he meant some time to resolve the matter in his own way. Revealingly, Faubus found it necessary to remind Ike that he wasn't a criminal. He undoubtedly was aware of how irritated the president was with him.[11]

That irritation soon manifested itself. Faubus would later say that Ike began to lecture him in a "rehearsed" manner. Eisenhower remembered it as less a lecture than a simple, straightforward plan for ending the stalemate. "I suggested to him that he go home and not necessarily withdraw his National Guard troops, but just change their orders...." Rather than keep the black students out of the school, Ike recommended that the governor "tell the Guard to continue to preserve order but to allow the Negro children to attend Central High."[12]

Then, in a shrewd proposal to a politician in a bind, Ike offered Faubus a deal too good to turn down. "I pointed out that at that time he was due to appear the following Friday, the 20th, before the Court to determine whether an injunction was to be issued."[13] Faubus stared at the president. If Faubus would cooperate by employing the Guard to protect the Little Rock Nine "the

Justice Department would go to the Court and ask that the governor not be brought into Court."

An adroit politician, Faubus knew how to phrase words to ensure maximum flexibility upon his return home. "He seemed to be very appreciative of this attitude and I got definitely the understanding that he was going back to Arkansas to act within a matter of hours to revoke his orders to the Guard to prevent reentry of the Negro children into the school," Ike recalled.[14] But "seemed" is very different from "committed." Faubus had managed to convince Ike that he basically agreed with him, without specifically saying so.

Not that Ike didn't have doubts about Faubus's next move. He gave the governor an explicit warning about the consequences of further resistance. "I further said that I did not believe it was beneficial to anybody to have a trial of strength between the president and a governor because in any area where the federal government had assumed jurisdiction and this was upheld by the Supreme Court, there could be only one outcome," Ike told him, "that is, the state would lose, and I did not want to see any sovernor humiliated."[15]

Faubus thanked the president. The private meeting ended twenty minutes after it had begun. Now it was time to bring in the others—Adams, Brownell, Morgan, and Hays. As the group expanded, Eisenhower announced in a matter-of-fact tone that the two men had agreed to allow the black children into the school.

Brownell was astonished. He couldn't imagine that Faubus could surrender when the white voters of his state were up in arms. He also perceptively noticed that Faubus had said nothing when Ike had finished recapping their meeting. Brownell believed that the governor's silence spoke volumes. He was convinced that Faubus was up to no good.

The attorney general, in a stern tone, spoke to make himself— and the law—clear to Faubus. Like a parent lecturing an adolescent, Brownell told Faubus that the desegregation law didn't have to be liked to be enforced. But it was the law, and it must be enforced. Ominously, Faubus said only that he recognized that it was the law. He made no comment about enforcing it.

It seems not to have occurred to Eisenhower that his presence and stature likely precluded a frank discussion. Faubus had practically admitted as much when he opened their private meeting with a description of his loyalty to the president and his World War II service. It was likely difficult for Faubus to tell Eisenhower that he disagreed with him, much less that the president of the United States should mind his own business. Instead, like any diplomat in an uncomfortable situation, Faubus said what he had to say in order to get the meeting over with. Brownell surmised correctly that Eisenhower had failed to change the governor's mind.

There are no lost causes, T.S. Eliot once wrote. This seemed to be Orval Faubus's guiding principle in September 1957. Segregation may have been a losing issue, but it was a winning political strategy in a Southern state. The man who had once feared losing office was now the darling of Arkansas's white society. And no president, not even the hero of D-Day, could change his mind about it.

Perhaps Congressman Hays realized that the vast gulf between the two men had not really been bridged. He brought everyone to laughter when he told a joke about the "Alabama Horse Deal" in which two men would sell a horse back and forth, each time raising the price, all the while thinking they were actually making money.[16]

◇

The extent of the governor's defiance become clear soon enough. After the meeting, Brownell excused himself for a reunion at Yale. Faubus, accompanied by Hays, slithered back to Providence. Like any summit, the plan was for a joint statement to be released to the press. Like many summits, finding common ground for a written statement proved to be more difficult than the talks that had transpired.

Press Secretary Jim Hagerty took a first crack at writing a statement based on Ike's account of the meeting. He reported the governor's intention to obey the law and to enforce the court rulings. So claimed the White House, anyway. Faubus remembered things differently. He was rather enjoying the attention, and he liked the role of the small state governor standing up to the big federal government.

Not more than two hours after Faubus left Ike's headquarters, Congressman Hays called with ominous news. The governor was already hedging. Sherman Adams insisted that he keep his word and issue a public statement along the lines agreed to in the meeting. But Faubus had played his hand well. He had been careful to leave himself some room. And now he was prepared to exploit it. Over the phone, Adams read Hays the version of the statement written by the president's team. Negotiations went back and forth.

The final text amounted to two statements: one from Ike and one from Faubus. To see the fault lines in the situation, only a quick glance at the differences in the two documents was necessary.

Eisenhower spoke of the governor's "intention to respect the decisions of the United States District Court and to give his full cooperation in carrying out his responsibilities in respect to these decisions."[17]

Faubus said that in carrying out those responsibilities "it is essential that...the complexities of integration be patiently understood by all those in Federal authority."[18]

Eisenhower stressed his conviction that it was "the desire of the Governor not only to observe the supreme law of the land but to use the influence of his office in orderly progress of the plans which are already the subject of the order of the Court."[19]

Faubus emphasized that in enforcing the court orders everyone should remember that the "changes necessitated by the Court orders cannot be accomplished overnight." In direct reference to Ike's somewhat conflicting statements that summer, he added: "As I interpret the president's public statements, the national Administration has no thought of challenging this fact."[20]

Most telling was Eisenhower's declaration of the "inescapable responsibility resting upon the governor to preserve law and order in his state."[21]

Faubus agreed, sort of: "It is my responsibility to protect the people from violence in any form."[22]

As Faubus left Rhode Island, reporters asked him about Eisenhower's insistence that he change the orders of the Arkansas National Guard. "That problem I will have to take care of when I return to Little Rock." On the whole, the scorecard showed Eisenhower winning the private meeting but losing the public debate afterward. Faubus's departing words were entirely consistent with his position before he had gone to Newport. He had not moved very much.

This became clearer still the following day, when Faubus appeared on CBS's *Face the Nation*. He again demurred on whether he would change the orders of the Guard. Viewers around the country, having heard the upbeat pronouncements from the White House, could be forgiven for their confusion.

At the White House, the optimism began to recede. Perhaps the president read the Faubus statement and compared it to his own. Perhaps Brownell had a few more harsh words about the dubious character of the man they were dealing with. Whatever it was, the Eisenhower team began to show signs of nervousness. Presidential secretary Ann Whitman wrote: "I got the impression that the meeting had not gone as well as had been hoped, that the Federal government would have to be as tough as possible in the situation. Governor Faubus seized this opportunity and stirred the whole thing up for his own political advantage. The test comes tomorrow morning when we will know whether Governor Faubus will, or will not, withdraw the troops."[23]

<><

More than anyone else, Eisenhower, as a career soldier, should have understood the limitations of a summit-style approach to resolving the standoff. Seldom do Munich-like agreements address the underlying issues in an evolving, emotionally volatile climate. The fundamental problem must be resolved, not massaged.

The pressure was rising. The *Arkansas Gazette* had reported earlier in the month that Secretary of State Dulles feared that the situation in Little Rock was "not helpful to the influence of the United States abroad."

Faubus wasn't concerned about world opinion. He was worried about local opinion. Upon his return to Little Rock, he bided his time. And after a couple of days, it became evident what he was going to do: nothing.

The troops remained at the school, and the governor remained silent. He didn't change the orders of the Guard, as he had hinted to Ike that he would. He didn't talk about finding a way out. Instead, he simply dug in his heels, perhaps hoping against hope that the national media attention—and more important, the president's attention—would fade away.

A shrewd surveyor of the local political climate, Faubus had spectacularly misjudged the president. As the days passed and the troops remained sentinels of segregation, Ike became convinced that Faubus had double-crossed him.

Until now, the issue was somewhat complicated, involving court rulings, school board plans, and local politics. Now, the issue was simple: Eisenhower had been lied to. It was personal. As he later wrote: "The troops stayed at Central High all the following week."[24] Eisenhower had used his office, his prestige, and his time to help find a way out for Faubus. In return, he felt that Faubus had taken advantage of him.

Now, at last, he was prepared to act. Enraged, he called Brownell in Washington. "You were right," he said, his anger obvious to Brownell even over the phone line, "Faubus broke his word."[25] He wanted to denounce the governor publicly. Both Brownell and Adams urged him to hold his fire. They reminded him that Faubus had a court date on September 20th with Judge Davies. They were certain the judge would order Faubus to admit the black students. It was just as likely that Faubus would remain defiant. In a memo written by General Andrew Goodpaster, Eisenhower was urged to wait for Faubus to defy Judge Davies. Let Faubus overplay his hand, Goodpaster essentially argued. Then, it would become the president's responsibility to use "whatever means may be necessary."[26]

<>

The drama escalated. On September 20th, in a Little Rock court room, Judge Davies convened the hearing with the words: "Civil Case no. 3113 on a motion for preliminary injunction." This was the case against Faubus. In his ruling, Judge Davies officially enjoined the governor. He said that Faubus ought to have used the troops to assist with integration rather than block it.

Not that it mattered to Faubus. Knowing full well what the ruling would be, he didn't even bother to show up. His lawyers represented him in the courtroom. And on cue, they got up and walked out even before the hearing started. Later, to reporters, Faubus vainly tried to portray himself as the victim of a heavy-handed federal court and federal government: "Now begins the crucifixion."[27] But no one was buying the Messiah routine. Even his most ardent local defenders knew that this was a crisis that Faubus wanted, even if it was not going as planned.

Faubus had a final card to play. Three hours after the court's ruling, the governor of Arkansas officially removed the National Guard troops from Central High School. He urged black parents not to send their kids to school on Monday. With that, he exited for the Southern Governors Conference in Sea Island, Georgia.

Eisenhower, monitoring the events from Newport, was concerned about possible mob violence when the schoolbell rang the following Monday morning. Publicly, he called the removal of the troops "a necessary step in the right direction" and urged that the order of the court be "executed promptly and without disorder."[28] Privately, he was very worried. He expected that a handful of police would not be enough if a riotous crowd were to show up, as they had on the first day of school. He discussed it with Brownell, saying he was "loath to use troops" to restore order even though he did not doubt his authority to do so. He hoped to enlist Brooks Hays on one last mission. He told Brownell that Hays should be told "just how low the governor has fallen in the president's estimation since he broke his promise."[29]

He also repeated his longstanding fear about what a local school district might resort to, once its back was against the wall: "Suppose the children are taken to school and then Governor Faubus closes the school? Can he do that legally?" Brownell said he would check.

That weekend, Eisenhower, realizing that he could soon find himself again sending troops into battle, tried as best he could to relax. Some of his gang of friends had joined him in Newport.

They played golf and bridge and devoured steaks cooked by the president. During a game of bridge, Ike complained about how hard he had worked to avoid a confrontation in Little Rock. And yet "…the agitators won't let it be that way." He compared the coming showdown to previous battles like D-Day and the Bulge. The general might not have wanted a confrontation, but he was ready for it.[30]

Meanwhile, Faubus and his wife, en route to Sea Island, stopped in Atlanta for the Georgia-Texas football game. If the governor was worried about the fate of the black children, it didn't show. "He's really lapping up the glory," another governor told reporters. "There were 33,000 people at the game, and every time they cheered a play, Faubus got up and bowed."[31]

After the game, the governor completed his journey and was feted like a conquering hero at the Silver Room of the Cloister Hotel. He drank and danced and signed autographs from well-wishers. One of those who danced with him was Mrs. James Karam, a friend who had been a part of the governor's entourage from Little Rock. Her husband was one of Faubus's best friends. He was also a professional strikebreaker who knew how to quickly round up enough brutes to cause trouble. Karam hadn't made it to Sea Island because he had business to take care of back home. That weekend, Karam spoke with Little Rock school superintendent Virgil Blossom about the upcoming Monday at Central High. "I like you personally," he assured Blossom, "but don't make a martyr out of yourself." He added, ominously, "Don't go out there tomorrow."[32]

◇

The first to arrive on Monday, September 23rd, were the police; some seventy Little Rock cops reached the school at 6:00 a.m. They put up sawhorse barricades. And then they waited for school to start.

It wasn't long until a mob a thousand strong began to assemble. Their taunts echoed the ugliness that had greeted the Little Rock Nine back on September 4th. Only this time, the crowd seemed angrier, nastier, meaner. An uneasy tension filled the air.

"Here come the niggers!" went the battle cry just after the schoolbell rang at 8:45 a.m. A roar from the crowd ensued. But the black students had yet to arrive. Instead, the crowd was incited by having spotted four black reporters who were on hand to record the day's events. A group of around twenty thugs went after the four men. One of the four, reporter Alex Wilson, chose to stand his ground. This was natural because he had served in the Marine Corps. He was also a large man, more than six feet tall. He was dressed sharply in a tan hat and dark suit, with the middle button fastening the jacket together. When the toughs approached him, he didn't back down. "I fought for my country, and I'm not going to run." One of the thugs surrounding Wilson held a brick in his hand. He raised it up and smashed it against Wilson's head. The proud reporter, with his immaculate suit still buttoned together, fell to the ground. (He survived the attack but died a couple of years later of complications from the wounds he received that day at Little Rock.)

Any semblance of order was now gone. It was mayhem. But it wasn't accidental. Right in the middle of the disorder was Faubus's friend, Jimmy Karam. He was no innocent bystander. He was directing the action. When police tried in vain to stop the chaos, Karam yelled out, "The niggers started it!" The crowd's intensity went up another notch.[33]

Unknown to the mob, the black students had already entered the school building. Distracted by the beating of the reporter, most people never saw the two cars that had delivered the kids to a side entrance. Daisy Bates, of the local NAACP, had planned the logistics for the Little Rock Nine, only this time even Elizabeth Eckford was included.

Inside, the kids found a climate nearly as hostile as it was outside. They were quickly ushered into the office, where they met with Principal Jess Matthews and Vice Principal Elizabeth Huckaby. "Here are your class schedules and homeroom assignments," Ms. Huckaby said, pretending that it was business as usual that morning. Soon, the door to the office opened, and a white student marched in. "You're not gonna let those niggers stay in here, are you?" he demanded.

Thelma Mothershed, one of the black students, collapsed on an office bench. The pressure was just too great. The other kids were told to make their way to their homerooms. When Melba Pattillo asked why all of the nine kids were going to different homerooms, a white officeworker gave her a less-than-reassuring answer: "You wanted integration…you got integration."[34]

As Melba walked down the hall to her classroom, another white school employee entered her personal space. "Nigger bitch," the woman said, "why don't you go home?" When Melba at last entered her homeroom, the white students who were already there recoiled at her sight. As she sat down, several of the kids around her picked up their books and moved to different seats.

"Are you going to let that nigger coon sit in our class?" a boy asked the teacher. His question was ignored. Melba's next class wasn't much better. At one point that morning, en route to another class, she was tripped by a white student and fell down on the floor, cutting herself. "What do you know?" snickered a white kid. "Niggers bleed red blood. Let's kick the nigger."

Throughout the ordeal, Melba and the other kids could hear the mob outside screaming insults. The crowd had grown tired of beating up on reporters. Now, they had finally learned that the Little Rock Nine were already inside the building. "Oh, my God, they're going in!" one woman screamed in horror. "The niggers are in!"

They wouldn't be for long. The mob began pushing forward, determined to break through the line of police in front. Karam continued his incitement. In fact, the crowd, perhaps having decided to share their anger with everyone, now turned on even the white reporters within reach. *Life* photographers Francis Miller and Gray Villet were each punched in the face. And the *Life* reporter, Paul Welch, had his face beaten and his neck cut. To add insult to injury, the three men were arrested by the police. The charge? Inciting a riot.

Finally, assistant police chief Gene Smith capitulated. Several of the protestors had pierced the police line and were angrily storming into the school building. At 11:30 a.m., Smith ordered the black kids removed. All nine were led out by police escort, placed in cars, and driven home. For the second time in three weeks, mob violence had prevented the integration of Central High School.

As the crowd celebrated its latest triumph, Daisy Bates began to plan her next move. The driving force behind the local NAACP's effort to integrate Central High, she was enraged by what had transpired that morning. Running out of options, she could only imagine one last resort that might just save the experiment.

When a reporter asked her that day whether the Little Rock Nine would return to Central the next day, she said no. She would instruct the black students to stay out of school "until the president of the United States guaranteed them protection within Central High School."[35]

◇

The stage was now set for the single most important constitutional showdown since the Civil War. Sides had been chosen. Lines had been drawn. Tension grew. Emotions filled the air. Anger. Fear. Rage. Hatred. Love. Hope.

Little Rock represented something else as well: the culmination of Eisenhower's own attitude toward racial justice.

As a young football player, he had instinctively sympathized with the black players on the other team. As an Army commander, he was willing to circumvent War Department policy to use his Negro troops. And as president, he had called segregation "criminally stupid."

But having the right instincts is different from doing the right thing. Sympathy is distinct from support; still more, it is far removed from identifying or enforcing a solution.

Until now, Ike had enjoyed the luxury of endorsing civil rights in broad terms, knowing full well that much of segregation law was a state and local matter.

Little Rock ended that. At last, the smoke had cleared, the battlefield was prepared, and Eisenhower could clearly see the line of attack that was needed. He had always said that where there was a federal issue involved, he would act. He had done so with the military and in the District of Columbia. Now, there was a federal issue in Little Rock. And he had to act. "The issue had now become clear both in fact and in law," he later observed.[36]

On the morning of September 23rd, 1957, while a howling mob raged in front of Central High School, Eisenhower was inside the serene confines of Washington's Sheraton Park Hotel. He was there to speak to the governors of the International Bank, the International Monetary Fund, and the International Finance Corporation.

Eisenhower's speech was a thoughtful, high-minded call to promote and sustain "prosperity in peacetime" for all the peoples of the world. "Our economies can help generate an ever better lot for our peoples if we are both forward-looking and prudent in our private and public policies."[37]

Black families in his own land would welcome such prosperity; but they were demanding justice. The violent scenes from Little Rock that morning soon overshadowed the president's eloquent words on the global economy.

Eisenhower returned to Newport later that afternoon. He received a call from Brownell. The attorney general didn't pull any punches in describing the deteriorating scene at Central High. Eisenhower was fed up with Faubus. He was ready to do something about it. He and the attorney general worked out a statement to be released to the press, putting the governor, the mob, and the nation on notice: "I will use the full power of the United States including whatever force may be necessary to prevent any obstruction of the law and to carry out the orders of the Federal Court." The federal law "cannot be flouted with impunity by any individual or any mob of extremists."[38]

Faubus offered his own commentary on the chaos. "The trouble in Little Rock vindicates my good judgment," he said, patting himself on the back for having originally used National Guard troops to keep the Little Rock Nine out.[39] Eisenhower was particularly irritated that Faubus continued to confuse the cause and the effect. He believed that Faubus "saw in the mobs not his duty but rather his vindication for having called out the National Guard in the first place."

Later that same day, in Newport, Eisenhower issued another public statement, this one a proclamation entitled "Obstruction of Justice in the State of Arkansas." In it, he ordered "all persons engaged in such obstruction of justice to cease and desist...."[40]

The mess in Little Rock left the president little choice. No less a source than Mayor Woodrow Mann had sent an urgent telegram to Newport describing the scene, as well as who he believed was responsible. "The mob that gathered was no spontaneous assembly," he wired. "It was agitated, aroused, and assembled by a concerted plan of action." He specifically fingered Jimmy Karam as the mastermind and informed the president that Karam was a "political and social intimate of Governor Faubus, and whose wife is now with the governor's party at the Southern Governor's Conference." Mann concluded that "Governor Faubus at least was cognizant of what was going to take place."[41]

School Superintendent Virgil Blossom called the Department of Justice and asked Brownell for federal intervention. When the call ended, the attorney general began working on a draft proclamation establishing the president's authority to use force to enforce the law. He called Newport and read it to the president on the phone. "I want you to send up that proclamation," Ike said. "It looks like I will have to sign it, but I want to read it."[42]

That night in Little Rock, events continued to deteriorate. Police broke up a racial fight at 15th and Main Streets. Bricks and bottles were hurled through windows. One hundred cars, filled with angry people and guns and dynamite, drove into Daisy Bates's neighborhood. After the police chased them off, Daisy's phone rang. "We didn't get you...," the voice threatened, "but we will. And you better not try to put those coons in our school."

In Newport, President Eisenhower retired to the sun porch of his living quarters to review the material that Brownell had sent him. Perhaps he reflected on the whirlwind of events that had led to this moment. The *Brown* ruling...the local integration plan put in place by Little Rock...the National Guard blocking the school doors...the federal court's injunction...the meeting at Newport with the governor...the duplicity of Faubus...the removal of the troops...the return of mob violence at the schoolhouse door.

Now, he was considering sending military troops into a Southern city for the first time since Reconstruction.

It was a lot to take in. The president retired to his bedroom. The executive order was left unsigned.

◇

A few minutes before 8:00 a.m. on the morning of September 24th, Dwight D. Eisenhower walked toward his office in Newport, breathing in the sea-kissed air of Newport. "There's a cold wind blowing up," he said, not making it clear whether he was referring to the Newport breeze or the political storm weather in Little Rock.[43]

At 8:35 a.m., Brownell called for the first of many updates that would come that day. The two men talked about issuing a statement in case hostilities continued in Little Rock, which they both fully expected would happen. Brownell thought it was important to point out that there had been previous disturbances in American history when a president had had to act, such as the Whiskey Rebellion. Eisenhower liked the reference and thought that it might be worth reminding the public of "like emergencies." He also thought it was important not merely to state that the "law has been defied." He wanted to express his personal sympathy.

The discussion moved to tactics. Brownell had already talked to General Max Taylor, Army chief of staff, about utilizing the National Guard troops in Little Rock. Eisenhower cautioned that this might create a "brother against brother" environment because they would be going up against their own families and friends in Little Rock. Instead, he recommended using National Guard troops from other parts of the state.[44]

Having given Brownell his preliminary orders, Ike turned to other business. His friend, General Al Gruenther, had urged him to return to the White House from his vacation. In response, the president wrote that the "White House office is wherever the president may happen to be." He then specifically addressed the tumult in Little Rock:

> I do not want to give a picture of a Cabinet in constant session, of fretting and worrying about the actions of a misguided gov-

ernor who, in my opinion, has been motivated entirely by what he believes to be political advantage in a particular locality.

Besides, Ike continued:

The Federal government has ample resources with which to cope with this kind of thing. The great need is to act calmly, deliberately, and give every offender opportunity to cease his defiance of Federal law and to peaceably obey the proper orders of the Federal court.

By pursuing this dispassionate course of action, Eisenhower hoped to avoid a situation where people like Faubus "are not falsely transformed into martyrs."[45]

Having completed this letter, Eisenhower now returned to managing the federal response to Little Rock. He called Brownell at 12:08 p.m. In the few hours since their first call that morning, Ike had changed his mind on tactics. "In my career," Eisenhower said, referring to his decades in uniform, "if you have to use force, use overwhelming force and save lives thereby." He would nationalize the Arkansas National Guard and take those troops out from under Faubus's command. But he would also send in perhaps the most famous military unit in America: the 101st Airborne Division. This same division had been visited by General Eisenhower in the hours before D-Day. He had counted on them before. And he knew he could count on them again. Plus, they were specifically trained for crowd-control challenges.

The conversation ended with another surprise from the president to his attorney general. "Meet me at the White House," he said. "I'm going to address the nation on TV."[46] In the meantime, Eisenhower issued an executive order federalizing the Arkansas National Guard and authorizing the use of active duty troops to enforce the law. He personally called General Taylor at 12:15 p.m. and told him to mobilize the 101st for duty in Arkansas.

Shortly after Ike gave the go-ahead, he received another telegram from Mayor Mann in Little Rock. "The immediate need for federal troops is urgent…," it read, since the "mob is much larger in numbers" than the day before. Mann described a chaotic scene in which the "police cannot disperse the mob...." Only military troops could do the job.[47]

At Fort Campbell, Kentucky, one thousand soldiers from the 101st Airborne prepared to leave that day for Little Rock. The first elements would arrive that afternoon, the rest by nightfall.

Still in Newport, Eisenhower conferred with Jim Hagerty on a speech. Having made the decision and issued the orders, he now had to explain it to the nation. A flight was scheduled to take him back to the White House. The communications facilities were better at the White House. But it was also important, Ike thought, to speak to the nation from the capital. The whole nation, indeed the whole world, would be watching. Eisenhower would have to marshal his words carefully, not just to give the moment clarity, but to give it meaning. The man who derided the role of speechmaking in the presidency would now have to give the speech of his life.

◇

Of all the myths in American politics, few are as enduring—and so misguided—as the power of the presidential speechwriter. Scholars and pundits enjoy regaling audiences with tales of surrogate presidents like Hughes or Sorenson or Noonan. Like a lyrical Svengali, a speechwriter is assumed to possess powers of hypnosis over those for whom he works. The speechwriter crafts the words, and the president reads them. Like most myths, this one has elements of truth, but it is largely untrue. Any honest presidential speechwriter will downplay his role.

The myth of the speechwriter doesn't factor in that a president is his own first and best speechwriter. No speech of any significance ever comes out of a president's mouth that didn't at least come in part from his hand, if not his heart or his mind. This was especially true for Eisenhower, who, as a career military officer, had written countless speeches for himself and others. As president, he was no less involved in the speechwriting process. "He reworked and revised his manuscripts endlessly," remembered one speechwriter, Art Larson. "Every open stretch of a few hours was pressed into service" for reworking and editing speeches. "No speech manuscript was finished until he carried it to the podium," Larson recalled.[48]

Eisenhower didn't reserve his involvement for the editorial backend of the process, as he demonstrated on the flight from Newport to Washington. The day he boarded the presidential plane, *The Columbine II,* air-traffic controllers were already calling it Air Force One. As president, Eisenhower had brought a sense of military decorum to the presidential plane. A desk had been placed there for him to work, along with a video projector to watch briefings from the Pentagon and State Department. A radio provided the news, and a safe was on hand, where he could securely store important documents. It was there in the confines of his plane that the president would craft one of the most important speeches of his presidency.

During the short flight to Washington, Eisenhower took out a piece of White House stationery with his initials "DDE" centered at the top. As the plane headed South from New England, the president began to scribble some basic principles that he wanted the speech to convey. Like all good writers, he began to narrow his focus, pulling the arrows out of his quiver, zeroing in on his target.

"Troops—Not to enforce integration but to prevent opposition by violence to orders of a court." Then, having established the theme of the speech, he drew a line to separate the rest of his thoughts. Beneath it, he added some more of the details that he wanted to cover in the speech:

"In Arkansas—Governor ordered out troops, armed and equipped and partially maintained by Fed Government with instructions to prevent execution of a plan proposed by School Board, approved by Fed Judges." Now that he had written out the general theme and the specific problem, he drew another line and began a third section. There, he hoped to outline the solution:

"President can stand by...or he can carry out his oath of office." The speech had to describe the choice that Ike had made and why he had made it. Troops would be sent into the South for the first time since Reconstruction. As he put it on the stationery while flying down to Washington, to allow mobs to disregard federal law would mean the "destruction of our form of government."[49]

The writing skills he had first tested as a young officer, honed with MacArthur, and perfected in World War II had served him well this day. On one sheet of paper, Eisenhower had written out a compelling and complete outline of the speech. He had a theme, a problem, a solution, and, most important for the dramatic effect necessary to hold an audience's attention, a choice. Eisenhower would portray his decision as a choice between lawlessness and the law.

Once he was safely returned to the White House, Eisenhower spent the remainder of the day preparing for his address, which was scheduled to be broadcast live to the nation that night at 9:00. Eisenhower took television seriously. He relied on actor Robert Montgomery for advice on everything from the use of makeup to camera angles. Long before Kennedy or Reagan, Eisenhower pioneered the art of creating a forceful image.

For this appearance on this night, stylistic concerns were less important than substance. Secretary of State John Foster Dulles was also very forthcoming with suggestions. Earlier that day, he had told Brownell that Little Rock was "ruining our foreign policy. The effect of this in Asia and Africa will be worse for us than Hungary was for the Russians." It was during this call that Brownell urged Dulles to add foreign-policy language to the speech. He did, later calling Eisenhower and suggesting that Ike add: "It would be difficult to exaggerate the harm that is being done to the prestige and influence, and indeed to the safety, of our nation and the world. Our enemies are gloating over this incident...."[50]

As Ike began editing the speech as prepared, he added many of Dulles's suggestions. He also had his own edits to make. In the section describing the Supreme Court's ruling of 1954, Ike, in his own hand, added: "Our personal opinions as to the accuracy of the decision have no bearing on the matter of enforcement." After all these years, he still wouldn't publicly say what he thought of the *Brown* ruling. It was the law; that's what mattered.

The speech then praised the desegregation efforts of other Southern communities. Ike added in his own hand that the willingness of these communities to cooperate with federal law was "the cornerstone of our liberties."

Toward the end of the speech, Ike added an entire paragraph making it "clear that Federal troops are not being used to relieve local and state authorities of their primary duty to preserve the peace and order of the community." And again, he added language to show that he was not trying to demonize anyone in the South: "The decision of the Supreme Court concerning school integration affects the South more seriously than it does other sections of the country. In that region I have many warm friends."

His edits finished, Dwight Eisenhower entered the Oval Office a few minutes before 9:00 p.m. and sat behind his desk. As the camera trained its eye on him, he greeted the country wearing a three-piece, gray suit, a dark tie, and the glasses needed to read the text in front of him. "For this talk, I have come to the president's office in the White House," he said in explaining his decision to leave Newport. But by coming to the White House and "speaking from the house of Lincoln, of Jackson, and of Wilson, my words would more clearly convey both the sadness I feel in the action I was compelled today to take and the firmness with which I intend to pursue this course until the orders of the federal court at Little Rock can be executed without unlawful interference."[51]

His pitch and tone were perfect: a strong hand tempered by a heavy heart. He read through the speech with evident conviction, occasionally looking down at the text, but often staring right into the camera. It was tightly crafted and well-delivered. Still, it was only a speech. And Ike understood that speeches don't win battles.

◇

More than a thousand miles away, his troops were taking care of that. That night, the 101st Airborne set up camp in a field just beyond the tennis courts. They had arrived from Fort Campbell in eight C-130 and C-123 transport planes. Jeeps and trucks soon carried them to Central High. A makeshift tent city was quickly erected to house the soldiers. Communications equipment and wiring were set up. Perhaps most impressive of all, no mob dared assemble to challenge the troops. In a matter of hours, the 101st Airborne, with spectacular military precision, had secured the school grounds. This was exactly why Eisenhower had ordered them—and not just National Guard troops—to Little Rock. He knew that their professionalism would be a warning against any agitators.

The next morning, September 25th, a crowd did gather. But it was outmatched, as it soon found out. The 101st had established a barrier at an intersection just east of the school. They called it "Roadblock Alpha," and it was there that a group of angry whites decided to engage the enemy. They were greeted by an officer's voice on a loudspeaker. "Please return to your homes, or it will be necessary to disperse you," Major James Meyers ordered.[52] The crowd refused to move. Twelve soldiers snapped into formation, pointed their bayonets forward, and began marching in perfect order toward the crowd. The crowd began to run. It was the first engagement in the battle that day. And the 101st had shown no problems toward winning it.

At 8:45 a.m., an Army vehicle entered through the barricade at South Park and 16th Streets. In front of the school, the car slowed down to let out nine black students. The youngsters were soon enveloped in a cocoon of soldiers, who escorted them up the steps and into the school. As they had done before, the angry white protestors bitterly complained that "the niggers are inside!" But this time, there was nothing to be done about it. One of the most powerful units in the entire U.S. military was protecting the Little Rock Nine.

Meanwhile, back at "Roadblock Alpha," the crowd had regained its nerve after being chased by the troops earlier. As the crowd grew in size and intensity, another order came over the loudspeaker from Major Meyers: "Let's clear this area right now. This is the living end!" The officer speaking added that this time "we're not going to do it on a slow walk," meaning that the crowd faced a real charge from the troops.

When the crowd didn't move, the charge began. Many of the protestors took refuge in houses, but the troops didn't care. They followed the resistors through the neighborhood until they were pushed well away from the school. Only one protestor tried to put up a fight. He was C. E. Blake, a switchman for the railroad. He tried to grab a soldier's gun and tumbled to the ground with him. He soon regretted it when another soldier took the butt of his gun and smashed it into Blake's head. An ample amount of blood soon flowed from his head. The crowd was now learning the hard way that these soldiers from the 101st were different from the police who had guarded the school earlier in the week. These boys didn't mess around.

Once inside the school, the black students fanned out to their homerooms. Each had an assigned soldier to follow and protect them. The soldiers had been briefed on their students. When Melba Pattillo first noticed a soldier following her, she turned and looked to him. Before she could speak, he did. "Melba," he said, "my name is Danny. I'll be waiting for you here. We're not allowed to go inside the classrooms. If you need me, holler." For the next few days, Danny served as a human metaphor for the federal government, walking behind Melba to make sure she was all right. "It takes a warrior to fight a battle and survive," Danny later told her. "This here is a battle if I've ever seen one." These little pep talks, often spoken from behind Melba as she walked down the hall, helped her to endure the ongoing insults from the white students. "In order to get through this year, you will have to become a soldier," Danny would say. "Never let your enemy know what you are feeling."[53]

Meanwhile, Faubus was again casting himself as the victim, even joking that he had been relieved of his job "like MacArthur." Harry Ashmore was not impressed. In the *Arkansas Gazette* he neatly summarized the strategic flaw inherent in the governor's strategy. Faubus "has by his actions and words dealt a major and perhaps a lethal blow to the cause of segregation which he purported to uphold."[54] Now that the federal government had been provoked, it had effectively settled the issue once and for all. Faubus may have scored some temporary political victories with his white constituents, but he had lost the war over integration.

Faubus was determined to go down fighting, anyway. He gave a televised address in which he portrayed C. E. Blake and himself as martyrs. He also cast aspersions on the character and conduct of the 101st. "In the name of God, whom we all revere, in the name of liberty which we hold so dear, which we all cherish, what is happening in America?" he asked.

Faubus realized how hopeless his cause was. He saw the profi-
ciency of the professional troops monitoring Central High. He saw
that the crowds no longer challenged the troops. He knew that it
was over. He began to wallow between defiance and self-pity. He
even referred to the head of the 101st, General Edwin A. Walker, as
the "Commander of the Little Rock Occupational Forces."

◇

While the 101st soldiers were escorting the kids into the school that
morning, Ike returned to Newport. On the plane ride, he gave a lift
to a reporter from *Time* magazine. John L. Steele was the magazine's White House reporter and knew Ike well; well enough to
coax the president into a candid post-mortem. The conversation
aboard the *Columbine II* that day was the closest thing to an after-
action report that Ike ever uttered on the subject. In an off-the-
record session, he spoke of the pain of the past few days.

Sending in troops "really doesn't settle anything." He paused,
then clarified: "It really doesn't settle anything except the supremacy of the federal government." Sending in troops to an
American city was the hardest decision he'd ever had to make,
save possibly for D-Day.

"Goddamn it," he said, "it was the only thing I could do. Just
a moment after I signed the order, I read an entirely irrational,
hysterical telegram from the mayor—what's his name?—in Little
Rock. It was nutty stuff."

Steele observed a "sad man flying back to Newport." It had
given him no joy to intervene militarily. "The issue here is *not*—
repeat: *not*—segregation," Eisenhower reiterated. "It isn't even the
maintenance of public order. It is a question of upholding the
law—otherwise you have people shooting people." Steele said that
Eisenhower worried that people would misunderstand his motives. No, it was not part of a crusade for racial justice. But neither
was it an effort to disperse with mob rule. Simply put, it was to
enforce the law of the land. This was an important distinction to
Ike, and one he would continue to emphasize for the rest of his life.

Ike expressed a particular animus for the agitators. "This
thing is going to go on and on and on in other places; these

damned hooligans...I was trying to speak last night to the reasonable people, the decent people in the South."

Ike felt that his speech just might have struck the right tone with his audience. He said that his former treasury secretary, George Humphrey, a man with considerable ties to the South, had called him to say that the speech had hit "exactly" the right tone. Still, Ike admitted that the whole ordeal had taken a toll on him, saying that it had "been nagging me day and night."

As the presidential plane landed at Quonset Point, the president turned to Steele: "Gee, it's been swell—wish we could do this more often, John. But damnit, there's so many of you." It was the first, and most detailed, account he had ever given on his decision to send in the troops. And it sounded themes that he would echo for years to come.[55]

As Eisenhower tried to resume his Rhode Island vacation, responses to his actions poured in from all over the nation.

"Please accept my congratulations," Jackie Robinson wired, "on the positive position you have taken in the Little Rock situation." Robinson's fervor for Ike had cooled considerably during the standoff. But he now confessed, "I should have known you would do the right thing at the crucial time."

Another icon of the black community who had also been restless with Ike's patience during the crisis was the great musician Louis Armstrong. He, too, wired his approval: "Daddy, if and when you decide to take those little Negro children personally into Central High School along with your marvelous troops please take me along...." Satchmo concluded by telling the president: "You have a good heart."[56]

Praise came as well from Martin Luther King, Jr. He waxed poetic about how eventually "justice must spring from a new moral climate." FDR's son, James, who had once sought to recruit Ike as a Democratic candidate for president, saluted Eisenhower's "firm and direct action...."[57] An associate of Fort Worth oilman Sid Richardson also approved. Monty Moncrief wrote that the "overwhelming majority of the American people are in full accord with the determined action you have taken."[58] Harry Ashmore took time out from a busy newspaper schedule to wire from Little Rock:

"Thank you sir for your masterful statement...."[59] And Woodrow Wilson's grandchildren sent words of approval.

Even Daisy Bates congratulated the president on his "forthright address...and decisive action."

Not all the mail was so kind. The man who had run against Ike in 1952 as Stevenson's running mate was particularly enraged. Senator John Sparkman spoke of the "resentment and disappointment that the troops were ordered in so soon after your command 'to cease and desist....'" He echoed Faubus's language in saying that "occupying Little Rock has brought about further deterioration of relations and further embitterment between our Negro and white citizens."[60]

Perhaps the deadliest venom came from Georgia senator Richard Russell. He explicitly compared the 101st Airborne troops to Hitler's stormtroopers. An indignant Eisenhower personally penned a response on a piece of White House stationery:

> I must say that I completely fail to comprehend your comparison of our troops to Hitler's storm troopers. In one case military power was used to further the ambitions and purposes of a ruthless dictator; in the other to preserve the institutions of free government.[61]

Some of the warmest applause for his action came from his own household. Mamie was particularly pleased, noting that those "folks have got to get an education, too."[62] Mamie and Ike spent time each day with Sgt. Moaney, who was still serving as the president's valet, and his wife, Delores, who served as the First Family's cook. Indeed, when traveling, the Eisenhowers refused to stay anywhere that refused to house the Moaneys. Mamie had even landed her own blows for racial equally. In 1953, she was saddened to see black children outside the White House gates, denied access to the Easter Egg Roll because of their race. She decreed an end to such exclusivity, integrating the beloved tradition around the same time Ike was pressing local authorities to desegregate the District of Columbia. Now, four years later, she had no doubts that her beloved Ike had done the right thing at Little Rock.

Not all of the responses about the crisis were directed toward Ike. Many others were made in the press or privately. Senate Majority Leader Lyndon Johnson, with his eye on the 1960 election, tried to stake out a middle ground by saying that "there should be no troops from either side patrolling our school campuses anywhere."[63] He elaborated, in a letter to former Secretary of State Dean Acheson, writing that Eisenhower "may find that getting the troops out is a much more difficult proposition than getting them in."[64]

Senator John F. Kennedy was even more skillful in navigating the Little Rock minefield. "The Supreme Court's ruling on desegregation of schools is the law of the land," he told a reporter, "and though there may be disagreement over the president's leadership on this issue, there is no denying that he alone had the ultimate responsibility for deciding what steps are necessary to see that the law is faithfully executed." In one sentence, Kennedy had reassured Northern liberals that he supported the *Brown* decision while hinting to Southern Democrats that he did not wholly approve of the president's handling of the crisis.[65]

◇

During the next several weeks, pressure mounted on Eisenhower to remove the troops. In October, he met in the Oval Office with four Southern governors. They suggested having Faubus send Eisenhower a declaration of his desire to cooperate with the law upon the removal of the federal troops. The president, undoubtedly remembering the experience a month earlier at Newport, told them to go ahead with it anyway. They did. In the Fish Room across from the Oval Office, the gubernatorial quartet worked on a statement. Yet, when they tried to engage Faubus, he did exactly what Ike had expected. A draft statement was sent to Little Rock, whereupon the governor began hedging. After seemingly endless negotiations, a single sentence was approved: "I now declare that I will assume full responsibility for the maintenance of law and order and that the orders of the Federal Court will not be obstructed."

Even still, Faubus couldn't help himself. At the last minute, and without notifying the four governors, he issued his own version of the statement, inserting the words "by me" at the end of it. It changed the entire meaning. Faubus was merely saying that he wouldn't cause trouble. This left him room to allow people like Jimmy Karam to do that for him.

"The statement issued this evening by the governor of Arkansas," Eisenhower answered in his own rejoinder, "does not constitute in my opinion the assurance that he intends to use his full powers as governor to prevent the obstruction of the orders of the United States District Court. Under the circumstances, the president of the United States has no recourse at the present time except to maintain Federal surveillance of the situation."[66]

Privately, his tone was harsher. The day after Ike met with the four Southern governors, he sent word to Vice President Nixon that he hoped to play a round of golf that afternoon. "If you already have a game, please don't think of changing your plans because mine are necessarily so uncertain because of the stupidity and duplicity of one called Faubus."[67]

Eisenhower continued to hope that patience and goodwill might change hearts and minds in the South. But he soon lost one of his closest allies in the fight. By prior agreement, Attorney General Herbert Brownell stepped aside later that month. Brownell's service would be missed. But his impact would remain. For years, the gentlemanly Brownell had gently nudged Ike forward on civil rights. One of his most successful—and least publicized—efforts involved the selection of judicial nominees. Brownell helped to ensure that Eisenhower nominated federal judges who were friendly to civil rights. He even persuaded Ike to appoint the grandson of Justice John Harlan—author of the famous dissent in *Plessy v. Ferguson*—to the Supreme Court in 1955. (Harlan's insistence on answering questions from the Senate during his confirmation process helped to set the precedent for all future Supreme Court confirmation hearings.)

But it was the lower-level judges who would make the greatest impact. For the next twenty years, the civil rights community would seek out these judges when taking their cases to court. "The best civil rights judges in the South," civil rights leader Andrew Young later remembered, "were the Eisenhower appointees...."[68]

Like lumberjacks in a vast, overgrown forest, these men would chop down segregation one ruling at a time. Still, Brownell would be missed, not least of all by the president. At the Department of Justice, Brownell's job would be filled his deputy, William Rogers, who shared his predecessor's passion for civil rights.

By October, the president began withdrawing troops. On October 23rd, the Little Rock Nine walked into school with no troops supporting them. It had taken a month, but Ike's troops had broken the resistance in Little Rock. The president was also able to defederalize large portions of the Arkansas National Guard. Without too many problems, integration continued throughout the remainder of the year. At the end of the school year, the only senior out of the original nine black students, Ernest Green, became the first black to graduate from Central High. So powerful was this moment to the civil rights community that Dr. Martin Luther King, Jr. flew in for the graduation ceremonies.

Faubus continued in his self-appointed role of Southern defender. Politically, his tactics were paying off. A Gallup Poll in 1958 revealed Faubus as one of the ten most admired men in America. And the man who had once feared a serious primary challenge was overwhelmingly nominated for a third term as governor in the summer of 1958.

Eisenhower had always hoped that moderate people of goodwill would solve the problem of racial injustice. At Little Rock, he learned just how naïve he had been. It wasn't just Karam's hoodlums who had chanted obscenities in front of Central High. It was some of the otherwise finest of Little Rock society—doctors, lawyers, and other professionals. Eisenhower, sensing that his faith in the people of the South may have been misplaced, complained bitterly to Oveta Culp Hobby. Hobby had left the Eisenhower administration and returned to Houston to care of her ailing husband in 1955. Ike told her that among influential newspaper editors only Ralph McGill of the *Atlanta Constitution,* had spoken up in support of the president's position at Little Rock.

Meanwhile, Ike's efforts at spiritual reconciliation were also failing. During the Little Rock crisis, a member of Billy Graham's staff penned an article called "No Color Line in Heaven," which showed that Graham generally opposed segregation. Graham himself enjoyed friendly relations with Dr. King. But when King asked Graham to stop including segregationist public officials on the platforms of his rallies, relations between the two men cooled a bit. Part of the power of a Billy Graham crusade was its quasi-official status, testified to by the presence on stage of elected officials. Graham was unwilling to kick these people off the stage, even though he didn't share their segregationist views.[69] Sadly for Ike, there was a limit to what white ministers were willing to do in confronting racism. Dr. King would learn this lesson anew six years later in a Birmingham jail.

And though he had tried to rally moderate editors in the South to his cause, very few seemed interested.

When the Supreme Court in 1958 unanimously upheld the federal government's actions in Little Rock, Faubus did what Eisenhower had always feared he would do: He simply closed down the public schools in Little Rock for the school year. But even politics is not a strong enough force to match economics. And since many white families couldn't afford to send their kids to private schools, the pressure soon mounted to reopen the public schools. In the late summer of 1959, the public schools of Little Rock were opened again. And they were operated on an integrated basis. At last, the Battle of Little Rock was over. But the fallout was just beginning.

CHAPTER ELEVEN

THE FALLOUT

"His conservatism was fixed and rigid, and any evil defacing the nation had to be extracted bit by bit with a tweezer because the surgeon's knife was an instrument too radical to touch this best of all societies."

—Martin Luther King, Jr.

THE PRESIDENT was in a foul mood. In the aftermath of Little Rock, Eisenhower said little publicly. Behind the scenes, he was more candid, and increasingly gloomy. The showdown at Central High had distressed him profoundly.

As husks of chaff are parted from grain during a threshing, so the violence in Little Rock had separated the good from the bad, the right from the wrong. The lines were now clear. Ike was on one side. Faubus was clearly on the other. Not that Ike was any happier about it all.

In October, he met with Arthur Larson, an aide who wrote speeches and worked on policy. Larson had written a memo on civil rights, and Ike was eager to discuss it. The president told Larson that it was important for him to enforce the law but otherwise not to appear personally connected to the issue, because he was essentially in the role of referee. Hence, he had never publicly stated an opinion on the *Brown* case.

He then shocked Larson with his candor: "As a matter of fact, I personally think the decision was wrong." Larson was stunned. To his knowledge, Ike had never said that to anyone before. He listened intently as Eisenhower explained that the Court should have focused on equal opportunities rather than on absolute equal integration. Here, again, was Eisenhower's—and the nation's— philosophical dilemma: opportunity versus outcome, freedom versus equality. Ike leaned toward creating opportunity and freedom. He worried that in an imperfect world it was impossible to reach the standard of equality. But he knew that in a democratic country with a free market, not everyone would reach the same station in life. It might not have been equal, but it was fair. He might not have liked it, but he could live with it.

Larson, a trained lawyer, was ready with a quick rebuttal that day with the president in the White House. He told the president that it was not as simple as a choice between opportunity and outcome. Rather, "separate educational facilities are inherently unequal." The court had to act. And it had done the right thing.

"Yes," Eisenhower sternly responded, "I am thoroughly familiar with that argument, but I do not find it compelling."

Larson shouldn't have been surprised. As the chief author of Eisenhower's 1956 convention acceptance speech, he had been chagrined by the number of changes the president had made on the speech's civil rights sections. Larson couldn't forget the president's comment that "political and economic opportunity did not necessarily mean that everyone has to mingle socially— 'or that a Negro should court my daughter.'" Larson was outraged that the president would rely upon a "cliché that was threadbare even at the time of the Lincoln-Douglas debates."

Larson concluded the president "felt that it was not his job to crusade generally for integration...he also felt that he should do a conscientious job of promoting integration within areas where the president had special legal responsibility." Larson was impressed with Ike's leadership in desegregating the military and the District of Columbia. But he fretted that Ike didn't do more to pursue a "program of legislative enactments designed to enlarge the areas of American life in which segregation was prohibited." To Larson, the reason for this reticence was simple: "He had little faith in legislation as a vehicle for promoting better race relations."[1]

◇

In the South, people were enraged that Eisenhower had used force at Little Rock. Ike's friend Cliff Roberts found that out firsthand when he went to Augusta that fall for some golf. Other than Bobby Jones, Ike was the most famous person who played golf in Augusta. The people loved him…until now. Roberts was "dumbfounded and chagrined to find supposedly sensible people who had become so bitterly critical of the president because he sent troops into Arkansas."[2]

In October, while the troops were still at Central High, the White House was deluged with mail. In a typical week, the mail ran nearly two to one against the president's use of troops in Little Rock. Though most people in the country at large supported the president's decision, all of the energy and passion was on the side of those who opposed it. They were outraged. And they let the president know it.

Even some of the reasonable voices in the South were angry. Fort Worth Congressman Jim Wright urged the president to visit Little Rock and experience the many "people of goodwill…." Perhaps this visit would clarify matters for the president. "I have every confidence that you are as fully anxious as anyone to find a basis on which the troops may be withdrawn and order restored at an early date." Wright candidly admitted that were Ike to pursue this course of action, it would look like a "surrender." Still, he urged the hero of D-Day to consider accepting his own Appomattox. He told the president that the average American considered "'saving face' less important than saving his country from a prolongation of the hideous and ugly spectacle" at Little Rock.[3]

Like Wright, Eisenhower wanted to remove the troops. But unlike Wright, he didn't think a surrender was such a good idea. Ike made this point explicitly in a response letter to the congressman. "No one is more determined than I that Federal troops be withdrawn as soon as possible from Little Rock," he wrote. "This will be done just as soon as such action is clearly consistent with the maintenance of law."[4] The president also rejected the congressman's suggestion that he pay a personal visit to Little Rock. It was a common theme emanating from friend and foe alike during the crisis. Countless people suggested that Eisenhower show up in Little Rock to solve the crisis.

Eisenhower realized what a bad idea this was. A presidential visit inevitably increases attention. That was exactly what he didn't want to do. He was attempting to still the stormy waters, not stir them even further.

Increasingly, Eisenhower became philosophical when discussing the events in Arkansas. "You disagree with the decision and tell me that I should show my disapproval by refusing to prevent violence from obstructing the carrying-out of the Court's orders," he said to one critic. "Let us take a different example. Suppose you had been thrown into jail by an arbitrary sheriff or United States marshall. Your lawyer asked for a writ of habeas corpus, and it is granted by the judge. But the feeling in the locality is such that the sheriff feels completely safe in telling you he will not obey the order, and you remain in jail." By this point, the parallel was obvious. "Would you consider I was doing my solemn duty as the president of the United States if I did not compel your release from jail?"

This was one of the most powerful analogies that Ike ever gave on the subject. From the time of the crisis until the end of his life, he would remain remarkably consistent in this argument: He didn't act to restore order but to enforce the law. "If the day comes when we can obey the orders of our Courts only when we personally approve of them," he wrote to his friend Swede Hazlett that fall, "the end of the American system, as we know it, will not be far off."

"The biggest worry of all," he wrote toward the end of a letter that covered a myriad of difficult issues, "is the constant question of 'doing the right thing.'"[5]

◇

On October 4th, 1957, as the shadow of Little Rock was just starting to recede, Eisenhower again found himself in the middle of a foreign policy crisis. The Soviets had designed and created the first-ever man-made satellite. Called "Sputnik" (Russian for "traveling companion"), it was fired successfully into orbit. It had little scientific or military value, as Eisenhower well knew. But it had a spectacular public-relations value, as he was about to find out.

Sputnik effectively ended the media obsession with Little Rock. The newspapers were filled with hysterical accounts of how the Soviets had beaten America into space. Thanks to the tilling of McCarthyism earlier in the decade, America was fertile ground for Communist hysteria. Americans had been told that there were Communists behind every corner. Now, they were in space, too! To many, it seemed the end of the world.

Eisenhower remained calm, reassuring the nation that it was still quite safe. Privately, he urged the military to get moving with its own lackluster satellite program. When the Navy's Vanguard rocket failed, Eisenhower met with his military chiefs to find out what their next move would be.

Afterward, Eisenhower's rage spilled over to an aide as he recounted the meeting: "And what do you think this goddamn three-star Army general said? He said it was a great day for the Army, because the Navy had fallen flat on its face!"[6] Like a latent volcano, Eisenhower's temper these days was mostly under control. Indeed, his doctors ordered him not to get too worked up. Yet, he was still capable of colorful explosions that witnesses did not soon forget. After the lava had stopped flowing, Eisenhower calmly told his staff that a "Manhattan Project" would be needed for space. They got busy laying the initial groundwork for what would eventually become NASA.

Still, as Eisenhower continued to deal with the aftermath of Sputnik, an ugly racial incident soon transpired that required his attention. Komla Agbeli Gbedemah, the finance minister of Ghana, visited the United States for a series of International Monetary Fund meetings. While in Delaware, Gbedemah was denied service at a Howard Johnson's restaurant. Outraged and embarrassed, Eisenhower quickly sought to limit the damage in the foreign press by personally inviting Gbedemah to breakfast with him at the White House.

Perhaps it was all too much for him: the 1956 campaign...the hard-fought legislative battles of 1957...the showdown at Little Rock...the Sputnik crisis. No one could tell, but it was all taking a toll on the president. On the outside, he was still the picture of health.

On November 25, 1957, the president was at the desk having lunch. He was in good spirits and, seemingly, good health. Suddenly, he rang for Ann Whitman. She immediately left her desk and entered the Oval Office. There, she found the president of the United States sitting behind his desk. He looked confused. As he tried to speak, his words made no sense. General Goodpaster was sent for. He quickly helped the president out of his chair and toward the residence: "Mr. President, I think we should get you to bed."[7] His doctors diagnosed a stroke. Yet his innate resilience again allowed him to bounce back quickly. Within a couple of days, his speech was functioning perfectly.

But he would have to pace himself for the rest of his term. He couldn't take many more years like 1957.

◇

Back in September, at the height of the standoff at Little Rock, the NAACP's Roy Wilkins wired the president at Newport to renew the "request of more than a year ago for a conference between you and the leaders of Negro organizations on the continued persecution of Negro citizens in certain areas of the South." Wilkins noted that Eisenhower had met with opponents of integration, like Richard Russell and Orval Faubus. Wasn't it time to meet with black leaders, too?

The logic was irrefutable even if the timing wasn't good. Ike's health, combined with the hysteria over Sputnik, soon pushed the meeting back. But it would happen; it was just a question of when.

Meanwhile, it was time to begin appointing members of the Civil Rights Commission provided for in the new law that Ike had signed in September. Congressman Gerald Ford of Michigan wrote the president to urge him that the appointments "be completed as soon as possible."[8]

Of all the provisions in the new law, this was perhaps the one closest to Ike's heart. By bringing together a bipartisan group of leaders from different fields and different parts of the country, he hoped that the hot issue of race could be cooled down a bit. "A sphere of action in which the Commission could be most helpful would be the highly explosive situations (e.g., the Autherine

Lucy matter and the Montgomery bus boycott)," Max Rabb wrote in a memo to Chief of Staff Adams that fall.[9]

The Commission would be chaired by John A. Hannah, who was then the president of Michigan State University and a former assistant secretary of Defense. Gordon Tiffany would be the staff director; he was an ally of Sherman Adams and a former New Hampshire attorney general. And the Commission itself would include one African-American: Ernest Wilkins, the assistant secretary of Labor, who had previously made history when he filled in for his boss, Secretary of Labor James Mitchell, and became the first black to attend a presidential Cabinet meeting.

One person who was not on the Commission was Ike's former rival Adlai Stevenson. Sherman Adams had sent word that Ike wanted Stevenson for the job. What better way to strike the tone on civil rights that Ike wanted—a tone that was above politics and tried to bring different people together. Stevenson asked his friends what he should do. Dean Acheson thought Stevenson should stay out of it. Arthur Schlesinger thought he should participate.

Stevenson had been thinking a good deal about race. When the Little Rock crisis first broke out, he told the press, "I don't suppose the president has much that he can do." And he had refused to advocate the use of troops to enforce the court order. But when Ike did send in troops, Stevenson had expressed mild support, saying that Ike "had no choice" but noting that it was at best a "temporary solution." He called on Ike to use the bully pulpit and "mobilize the nation's conscience as he has mobilized its arms." Nevertheless, Stevenson declined to serve on the Civil Rights Commission.[10]

Dr. Hannah said the purpose of the Commission was to study ways of combating discrimination and promoting "domestic tranquility" and "long-term relationships with the uncommitted areas of the world that are so vital" to the United States. Like the president they served, the commissioners would address discrimination but with a profound appreciation for the Cold War environment in which they lived.

By the Spring of 1958, as the Civil Rights Commission was fighting Southern congressmen and senators for funding needed to get started, Max Rabb resigned from the president's staff. He had served the president long and well. But if presidents run marathons, staffers run sprints. Five years in any White House is a long time, indeed. To replace him, the White House chose a young special assistant for personnel management named Rocco Siciliano. A veteran of World War II, Siciliano was a lawyer who was eminently capable, competent, and committed to the president.

As he went through Rabb's files, Siciliano noticed a high number of meeting requests from various black leaders that had accumulated over the years. "I went through the letters and found a recent request from the Reverend Martin Luther King, Jr.," he later remembered. "After thinking it through, I went in to see Governor Adams, and I proposed the president meet with a few of the black leaders."[11]

"Go ahead," Adams responded. Siciliano immediately set out to arrange a meeting between a president of the United States and an official group of black leaders. He first met with Fred Morrow. Morrow saw Siciliano's leadership as manna from Heaven because he had toiled for years in the desert trying to set up such a meeting himself.

Siciliano called Dr. King personally and urged that they get together and talk. King readily agreed. On June 9th, 1958, King met with Siciliano, Fred Morrow, and Deputy Attorney General Lawrence Walsh. The meeting was essentially a trial run before going to see the president. It went well. King assured everyone that the most important part of meeting with the president was the meeting itself. Reasonably assured that expectations were not too high, the staffers agreed to pursue an event with the president.

June 23rd, 1958, was set as the date for the meeting. That day, Siciliano first met with Attorney General William Rogers and Fred Morrow. The men went into the Oval Office to brief the president in advance of the meeting. The president seemed to be in a fine mood. But Siciliano felt that it was important to warn the president about two possible semantic pitfalls that he should avoid.

"Mr. President," he nervously said, "there are two words that generally cause some negative reaction, that I might suggest you not use when you meet with them. These two words are 'patience' and 'tolerance.'"

Ike was immediately irritated. "Well, Siciliano," he shot back, "you think I'm going to avoid good English words?"[12]

Within a few minutes, the meeting began. Entering the room were Martin Luther King, Jr., A. Philip Randolph, Roy Wilkins, and Lester Granger of the Urban League. Eisenhower warmly greeted the men and invited them to sit down. But the sunny mood in the room soon turned a bit darker. Randolph read a nine-point plan on civil rights that they wanted the president to enact. King soon followed, urging the president to declare forcefully "that the law will be vigorously upheld." He also asked the president to use the bully pulpit to encourage white Americans to accept an integrated society.

Wilkins was next. He praised the president for desegregating the military and helping to secure the 1957 civil rights law. He also questioned the justness of a court ruling, from a week earlier, that gave the Little Rock Board of Education a stay before completing integration (the ruling was soon overturned). But it was Granger who caused the temperature in the room to rise considerably. He told the president that the anger and bitterness in the black community was higher than he had ever seen it.

Attorney General Rogers was the first to respond when the four civil rights leaders were finished. He had been reading the written statement that the four men intended to release to the press. He pointed out that its tone was harsh and that it did not include any of the praise that Randolph in particular had been careful to make during the meeting. He also pointed out that previous administrations had been long on speeches but short on action. The Eisenhower White House had reversed this.

At this point, Ike jumped in. He was "extremely dismayed" to learn of the bitterness in the black community after what he saw as five years of positive results from his White House.[13] Would more action on civil rights continue to leave black Americans discouraged? Not all, Granger responded. Indeed, any bitterness that was felt was in no way directed at the president.

As to King's longstanding desire that the president convene a summit-like meeting to discuss race, Ike said there might be some value in it, though he doubted it would solve the problem. The president then ended the meeting by renewing his pledge to support stronger voting rights legislation. As King prepared to leave, the president reached out for his hand: "Reverend, there are so many problems...."[14] He perhaps thought that reminding King of the myriad of issues facing the president might provide some useful context. Instead, King felt that it showed Ike wasn't terribly interested in moving forward on civil rights.

After the meeting, the four civil rights leaders went into the Fish Room in the West Wing to meet the press. "The president manifested a profound interest in this whole question," Randolph told the assembled reporters.[15] The men were so positive about the meeting that one black reporter asked whether the president had "brainwashed" them. The press conference soon ended.

Years later, Martin Luther King, Jr., reflected on his meeting with Eisenhower and his views about the president's commitment to the cause of ending discrimination. It was a nuanced, complicated portrait that King drew of the president. "No one could discuss racial justice with President Eisenhower without coming away with mixed emotions," he wrote. "His personal sincerity on the issue was pronounced, and he had a magnificent capacity to communicate it to individuals."

Still, while King recognized Ike's commitment to evolving change, he was disappointed that the president could not embrace a little more revolution. "President Eisenhower could not be committed to anything which involved a structural change in the architecture of American society. His conservatism was fixed and rigid, and any evil defacing the nation had to be extracted bit by bit with a tweezer because the surgeon's knife was an instrument too radical to touch this best of all societies."[16]

<>

Eisenhower was a tired man. Beset by domestic problems and a string of health issues, he began to conserve his time and energy for the area that he had always cared about most—foreign policy. This was the age of nuclear buildups, and Ike wanted to know what the Soviets were up to. He had first proposed an Open Skies Initiative, whereby both American and Soviet planes could fly over the other's airspace and monitor their missile capability. But the Soviets rejected it.

Now, Eisenhower turned to one of his favorite assets in waging peace: the intelligence community. Ike had already used covert operations to topple the pro-Soviet leader of Iran and had staged a successful coup in Guatemala to remove the democratically elected Jacobo Arbenz Guzman because he was sympathetic to the Communists.

Now, Eisenhower turned his intelligence operation toward the heart of the Soviet empire. He approved a new spy plane, the U-2, which could fly at such altitudes in Soviet airspace as to not be detected. Pictures could be taken from the plane, giving Ike the intelligence he needed on his adversary.

All seemed well. The planes produced a stream of valuable intelligence. But in May 1960, Gary Powers's plane was shot down by the Soviets. Ike manfully told the public—and the world—that of course he was spying on the Soviets, just like they were spying on America. Had he not been doing so, he would not have been doing his job.

The end of the second term also saw Eisenhower traveling the world. Ike felt that these tours were good for the image of the United States. One thing that was not good for the image of the United States was continuing racial unrest in the American South.

Eisenhower also had more staffing issues. All presidential staffs fall victim to the attrition that inevitably builds over the years. Perhaps the most painful loss was that of his chief of staff, Sherman Adams. A New England businessman named Bernard Goldfine had paid some hotel bills for the chief of staff. He also had given Adams other gifts, including expensive coats. Though Ike hated to lose him, Adams had to go. And he did, to be replaced by General Jerry Persons.

One of Persons's first acts as chief of staff was to reach out to Fred Morrow. The two men were indeed an odd couple. Persons was a white Southerner, and Morrow was a black Northerner. But they had always gotten along fairly well. Once the meeting began, Persons got right to the point: "Fred, I have a tough job to do now; I need all the help I can get. I just want to ask you to do me a favor. If you have any more Little Rock problems...don't come to me with them. Go to anybody else."[17]

Persons complained that "this damn civil rights, black business has broken up my family!" He again asked Morrow, "Just don't ever come to me."

Morrow, appreciative more than angry, responded: "I won't, general." He couldn't help but notice that implicit in Persons's words was a downgrade in the issue. At least when Adams had been around, the top staffer had been concerned about the issue. The new chief of staff didn't even want to know about it.

◇

Eisenhower was not the only public figure to have mixed feelings about the pace of the civil rights movement. Around this time, former President Harry Truman paid a visit to Yale University. The self-educated Truman felt totally at ease in New Haven. At a private meeting with a small group of faculty and students, the subject of civil rights came up. One of the students present, Fred Greenstein, remembered that Truman had spoken with pride of his role in pursuing equal rights for all Americans. "But personally," Truman continued, "I don't care to associate with niggers."[18]

On February 1st, 1960, a new weapon was introduced into the civil rights arsenal. Joseph McNeill, a black student at North Carolina A&T State University, walked into a Woolworth's store restaurant and sat down at the lunch counter. When he was refused service, he refused to leave. The power of his protest lay in his direct confrontation with his oppressor. McNeill could literally stare down the segregationist. Plus, he could continue to take up a seat until the police came. At that point, the sit-in strategy became dicey as cops would typically not be in a good mood when they arrived to break up the demonstration.

By the spring of 1960, civil rights leaders were asking the federal government to protect the protestors against police brutality.

On March 16th, Edward Morgan of ABC asked the president what he thought of the "current Gandhi-like passive resistance demonstrations of Negroes in the South...."

Though he refused to make any "sweeping judgment" Ike remarked of the protests that "some are unquestionably a proper expression of a conviction...." He added that he was "deeply sympathetic with the efforts of any group to enjoy the rights, the rights of equality that they are guaranteed by the Constitution." He concluded that "if a person is expressing such an aspiration as this in a perfectly legal way, then I don't see any reason why he should not do it [sit in]."[19]

Meanwhile, members of Eisenhower's Department of Justice, led by Attorney General Rogers, sat down with representatives of several major store chains, including Woolworth's, to try and find a compromise. The agreement that they later reached ended segregation in lunch counters in sixty-nine Southern communities.

The sit-ins had worked. They also had roused the ire of an increasingly irritable Harry Truman. The former president said publicly that if anyone were to stage a sit-in at a store he owned, "I'd throw him out." He wondered aloud whether the Communists weren't somehow responsible for the sit-ins. But even ex-presidents need strong-willed friends to tell them when to be quiet. After Dean Acheson urged Truman that his recent comments had been "wholly out of keeping with your public record," Truman put a lid on it.[20]

◇

In September 1959, the Civil Rights Commission issued a report criticizing the lack of voting rights in the South. A bright, young CRC staffer named Harris Wofford noted that even the Southern press could not help but condemn voting discrimination even though they generally opposed the report's recommendations. Voting rights, Wofford decided, would be the next great civil rights battle. "Here it seems to me," he wrote in a memo, "is the open door. The solid South is split on the issue."

Eisenhower agreed that suffrage was paramount. It was consistent with his conservative philosophy—it was a federal issue, plus it was an area where he could push for greater opportunities to vote, rather than try to equalize outcomes and resources, which the school-integration cases demanded.

In 1960, legislation was approved that, though watered-down, still provided increased guarantees for voting rights. It offered referees, appointed by the courts, to oversee voting procedures, and it laid down tougher penalties for obstruction of voting rights. On May 6th, 1960, Eisenhower signed the bill, seeing it as a step toward protecting the vote for all citizens.

1960 was an election year. Eisenhower was not ready to see a Democrat succeed him. After John Kennedy emerged as the Democratic nominee, Ike was even more determined to see Vice President Nixon win. He viewed Kennedy as a pretty boy; a rich, young man in too much of a hurry.

To win, both parties courted the black vote that year. And the key, many experts thought, was not Martin Luther King or Ralph Abernathy. It was Jackie Robinson. The legendary slugger had supported Eisenhower, but he was disillusioned about the president's commitment to civil rights. "Could it be that his frequent trips for golf and hunting in Georgia bring him in contact with people whose rigid opposition to equal rights he is affected by?" Robinson asked.[21]

Still, if he was dissatisfied with Republicans, Robinson was distrustful of Democrats. In July, Robinson met with Kennedy. For once, the senator's fabled charms failed him. Robinson complained that Kennedy wouldn't look him in the eye. And he was offended when the senator asked what it would take to win his support. "I don't want any of your money," he responded. "I'm just interested in helping the candidate who I think will be best for the black American." When Kennedy chose Lyndon Johnson as his runningmate, Robinson saw it as a complete surrender to the Dixiecrats. He labeled it a "bid for the appeasement of Southern bigots."[22]

Robinson declared his support for Nixon, whom he believed was more progressive on race than Eisenhower. During a personal meeting in the vice president's office, Nixon assured Robinson that he was committed to fighting segregation. Yet, years later, what Robinson remembered most about the meeting was a phone call that Nixon received. As the baseball legend watched, the vice president answered the phone. "No, well, I can't do that," Jackie recalled hearing the vice president say. "I'm tired of pulling his chestnuts out of the fire. He'll have to work his own way out of this one." Nixon hung up, telling Robinson that he had been referring to the president. Robinson felt that Nixon was trying to demonstrate his independence from Ike, who, he correctly surmised, was not wildly popular with the black public. Still, Robinson was a team player. He didn't always agree with Ike. But he was the leader of the team at that time. Nixon likely meant no harm. He was with a friend and was speaking candidly. But Robinson found Nixon's action that day to be disloyal. "It had the feel of a cheap trick," he wrote. As the campaign wore on, Robinson felt he had cause to regret his endorsement.[23]

That fall, Ike called Nixon on the campaign trail for updates. The vice president said that the crowds in the South had been fantastic. Ike asked what parts of the stump speech had been getting the most response. Nixon answered that what "appeals most is a statement to the effect that we are not going to weaken states' rights but we are going to strengthen them." This may have raised cheers from the white Southern crowds, but it also raised concerns from many in the black community.

In October, a judge in De Kalb County, Georgia, sentenced Martin Luther King, Jr. to four months of hard labor for his role in a sit-in. Robinson, on the road campaigning for Nixon, urged the campaign to speak out about this injustice. "He has to call Martin right now, today," he told campaign aide William Safire. "I have the number of the jail." Safire arranged for Robinson to speak to Nixon personally. Robinson left the meeting depressed. "He thinks calling Martin would be 'grandstanding,'" he told Safire with tears in his eyes. Then he revealed a changed mind: "Nixon doesn't deserve to win."[24]

Nixon wasn't alone in his reluctance. Deputy Attorney General Lawrence Walsh had drafted a statement for the White House to issue: "Dr. Martin Luther King was ordered imprisoned for driving without a license in Georgia after participating in a demonstration to end discrimination (segregation) in the dining room of Rich's Dept. Store, Atlanta, Ga," Walsh's proposed statement began. "Seems unjust that a man be imprisoned on an unrelated and insignificant charge. Attorney general has been asked to take steps to vacate charge."[25]

But Eisenhower held back. "He thought the charges were ridiculous," Walsh later remembered, "but he thought his involvement in the case would look like grandstanding."[26]

One group of people who didn't think it would look like grandstanding was the Kennedy campaign. Harris Wofford had left the Civil Rights Commission and was now working full-time for Kennedy. When he heard about King's arrest, he called his boss, Sargent Shriver. "If the senator would only call Mrs. King and wish her well it would reverberate all through the Negro community in the United States."[27] Shriver agreed. As the candidate's brother-in-law, he was the perfect messenger to broach the subject. Alone with Kennedy, Shriver described the "lousy treatment" King was getting in jail. "I think you ought to give her a call, Jack," he said, urging the senator to reach out to Mrs. King, who was terribly worried about her husband.

"What the hell," Kennedy responded. "That's a decent thing to do. Why not? Get her on the phone."

"I know this must be very hard for you," Kennedy told Coretta Scott King. "I understand you are expecting a baby, and I just wanted you to know that I was thinking about you and Dr. King. If there is anything I can do to help, please feel free to call on me."[28]

Though his brother Robert later called the judge who was involved, it was the candidate's call to Coretta that made the difference. Kennedy's phone call, juxtaposed with the Eisenhower-Nixon silence, illustrated why Eisenhower received little credit on civil rights. Ike preferred actions to speeches. But what Kennedy instinctively understood is that sometimes symbolism is substance. Calling a grieving wife on the phone was not grandstanding—it was a great act of sympathy and compassion. Sometimes, a symbolic gesture can transcend politics and even policy. "If there is anything I can do to help" is hardly a specific plan of action. But it does connect a political leader to a person in need.

Wofford understood this better than most. He now prepared to make the most of it. He and Shriver prepared a pamphlet called "'No Comment' Nixon Versus a Candidate with a Heart, Senator Kennedy." It contained quotes from the King family and other black leaders about the King imprisonment. More than two million copies were printed on blue paper, giving it the nickname of the "blue bomb." The documents were discreetly distributed to black churches.

Kennedy himself knew nothing of the clandestine politics that Wofford and Shriver were orchestrating. However, he had read that King's father had endorsed him even though he was Catholic. Kennedy was outraged. "That was a hell of a bigoted statement, wasn't it?" he asked Wofford as he walked with him to the campaign plane, carrying his daughter, Caroline, on his back. "Imagine Martin Luther King having a bigot for a father." He paused, then smiled at Wofford and joked, "Well, we all have fathers, don't we?"[29]

<>

On Election Day, John F. Kennedy was elected president of the United States in one of the nation's history's closest contests. A majority of black voters helped to put him over the top. Plus, the attitudes of the majority were at last beginning to change a bit on race. Throughout the 1950s, Gallup Polls consistently showed that just over half of the public supported the *Brown* decision and that a consistent forty percent opposed it. But a Gallup Poll in 1959 showed that nearly sixty percent of Americans supported it and that fewer than thirty-five percent opposed it.[30] A small, but significant, change. Eisenhower had always said that hearts and minds would have to change and that it would take time. By 1960, it appeared that they were beginning to change.

The morning after the election, Ike flew on Air Force One to Georgia for a vacation. He told his friends during a bridge game on the plane ride that the election had been the "biggest defeat of my life." He was critical of Nixon: "Dick never asked me how I thought the campaign should be run."[31] Ike regretted that Nixon hadn't used the president's Hollywood advisor, Robert Montgomery. "I offered him Montgomery, who would never have let him look as he did in that first television debate." Then, Ike suggested that Nixon's runningmate, Ambassador Henry Cabot Lodge, Jr., should shoulder much of the blame. The ambassador had promised that, if elected, he and Nixon would place a black in the Cabinet. Nixon had publicly demurred, creating a situation where whites in the South were enraged by Lodge, and liberals in the North were enraged by Nixon. "Cabot Lodge should never have stuck his nose into the makeup of the Cabinet," Ike fumed. "Promising a Negro cost us thousands of votes in the South, maybe South Carolina and Texas."

Five weeks after the vote, Eisenhower was still fuming. He convened a meeting in the Oval Office with Vice President Nixon, Chief of Staff Persons, and Senator Thurston Morton, who also served as chairman of the Republican National Committee. This was to be the group's official post-mortem on the election results.

Eisenhower began by telling the group that he was "nonplussed" by the election results and then praised the efforts of Nixon. When the conversation turned to civil rights, Eisenhower observed that the attorney general was to his left on the issue. In the next breath, he noted that his White House had "made civil rights a main part of our effort these past eight years," but that his administration had "lost Negro support instead of increasing it." The president was angry, even bitter. In spite of what he saw as his achievements on civil rights, black voters "just do not give a damn."[32]

Nixon, reflecting his innate color-blind outlook, noted with pride that he had received "slightly more Negro votes" than the ticket had gotten in 1952. Still, he acknowledged the political realities of the South. The vice president agreed that Lodge's promise to appoint a black to the Cabinet "just killed us in the South."

Senator Morton was perhaps the angriest. In referring to black voters, he simply said, "The Hell with them," a strange comment from a man charged with building coalitions and winning votes.

For his part, the president argued that "nobody is more sincere" in improving "the opportunities of these people...." Again, however, he stated his belief that more than the law was needed to create a more just society.

Christmas is a beautiful time at the White House. A grand pine tree takes up residence in the Oval Room on the second floor of the residence in the White House. Outside, just beyond the South Lawn, another huge tree occupies some prime real estate in back of the White House for visitors to see. All around the town, lights and mistletoe can be seen.

But it was a sad Christmas at the White House that December of 1960. A melancholy mood filled the place. At the staff Christmas party, Eisenhower sought out Fred Morrow, who had served him so long and so well since they had first met on the campaign train in 1952. He took Morrow aside and spoke to him about his future.

"Son, I've done my damnedest to try to help you find a job. Unfortunately, industry in this country is not yet ready to accept Negro men like you on the level that you ought to be used." Eisenhower was genuinely pained as he talked to Morrow. "I've tried everything; friends, everything else, and they all say, 'Yes, he's qualified, but....'" With tears in his eyes, the president said simply, softly, "I'm sorry."[33]

Morrow was touched by Ike's emotion, and by his efforts. Perhaps the president hadn't noticed that his failure to secure a job for Morrow was proof of just how far America still had to go in the struggle for equality. Eisenhower had often talked about the power of persuasion in fighting racial ills. And yet, even he couldn't persuade his many business friends to hire Fred Morrow, a man who was a lawyer, a military veteran, and a White House staffer. But a man who also happened to be black.

As he prepared to leave the White House in Washington for the greener pastures of his farm at Gettysburg, Eisenhower was a mix of pride and regret—pride of what he had accomplished, and regret that he couldn't have done more. During his presidency, he had tried to manage the civil rights issue. He had wanted to do it right. Had he had gone any faster, expectations might have been raised to exorbitant levels for blacks, while Southerners would have been angered and rebellious. There might have been even more Little Rocks. Instead, there had been one. Conservatives often judge success by that which doesn't happen. And for Eisenhower, the lack of more widespread racial violence was an argument for his policy, not against it.

His job, as he saw it, had been to be president of the people...all the people. He had tried to reconcile competing interests, protecting minority rights while respecting the will of the majority. This was the American system bequeathed by the Founding Fathers. If American government moves slowly, that's because it was designed to do just that.

Eisenhower had tried hard to balance it all—the progress of civil rights with majority rule. In the seesaw of American politics, Eisenhower had tried to ensure that no one hit the ground too hard.

More important than where Eisenhower stood was where he was heading. At a time in life when attitudes and actions harden for most people, Ike was rethinking the values of a lifetime.

Like the country he had served so long and so well, he was growing, evolving, and changing.

PART THREE

TAPS

"What lies behind you and what lies in front of you,
pales in comparison to what lies inside of you."

—Ralph Waldo Emerson

CHAPTER TWELVE

THE ENDING

*"Is this pretty much what Ike signed in 1957
with the Little Rock thing?"*

—John F. Kennedy

A FEW MILES EAST of Pennsylvania's South Mountains, nestled comfortably into green and fertile farm land, resides the little town of Gettysburg, immortalized by three bloody days in July 1863. General Robert E. Lee was confident—too confident, it turned out—that his Army of Northern Virginia could again perform miracles. He ordered a suicidal, fateful charge that failed to break the Union line. It was the high-water mark of the Confederacy, and its death knell.

One hundred years later, visitors still made pilgrimages to this hallowed Pennsylvanian ground. Not all of the battlefield was covered by the National Park. Many local people owned land either on or adjacent to the battlefield itself. There, cannon and crops were neighbors.

One of these local landowners was a man in his seventies, whose weathered head was rimmed with white hair, and whose walk had been slowed a bit by years of health struggles. He was a former five-star general and president of the United States.

Dwight Eisenhower owned 246 acres and leased another 305. He grew oats, corn, and barley. And the hay fed the black Angus cattle that he raised.

When he wasn't in his fields, Eisenhower could be found in the house. A white, two-story, colonial home, it had a glassed-in sun porch that was shaped like a rectangle.[1] This was the former president's favorite room. There, he could look out over Seminary Ridge to the east, where, a hundred years earlier, Confederates assembled for Pickett's Charge. Perhaps Ike sat and wondered about how his hero Lee could have talked himself into such a colossal blunder.

Mostly, Ike sat in the sun porch and read, wrote, even painted. To tend to his business matters, he traveled a short distance to Gettysburg College, where an office was set up for him. The office, as always, was simple. A wooden desk sat in the corner, with a rug posted in front and an American flag directly behind it. The walls were a pale green, the curtains a faded gold. Paintings of nature decorated the walls. There, Ike answered correspondence, worked on his memoirs, greeted visitors, and kept an eye on politics. When the weather in Pennsylvania turned cold, Ike and Mamie would spend a few months in sunny Palm Springs, California. Usually, they took their personal staff along with them. And that meant John and Delores Moaney. The African-American couple were still proudly and loyally serving the Eisenhowers, as they had for years.

The general in winter was a restless soul. Like other ex-presidents before and since, he found prestige a poor substitute for power.

Presidents convince themselves that they alone understand the job and how it should be done. Ike was no different. Like a skilled engineer, he had spent a lifetime studying how the gears of the engine meshed to make the vehicle operate. He viewed his dashing, young successor as something closer to a hot-rod driver.

And like all ex-presidents, Ike was fighting old battles. Still a keen observer of the global and domestic political scene, he couldn't help but overlook the domestic issue that had caused him so much difficulty and that showed no signs of abating in the 1960s. The civil rights movement was fast becoming a revolution.

<>

As a senator, John Kennedy had criticized Eisenhower's handling of the Little Rock crisis. Now, as president, he was reconsidering. In the fall of 1962, a young black student and military veteran named James Meredith attempted to enroll at the University of Mississippi. As at Little Rock, the court had ordered that he be allowed to attend the school. As at Little Rock, a defiant governor vowed to stop it.

Voltaire observed that common sense isn't always common. And so it was at Ole Miss in 1962. Chaos reigned. Tension escalated. President Kennedy could not talk sense into Governor Ross Barnett.

The Kennedy administration relied on U.S. marshals to protect Meredith. But the marshals were no match for mobs of angry white people swarming over the Ole Miss campus. The scene was made even more chaotic by the bizarre cameo appearance of former Major General Edwin Walker. Five years earlier, the general had commanded the 101st Airborne at Little Rock. But now, having resigned his commission, Walker had officially switched sides. He joined with the protestors, accusing the civil rights leadership of "collusion with the international Communist conspiracy." He praised Governor Barnett and denounced the red agenda he thought he saw: "Barnett, yes; Castro, no!" he yelled in rallying the crowd.

At a White House strategy session, Kennedy talked his options over. He also called his favorite wordsmith, Ted Sorenson, who was in the hospital. He suggested that Sorenson put down some words on paper in case a speech were needed. The wordsmith wanted the president to blame Republicans for "taking the straight Ross Barnett line."

Kennedy couldn't help but notice the irony. With a laugh, he corrected his speechwriter: "Except Eisenhower. Eisenhower's taking a little away from 'em."[2]

Indeed, Eisenhower was appalled at the scene in Mississippi. On September 27th, the elder statesman was quoted in the *New York Times* condemning Barnett's actions as "absolutely unconscionable and undefensible...."[3] Ike could not have missed the similarities between Ole Miss in 1962 and Little Rock in 1957. It probably brought back a lot of painful memories of another demagogic governor who had made his life miserable five years earlier. With the perspective of time and experience, he was much quicker to denounce the Dixiecrats, calling on the orders of the court to be fully enforced.

The mobs in Mississippi continued to riot and block Meredith's entrance. As September ended, gunfire erupted; 375 were wounded, and two were killed. Kennedy had finally had enough. He would send in federal troops. At the White House, an aide placed the necessary paperwork for the president to sign. "Is this pretty much what Ike signed in 1957 with the Little Rock thing?" Kennedy asked.

After signing the documents, Kennedy noted, "That's General Grant's table." Catching himself, he cautioned his aide: "Don't tell them [the press] about General's Grant's table." The president may have appreciated the history involved. Many Southerners would have resented it.[4]

Kennedy finally ended the standoff by sending the troops. Why did he hesitate? Why did he insist on using marshals even when it was obvious the crowds could and would overwhelm them? Part of the answer is that Kennedy, like any president, didn't relish the thought of sending regular military troops into a community, especially a Southern community.

But there was more to it than that. Kennedy was haunted by the memory of Little Rock. He had criticized Eisenhower for allowing Little Rock to escalate to the point that troops were necessary. He was determined to prevent history from repeating. But his charms failed to change Governor Ross Barnett. And in the end, when he could delay no longer in dispatching troops, he even asked that the papers he signed be similar to those of Eisenhower's—a small admission that he had been too quick to condemn his predecessor about the events of September 1957.

James Meredith at last was enrolled in the University of Mississippi. A few days after the crisis subsided, *Time* magazine criticized Kennedy's handling of it and unfavorably compared it to another president's dealings with a similar uprising. "President Kennedy could have learned from Eisenhower's performance in the Little Rock crisis," the magazine opined. If intervention was needed, "then intervene with sufficient force. That's what Ike did, and there was no death toll in Little Rock, nor any serious casualties."[5]

◇

If Mississippi had challenged Kennedy's views on civil rights, Birmingham would change them forever. By 1963, the civil rights movement was a full-scale revolution. No longer willing to accept scraps from the table, civil rights leaders demanded full equality across a whole cross-section of issues: education, transportation, and increasingly, public accommodations.

In Birmingham, Martin Luther King and his associates were upping the ante. King was now reaching the height of moral authority. Part of his power stemmed from his untouchability. The movement had always been careful to put ministers in charge. A black leader who worked in a white-owned business or taught school could easily be fired. A black minister answering to a black church had no fears of job security.

King's personality galvanized the movement. The sun around whom the civil rights world revolved, he was a celebrity who traveled the country, speaking at churches, signing autographs and appearing in the newspapers on an almost daily basis.

But King's powers also derived from his sense of grand strategy. His plans for the civil rights movement were as attentive to detail as they were ambitious in reach. Traditionally, protests had been geared toward sympathetic national reporters as well as local people of goodwill. No more. By 1963, co-option was giving way to confrontation. Indeed, in March of 1963, King and his team launched "Project C"—for confrontation—in Birmingham. The goal was to directly target businesses in the downtown area. King hoped to convince mainstream America to expunge the odious scent of segregation and disinfect a racist society.

King had chosen his target well. Easter was fast approaching and Birmingham's business community did not want any boycotts. Some friends of the civil rights movement even urged King to re-think his high-stakes gamble in Birmingham. Wasn't he already winning? Wasn't segregation losing? The only question was how long it would take to finish it off.

But King saw it differently. He feared that the very successes of the civil rights movement might trigger failure. King wanted to re-ignite the movement by taking on an even bigger challenge in Birmingham.

Besides, King was dissatisfied with the Kennedy administration. Earlier that year, the president refused to issue an Emancipation Proclamation for the 20th century, as King had urged. In January, King had listened in horror to the words of the new governor of Alabama, George Wallace: "Segregation now! Segregation tomorrow! Segregation forever!"

Like his predecessor, President Kennedy seemed content to focus his energies on fighting the Cold War. And so King decided the time had come to try and force the administration's hand.

When the protests began in earnest that spring, policemen led by Eugene "Bull" Connor did exactly what King expected, and secretly hoped for. They overplayed their hand. With nightsticks and dogs, they viciously attacked the peaceful, unarmed protestors in the streets of downtown Birmingham. King himself was soon arrested. Turning tragedy into triumph, he penned the immortal "Letter From a Birmingham Jail." It was written in response to a public appeal from white ministers who called on King to exercise patience.

"This 'Wait' has almost always meant 'Never,'" King angrily rebutted. "We must come to see with one of our distinguished jurists that 'justice too long delayed is justice denied.'"[6] The letter created a sensation around the country and around the globe. It was a battle cry for freedom and it galvanized countless people who read it.

Eventually, King was released. He immediately returned to the front, planning the next phase in "Project C." His next move would shock the country. He organized little armies of young students to go downtown and be arrested. King knew this was a risky strategy—putting children into the middle of the fight. But he again gambled that Bull Connor would overplay his hand and mistreat the kids. With the media on the scene in Birmingham, King hoped images of kids being beaten by police would finally arouse the national conscience.

Connor did not disappoint. His cops not only beat the kids but, in a new tactic, turned one hundred pounds of water pressure on them from fire hoses. As the protests continued and the violence grew, President Kennedy sent 3000 federal troops to a position not far from the city. Though they kept their distance, their presence calmed the tensions inside Birmingham.

Soon the businesses of Birmingham bowed to public pressure. "WHITE" and "COLORED" signs soon came down. In the spring of 1963, segregated lunch counters in Birmingham were desegregated. And King was again hailed as a master strategist. The movement, and the issue, could not be ignored.

At the White House, Kennedy decided that he could no longer try and manage the crisis. It was time to lead. He would introduce sweeping new civil rights legislation. To get it passed, he thought he might need the help of his predecessor.

<>

On June 12th, 1963, Dwight Eisenhower returned to the White House for a meeting with President Kennedy and Vice President Johnson. The men had kept a low-profile, though cordial, relationship since the transition in 1961. Kennedy sent Ike golf balls and even visited the general in Palm Springs.

Until now, foreign policy had dominated their discussions. Now, Kennedy asked Ike for help on the most pressing domestic matter of all—race. With the searing images of Birmingham still fresh on everyone's minds, the men discussed how to pass a new civil rights bill, and what form it should take.

Eisenhower, though generally supportive, was careful to avoid specific suggestions. "I expressed the conviction that the race question has become one that involves the conscience of both the nation and the individual," Ike later recalled, "but concerning additional laws, I as a layman, was not able to suggest the details that might be useful in solving the bitter problem with which we are faced."[7]

Then Kennedy raised the ante. He specifically asked Ike's assistance in rounding up Republican votes for the bill once it was written. "Mr. President," Ike demurred, "you have got two-thirds of the Senate right now."

Kennedy pushed back. "Well, you know what is going to happen to my party," a none too veiled reference to the continuing resistance of Southern Democrats.

Ike agreed that the bill should not be killed by parliamentary maneuver. "I think this thing should finally, as a matter of policy, be voted on on its merits rather than just on this problem of cloture."

Eisenhower offered some tactical advice. "In 1957 when I was working on civil rights legislation I had to take decisive steps" but he recalled that he "didn't get nearly as much as I wanted in 1957." Ike suggested that Kennedy's bill start with the most important proposals. That way, he could more easily beat back the inevitable cloture attempts by Southern Democrats. Then, he could add in the rest of his proposals.

Before leaving, Ike pledged to help out with Republicans. "Well," he told Kennedy, "I haven't talked to my people, and I have no authority over them. I can see what they would like to do, and then suggest to them what I believe."[8]

When Ike returned home to Gettysburg, he had a letter from the White House that had already been in the mail before the men met on June 10th. In it, Kennedy sought Ike's help and specifically compared his upcoming civil rights bill to "the measure you sent to the Congress in 1957."[9]

Eisenhower wrote back, renewing his pledge to work with Republicans and "not hesitate to let them know of my personal convictions...."[10] Eisenhower's lobbying of Senate Republicans took the form of a letter to Republican Leader Everett Dirksen on June 14th, 1963. Eisenhower, though measured in his words, expressed his desire to "strive in every useful way to assure equality in economic and political rights and opportunities for all...." Still, he couldn't help notice the irony of the Democrats becoming "immersed in a hopeless civil war when anything remotely touching the race question is brought up in the Congress."[11]

This is likely the key to deciphering Ike's maneuverings with Kennedy on race. As always, he was broadly sympathetic on civil rights and was willing to support new legislation. But he likely thought it was odd for Kennedy to summon him to the Oval Office for a presidential sales pitch. Most Republicans would vote for it. They weren't the problem. The problem was the Southern Democrats. And Ike undoubtedly believed Kennedy should spend his time in meetings with them, not a former Republican president. For his part, Kennedy wasn't sure how willing Ike was to help out.

Since Birmingham, Kennedy seemed to have changed on civil rights. So did the country. In the 1950s, Eisenhower confronted huge numbers of Americans who opposed civil rights. Now the numbers were shifting. A Gallup Poll in July of 1963 showed that eighty-three percent of Southerners believed the day was coming when whites and blacks would live in equality. Kennedy could afford to move forward on civil rights. The country was moving that way.

On August 28th, the president hosted Martin Luther King at the White House following his magnificent "I Have a Dream" speech at the March on Washington. An impromptu strategy session ensued as the leaders of the march met with the president and his staff to discuss civil rights legislation.

Toward the end of the meeting, King suggested that Eisenhower be recruited to lobby House Minority Leader Charles Halleck. King thought that maybe a personal, moral challenge to Ike from a minister might get him more involved and make a difference.

"No, it won't," Kennedy disagreed. "No, it won't." But King persisted. He joked that Ike "happens to be in the other denomination." But he asked: "Isn't he a Democrat when he goes to church?"

Laughter filled the room. Then Eugene Carson Blake, a minister with ties to Eisenhower, suggested that the former president "can be got at on that ground." Blake suggested that a group of ministers visit Ike at Gettysburg. Kennedy liked the idea. Then he looked over at Walter Reuther, whose own speech at the March on Washington that day had blistered the Kennedy administration for not doing more on civil rights. With a wry smile, the president said: "And keep Walter in the background."[12]

That fall, Rev. Blake did visit with Eisenhower. The general again pledged his support for "equal rights and opportunities for all our citizens." He expressed some concern about the clause in the Kennedy bill requiring equal access to public accommodations. Since these accommodations were in many cases private property, many conservatives worried that perhaps the heavy hand of the federal government was a bit too strong on this point.

Ike also suggested that for any meaningful change in civil rights policy to occur, unity must be achieved. To do this, he suggested a "common platform" be written by both parties on civil rights.[13]

Blake relayed Ike's ideas to Kennedy. The president, perhaps amused at the naiveté of a common platform, told the minister to thank Ike for the idea but to point out that the new civil rights bill could not wait for a unity plank.

<>

Kennedy's death that November changed everything. Seizing the opportunity to make history, almost overnight, Lyndon Johnson, the Southern Democrat, transformed into a civil rights statesman. Marshalling all of his considerable legislative skill, he challenged the mourning nation to honor JFK's memory by supporting civil rights.

Meanwhile, as the election year of 1964 began, Eisenhower was brooding over the possible Republican candidates for president. The GOP base was rallying to Arizona senator Barry Goldwater. With his black-rimmed glasses and his unsmiling face, Goldwater was hardly a natural in the television age of politics that Ike himself helped launch.

But Goldwater was a man of conviction. His principled stand on issues attracted friends, as well as enemies. The growing conservative base of the party revered him as a plain-spoken, tough-talking Westerner who would right the wrongs of Washington.

Conservatives of the 1960s were animated by a palpable sense of grievance—Eastern Europe had been stolen, China had been lost, Korea was surrendered, and the New Deal was expanding. Anger was the emotion that defined conservatives of that era. When William F. Buckley had launched the first edition of his new magazine *National Review* in the 1950s, he wrote that its purpose was "standing athwart history, yelling Stop."

Eisenhower found this thinking inherently backward. Talk about rolling back Social Security or education spending struck him as political suicide. Furthermore, he found the Goldwaterites too strong, too harsh, too unelectable. He was still temperamentally a conservative, less concerned with how society ought to be than with how it was.

Still, Eisenhower understood that the United States had been fundamentally altered by the New Deal and the Cold War. In this sense, Eisenhower was more conservative than the Arizona senator—he was the one who accepted the reality of American politics where Goldwater was the dreamer, planning huge changes for the country in both domestic and foreign policy.

Eisenhower told an aide that Goldwater's vaunted conservative philosophy brought to mind an Indian River: "an inch deep and a mile wide—too deep to plow and too shallow to drink." That was when Ike was in a good mood. At other times, he would simply say: "The guy is nuts."[14]

One issue that particularly concerned Eisenhower was civil rights. By 1964, he, like much of the country, had decided that civil rights could no longer wait. Before now, like Hamlet, he had tried to balance competing interests. He had tried to temper his desire for greater freedom for blacks with his respect for the rule of law and the will of the majority. Now, in the aftermath of Birmingham, the Kennedy assassination, and media images of police dogs mauling black children, it was time to choose sides. The issue was no longer *how* to do civil rights, as it had been during the 1950s. The issue was *whether* to do civil rights. And Ike, like much of the country, came down squarely on the side of civil rights. To paraphrase one of Dr. King's favorite metaphors, the time for thermometer politics was over. It was time for a thermostat to set the climate for the country.

On July 2nd, the Civil Rights Act of 1964 was signed into law by President Johnson. It included the public accommodation clause, which gave Goldwater a reason to vote against it though not before he journeyed to Gettysburg to explain his vote to Eisenhower. Ike was enraged. Not long after, Pennsylvania governor William Scranton got a phone call from his state's most famous resident.

Eisenhower and Scranton were old friends. Ike had supported Scranton for governor in 1962. They had also talked about a possible Scranton bid for the presidency. In an earlier conversation, Ike seemed to imply support. But once Scranton entered the race, Eisenhower remained neutral, thereby killing one of the best chances to stop Goldwater.

Now, as the two men discussed the civil rights vote, a touch of regret could be heard in Ike's voice. He asked Scranton what he thought of Goldwater's vote. Scranton told him that "I feel rotten" about it. Scranton asked what the former president thought about it. "I'm sick," he responded.

The two men talked for a while. Eisenhower said he was "very concerned" about how Goldwater's vote would be interpreted and what it meant for the long-term health of the party. The conversation ended with Ike telling the governor he feared "the Republican Party will become a white supremacist party."[15]

◇

But Eisenhower remained a team player. And if Goldwater was the nominee, he would support him, painful though it may be. On August 6, Ike met with the candidate and his running mate, Bill Miller. Ike laid out the conditions for his support. It is a measure of how little he thought of Goldwater that one of his conditions was for the nominee to renounce all support from racist groups. Goldwater agreed, pledging he would reject "the backing of the Ku Klux Klan."[16]

As the campaign unfolded, Goldwater realized he would have to do something dramatic to demonstrate that he was in the mainstream ("a meandering stream" Nelson Rockefeller joked). He arranged to record a short film with Eisenhower at Gettysburg in which the two men would discuss Goldwater's qualifications for office.

Ike agreed, unhappily, to do it. The day of the filming, the producers briefed the two men on the taping and told Ike the key was to rebut the charge that Goldwater wanted to start a nuclear war.

"Oh, you know I'd say that's a lot of bullshit," Ike proposed. "But I can't say that on TV, can I?" Told that he couldn't, Eisenhower decided to use the word "tommyrot" instead. With the rolling green fields of Ike's farm in the background, the two men prepared to tape the spot. True to his word, when the cameras rolled, Eisenhower responded to a question from Goldwater about his perceived eagerness to start a war: "Well, Barry, in this mind, this is actual tommyrot."[17]

But all was not well during the taping. When the crew broke for lunch, Eisenhower left for the house to eat with Mamie. He did not invite Goldwater to join him.

But Goldwater got his campaign commercial. He was pleased with it. When he found television time had been purchased to broadcast an endorsement speech from a rising star, Goldwater suggested using that air time to re-broadcast the Ike video.

"Barry, I can't just turn the time over to you, because it's not mine to give," said the rising star, Ronald Reagan.[18] He told Goldwater that he was planning to give his standard stump speech and that "a private group bought this time."

"Well, I haven't seen the speech or heard it," Goldwater responded. "Let me call you back." Reagan's stirring oratory no doubt impressed the candidate. Perhaps he even liked Reagan's evocation of FDR's "rendezvous with destiny" for the conservative cause. And who could not help but be impressed with the commanding presence the former Hollywood actor displayed, as well as his resonate cadence that had been honed during years of radio work? "Well, what the hell's wrong with that?" Goldwater asked his staff after reviewing Reagan's performance. Reagan's speech went on the air. But to no avail. No one could save Goldwater. Not Ike. Not Reagan. Lyndon Johnson won in a huge landslide. But he did lose most of the South, which voted Republican in protest of the Civil Rights Act of 1964.

There was little Eisenhower could do. Like all ex-presidents, he was learning that he could still give orders, but no one was required to follow. And the Republican Party of 1964 showed no signs of following his lead, least of all on civil rights.

In his phone call to Governor Scranton that summer, Ike had voiced his fear that his honorable, if moderate, record of progress on civil rights as president would now be forgotten in the face of Goldwater's racial policies. He was right. The party of Lincoln was now the party of Goldwater. It would never again win more than a fraction of the black vote.

◇

Civil rights was much on Ike's mind these days. In 1963, Fred Morrow's memoir of his years inside the Eisenhower White House had been published. Morrow may have had trouble finding a job, but he had no trouble finding a publisher eager to print the story of a high-level African-American working for Ike.

Morrow's portrait, *Black Man in the White House*, offered a balanced look at what he saw as the successes and failures of his time in Washington. Though tinged with regret that more wasn't done, it presented Eisenhower as a good boss and a fair man who cared about civil rights.

But Eisenhower was a bit spooked about former staffers' memoirs. Emmet Hughes's 1962 *The Ordeal of Power* had presented Eisenhower as a vacillating man who reserved his energy for the golf course. One chapter was entitled "Thrusts and Tremblings." It could hardly have been any other way. A lifelong Democrat, Hughes admired Eisenhower in some ways. But he found Ike severely wanting next to FDR and his activist agenda.

In his old age, Eisenhower retained a thin skin. Perhaps knowing that Morrow might have an even stronger case to make, he was nervous about his book. Years later, Morrow would recall a retreat in Hershey, Pennsylvania where Ike gathered with some of his former staff to discuss ways of re-building the Republican Party. During one session, Ike announced that after the group took a break, a conversation about civil rights would follow. He then walked over to Fred Morrow. He said he wanted Morrow to lead the discussion on civil rights since "you were always ranting about this thing."

Morrow was shocked. As the break ended, his shock turned to horror when Eisenhower addressed the group. "There is a man

292

here today whom I felt was my friend," Eisenhower said, "but he wrote a book. I don't know whether he's my friend now or not."

Staggered by the introduction, Morrow made his way to the front of the room. "Mr. President," he began, "I am certain you have not read my book, because if you had, you could not have introduced me the way you did this morning." Morrow looked out over the crowd and continued: "I'm devastated, because in my book I bent over backwards, sir, to let the world know what a great, honorable, decent man you were and how, together, we sweated blood to try to make this country a better place, not only for blacks but for everybody."

An uncomfortable silence filled the room as Morrow concluded: "The only reason why I wrote that book was because I caught unshirted hell for being loyal to you, and that was the only way I could let the world know that I had tried to serve and serve decently and honorably." With that, Morrow sat back down.

Eisenhower's relationship with Morrow soon returned to its normally warm status. "Of course he hadn't read the book," Morrow explained later. Yet, it was obvious to Morrow why Ike was so nervous on the subject: "This was guilt!" The president, Morrow later said, "knew darned good and well the things that hadn't been done..." and perhaps felt he could have and should have done more.[19]

◇

As the long, dark shadows began to creep ever closer, Eisenhower remained active in those final years. Like all ex-presidents, he devoted considerable time to refighting old battles. It was Churchill who had joked that history would treat him well because "I intend to write it." Now Ike was writing his own history.

The first volume of his presidential memoirs, *Mandate for Change*, had been released in 1963. Now, he was working on the second volume, which would cover the second term of his presidency. When his editor read a first draft and suggested that more be written on civil rights, Ike readily agreed. "I particularly appreciate the criticism on the lack of comment on the civil rights issue," he somewhat sheepishly wrote back. "That was just an oversight because I have always felt very strongly on the matter."[20]

All memoirs are, at some level, a final act of spin. Ike's was no different. Interestingly, he wrote about his views on the *Brown* case in the second volume of his memoirs, not his first, which had been released in 1963. Since then, in the wake of Birmingham, the nation was increasingly supportive of civil rights and the most sweeping civil lights law in history was passed in 1964.

But now, in the mid sixties, and with the nudge of his editor, he was ready to re-visit the issue. He wrote in the second volume of his memoirs that he had asked a number of lawyers about the *Brown* decision at the time and that they had all told him it was a good decision. Eisenhower wrote that "I definitely agreed with the unanimous decision."[21]

This probably came as news to Emmet Hughes, Art Larson, Ann Whitman, Max Rabb, and even Herbert Brownell. None of them ever recalled Ike saying this at the time. Indeed, in the case of at least one of them, it was recalled that he said he opposed the decision. To another, he said the ruling had set the cause of civil rights back. And to all, his words and actions were consistent with one doing a duty rather than carrying out a decision he agreed with.

Still, Eisenhower's revision was indicative of his current mind-set. He really did think people deserved fair treatment. He really did think he had done the right thing at Little Rock. And he really did think Goldwater was wrong to oppose the 1964 bill.

Eisenhower's recollections for his second volume of memoirs were insightful. Not because they showed how he really felt in 1954; they didn't. But because, more important, they showed how he felt in 1964.

What Eisenhower said about the issue was less important than what the issue said about him. That he made an effort to deal directly with civil rights in his memoirs is a good indication it was much on his mind.

In the aftermath of Birmingham, the Kennedy assassination and LBJ's all-out blitz for a new civil rights law in 1964, the country had finally crossed the Rubicon. Ironically, after the sweeping 1964 Civil Rights Act, King approached President Johnson about pursuing a single focus that Eisenhower had long argued was most important: voting rights. In 1965, the Voting Rights Act became law.

In the meantime, when he learned that Anthony Lewis of the *New York Times* was writing a book critical of his leadership—or perceived lack thereof—on the 1957 civil rights bill, Ike indignantly wrote to Brownell that either "my memory is nuts" or Lewis was making the story up "out of whole cloth." Brownell offered reassurances, essentially telling Ike to consider the source of the book.[22]

Brownell remained a favorite of Ike's to the very end. As Richard Nixon again entered the national stage, and the chief justice's seat was again open to be filled, Ike urged his former vice president to consider Brownell for the nation's top judicial job. But old resentments died hard. Ike told historian Stephen Ambrose that he regretted "the appointment of that dumb son of a bitch Earl Warren."[23] Indeed, Warren was aware of Ike's animus toward him and went so far as to confront him about it. Aboard Air Force One, en route to Churchill's funeral, Warren approached Eisenhower and asked which cases had so upset him.

"Oh, those Communist cases," he answered.

"What Communist cases?" the Chief Justise asked.

"All of them," Ike replied. Warren responded with a description of the legal rights entitled to all Americans. The former president was not persuaded.

"What would you do with Communists in America?" he asked Eisenhower.

"I would kill the S.O.B.s," Ike answered.[24] Curiously, the conversation between the two men contained no mention of the *Brown* ruling. By this time, Eisenhower appreciated both the importance and the rightness of the decision, though he didn't bring it up with Warren. His anger with the chief justice stemmed from what he saw as liberal rulings on cases involving national security.

◇

Ike suffered a series of heart attacks, starting with one in November of 1965 while he was in Augusta for golf. As his health deteriorated, so too did the national mood. Eisenhower was increasingly concerned about Vietnam. As president, he had skillfully kept America out of any major involvement in the Southeast Asia country. Now that his successors had committed half a million troops to the struggle, the old soldier counseled LBJ to go all out for victory. Meanwhile, he was outraged by the racial rioting that took place in Los Angeles, Detroit and other cities.

He blamed the violence, in part, on the heightened expectation levels produced by the New Frontier and the Great Society. "One of the worst things has been the glib assurances that have been given to so many disadvantaged people that all their difficulties will disappear by magic just as soon as a particular speaker is elected to office," he wrote to George Humphrey in 1968. "If the problems of the slums had been properly presented to the people in terms of needed objectives but with an accurate account of the time and work—including also work by the disadvantaged themselves—I am sure that many of the riots that we experienced last summer would never have occurred."

He recalled that he had been preaching that "laws alone" were not enough for a long time. And he despised what he saw as the casual pandering of the War on Poverty. He wrote that "when leaders become so personally ambitious that they paint rosey pictures of early perfection, they have only themselves to blame for the ensuing disappointments, resentments and riots."[25]

In an almost Hegelian manner, Eisenhower's philosophy on race was now complete. Like a journey up a steep mountain, only at the end, from the summit, could the entire ascent be viewed and understood.

He still held the nature of man to be sinful and therefore not easily perfected. He still believed incremental evolution was preferable to immediate revolution. And he still thought that changing laws was only part of the solution.

On matters of race, he had always preferred the velvet cords of persuasion to iron bonds of federal law. He had always been more interested in leveling the playing field than in dictating scores. As long as people had a fair shot at the starting line he wasn't too worried about different outcomes at the finish line.

He had accepted that freedom sometimes brings ugly truths: in a free society, some will achieve more than others. Fair did not mean equal, in Eisenhower's eyes. It couldn't, because absolute equality could never be achieved. He shared the ancient conservative view that those who seek heaven on earth can inadvertently end up creating hell.

Here is the classic conservative critique of liberalism: That utopia can never be reached is evident; less apparent, but even more dangerous, is that the pursuit of utopia requires such heavy-handed measures as to make life worse, not better. Revolutionaries like Thomas Paine may have believed that we "have it in our power to begin the world over again," but Eisenhower didn't want to start the world over. He was content to leave it a little better than he found it.

But civil rights may well have been an issue where conservatism simply didn't have enough to offer. The promise of incremental change over time was little solace to a poor black family in Selma or a young child of color in Albany. If ever an issue cried out for dramatic, federal action it was racial justice. If ever policymakers should have sought to "begin the world over again," it was on civil rights.

And so Eisenhower now genuinely believed in and embraced the cause of racial justice. He had been outraged by Goldwater. He had quietly worked with Kennedy to support civil rights. He even campaigned for black candidates for office and served as honorary chair for a fundraising drive to benefit the Tuskegee Institute. When Harvard's first black professor willed that his life's savings go the establishment of a "Dwight D. Eisenhower Scholarship Fund," Ike "could not recall a personal distinction that had touched me more deeply."[26] And later, in the spring of 1968, while admitting he didn't always agree with his tactics, he mourned the loss of Dr. King as a "disaster."

What to make of these seemingly disparate pieces? As Hegel would put it, this was a "truth as a whole," a synthesis of Eisenhower's goals of freedom and equality of opportunity with his preferred means of government when necessary, but not necessarily government. But as the years grew, so too did Ike's sympathy with more government action.

His journey had brought him a long way, indeed. Eisenhower's strength came from his ability to speak for—not to—the country as a whole. As president, he had been an effective emergency room doctor who could successfully perform triage. He could quickly evaluate an incoming crisis, make an accurate diagnosis, and write out a powerful prescription. This was most evident at Little Rock where he skillfully and decisively managed an explosive situation and brought it to a peaceful conclusion.

If he made a mistake, it was not a lack of leadership or commitment or vision.

His shortcoming was a lack of imagination. "Nothing happens unless first a dream," the poet and historian Carl Sandburg wrote. Some important things did happen in the 1950s on civil rights. But they sprang from the dreams of others, not from the president.

Eisenhower found it difficult to imagine what the world would look like if the radical changes proposed took effect. It was hard to imagine how the government would or could desegregate every public school in America. The logistics alone must have seemed overwhelming. How would you ensure that schools were equal especially when schools were built in neighborhoods which were themselves segregated? This is perhaps what he was getting at when he complained to his speechwriter that the Court should have focused more on equal opportunity. It was not an unreasonable concern. Years later, it would take a fleet of yellow school buses to solve this issue by transporting kids from one neighborhood to a school in another.

The only crusade he had ever wanted to lead was liberating Europe in World War II. He was not a revolutionary and didn't want to radically change what he saw as a fundamentally good society. He was what political scientists call a "stewardship" president—more concerned with managing change than with boldly taking the initiative and righting wrongs.

He didn't much care for philosophers and he certainly wouldn't have liked Rousseau, who helped launch the French Revolution with his theories that mankind is essentially good by nature and had been corrupted by civilization. Eisenhower saw American society as a place where people would reach different stations in life depending on their effort, talent, and determination. He accepted that the nature of man was flawed and had been since the Garden of Eden. The world could be improved, perhaps, but not perfected.

Unlike Dr. King, Eisenhower did not "have a dream." But he did have a plan. Once the *Brown* ruling had been handed down, Eisenhower began, in his own methodical, incremental way to accept the ruling and do his part to enforce it. Had Faubus succeeded at Central High, it is hard to imagine how the movement could have gone forward, much less how it would have achieved its successes in the 1960s.

Little Rock was a defining battle. After it was settled, the outcome of the civil rights struggle was not in doubt. It would take time, yes, and more battles. But once the federal government effectively broke the back of segregation with the use of troops, there was no hope that segregation could hold on and preserve itself.

When the poet Robert Frost visited Eisenhower in the Oval Office, he handed the president a book of his poetry. Inside it, the silver-haired sage from New England had inscribed words that could have been written about Little Rock: "The strong are saying nothing till they see."

Through it all, Eisenhower hadn't always taken the right position on every issue nor done everything asked of him by the civil rights community. If at times his tongue seemed fixed to the roof of his mouth, it was by design. He measured his words on purpose, trying not to inflame an already volatile climate. And if he appeared at Little Rock uneager to use force, that is at it should have been. No president should employ troops against American citizens with any less deliberation than that which was shown in the autumn of 1957.

He was not kidding when he later said that his decision at Little Rock ranked with D-Day as the hardest of his life. Thanks to his skill, America successfully passed the gravest constitutional test since the Civil War. Eisenhower helped prove to the world that a government of majority rule could still be a society that protects minority rights. Steady was the hand that guided the tiller of America in the 1950s.

But more important than where he stood at a particular time was the course he charted for all time. Dwight Eisenhower, like most of his countrymen, was traveling toward a more just society. In the fight for civil rights, he was always extending his front, step by step, skirmish by skirmish.

Above all, his handling of civil rights serves as a profound rebuttal to the caricature of him that was created by his critics. No, this was not the genial, slightly doddering grandfather whose steps were slow, whose spirit was soft, and whose mind was tired.

This was a thoughtful, careful, methodical man who tried to first prevent a crisis and then, once it had begun, tried to effectively and decisively settle it. He was a career soldier whose entire training was to avoid battle when possible but to fight and win unavoidable battles when necessary. Through it all, he was informed and involved, engaged and energetic. In every way he was a president; in every way he was a human. His record, like all records, is mixed, but is clearly marked with more positives than negatives. It is not claiming too much to contend that his record on race is largely good and entirely honorable. Herbert Brownell had been right all along: his mind and his hands may not have immediately followed, but his heart was always in the right place.

In the final analysis, Eisenhower's last, longest, and perhaps greatest battle was ultimately a struggle within himself. He had to overcome his own background and his own doubts. In the end, like every battle he ever waged, he fought it with his heart, mind, and soul. And like every battle he waged, in the end, he won. Ike's final battle ended in victory.

◇

The last few months of Ike's life were lived inside Walter Reed General Hospital in Washington, D.C. The hospital was, appropriately enough, named for an Army legend. Major Walter Reed helped to cure yellow fever and thus had helped to make the creation of the Panama Canal possible. The hospital was a stately structure with huge white columns in front and a red brick texture all around it. There, soldiers and former soldiers went to heal. There, Eisenhower went to die.

He knew the end was near. The heart attacks were taking a toll on him. Still, he tried to keep a busy routine for as long as possible. And his political judgment was still quite good. He had told Nixon in 1967 that he was particularly impressed with his friend Prescott Bush's son, George. Ike said that the younger Bush was a "comer."[27] And when Nixon visited with Ike in 1968, the general was pleased to see that Bush was on the list of possible vice-presidential nominees. Eisenhower even dressed up in his hospital room so that he could be beamed to Miami and briefly address the delegates of that year's Republican National Convention. He was thrilled to see Nixon win the White House. Sadly, there was no chance of his attending the inauguration, though he had been able to watch on closed-circuit television the December wedding of his grandson David to Nixon's daughter Julie.

By 1969, it was obvious that it was only a matter of time. On the morning of March 28th, 1969, Eisenhower took command of one last engagement. The approach of death has a way of stripping away the veils of life until all that remains is the essence of the man. And so it was that day. Ike became, again, a commander.

"Lower the shades!" he ordered, as if calling up reinforcements at the Bulge. "Pull me up," he instructed as though he were commanding at Normandy. When the doctor and John Eisenhower had failed to raise him to the desired level, Ike's temper flared one last time: "Two big men—*higher*." They complied. At last, all was set. His struggle was over. His work was done. His time had come.

"I want to go," he said quietly, looking at his son John. "God take me." He was seventy-eight years old.[28]

Outside, the light of Heaven had dawned bright and broad, peeling back the curtain of dusk to unveil a crystal sky unbroken by clouds.

BIBLIOGRAPHY

Abdul-Jabbar, Kareem, and Anthony Walton. *Brothers in Arms*. New York: Broadway Books, 2004.

Abels, Jules. *Out of the Jaws of Victory*. New York: Henry Holt & Co., 1959.

Adams, Sherman. *Firsthand Report: The Story of the Eisenhower Administration*. New York: Harper and Bros., 1961.

Ambrose, Stephen E. *Eisenhower*, Vol.1, *Soldier, General of the Army, President-Elect 1890–1952*. New York: Simon and Schuster, 1983.

------. *Eisenhower: The President*. New York: Simon and Schuster, 1984.

------. *The Supreme Commander: The War Years of General Dwight D. Eisenhower*. Jackson: University Press of Mississippi, 1999.

Baker, James T. *Brooks Hays*. Macon: Mercer University Press, 1989.

Bates, Daisy. *The Long Shadow of Little Rock: A Memoir*. Fayetteville: University of Arkansas Press, 1987.

Beals, Melba Patillo. *Warriors Don't Cry*. New York: Pocket Books, 1994.

Beschloss, Michael R. *Eisenhower: A Centennial Life*. New York: HarperCollins Publishers, 1990.

Black, Conrad. *Franklin Delano Roosevelt: Champion of Freedom*. New York: Public Affairs, 2003.

Bradley, Omar N. with Clay Blair. *A General's Life: An Autobiography by the General of the Army*. New York: Simon and Schuster, 1983.

Branch, Taylor. *Parting the Waters: America in the King Years 1954–63*. New York: Simon and Schuster, 1988.

Brendon, Piers. *Ike: His Life and Times*. New York: Harper and Row, 1986.

Brinkley, Douglas and Ronald J. Drez. *Voices of Valor: D-Day: June 6, 1944*. New York: Bulfinch Press, 2004.

Brownell, Herbert with John P. Burke. *Advising Ike: The Memoirs of Attorney General Herbert Brownell*. Lawrence: University Press of Kansas, 1993.

Bryant, Nick. *The Bystander: John F. Kennedy and the Struggle for Black Equality.* New York: Basic Books, 1983.

Burke, Edmund. *The Best of Burke.* New York: Gateway Editions, 1999.

Burns, James McGregory. *Roosevelt: The Soldier of Freedom 1940–45.* New York: Harcourt Brace Jovanovich, 1970.

Butcher, Harry. Papers. Dwight D. Eisenhower Library, Abilene, Kansas.

Caro, Robert A. *Master of the Senate: The Years of Lyndon Johnson.* New York: Alfred A. Knopf, 2002.

Childs, Marquis. *Eisenhower: Captive Hero.* New York: Harcourt, Brace and Company, 1958.

Claridge, Laura. *Norman Rockwell: A Life.* New York: Modern Library, 2003.

Clements, Kendrick A. *Woodrow Wilson: World Statesman.* Chicago: Ivan R. Dee, 1999.

Cray, Ed. *Chief Justice: A Biography of Earl Warren.* New York: Simon and Schuster, 1997.

Dallek, Robert. *An Unfinished Life: John F. Kennedy 1917–1963.* New York: Little, Brown and Company, 2003.

Davis, Kenneth S. *Soldier of Democracy: A Biography of Dwight D. Eisenhower.* Garden City, New York: Doubleday and Company, Inc., 1945.

D'Este, Carlo. *Eisenhower: A Soldier's Life.* New York: Henry Holt & Co., 2002.

Donovan, Robert. *Confidential Secretary: Ann Whitman's Twenty Years with Eisenhower and Rockefeller.* New York: E. P. Dutton, 1988.

------. *Conflict and Crisis: The Presidency of Harry S Truman 1945–1948.* New York: W.W. Norton and Company Inc., 1977.

Duram, James C. *A Moderate Among Extremists: Dwight D. Eisenhower and the School Desegregation Crisis.* Chicago: Nelson-Hall, 1981.

Edwards, Lee. *The Conservative Revolution: The Movement that Remade America.* New York: The Free Press, 1999.

Eisenhower, David. *Eisenhower: At War 1943–1945.* New York: Random House, 1986.

Eisenhower, Dwight D. *At Ease: Stories I Tell to Friends.* New York: Doubleday and Company, Inc., 1963.

------. *Mandate for Change: The White House Years 1953–1956*. Garden City, New York: Doubleday and Company, Inc., 1963.

------. *Waging Peace: The White House Years 1956–1961*. Garden City, New York: Doubleday and Company, Inc., 1965.

------. Personal Diary. Dwight D. Eisenhower Library, Abilene, Kansas.

------. *Public Papers of the Presidents*. 9 vols. Washington, D.C.: Library of Congress, 1953–61.

------. *The Papers of Dwight David Eisenhower*. 17 vols. Baltimore, MD: The Johns Hopkins University Press.

------. *Eisenhower: The Prewar Diaries and Selected Papers, 1905–41*. Baltimore, MD: The Johns Hopkins University Press, 1998.

Eisenhower, John S. D. *Strictly Personal*. Garden City, New York: Doubleday and Company, Inc., 1974.

------. *The Bitter Woods: The Battle of the Bulge*. New York: Da Capo Press, 1995.

Eisenhower, Susan. *Mrs. Ike: Memories and Reflections on the Life of Mamie Eisenhower*. New York: Farrar, Straus and Giroux, 1996.

Ellison, Ralph. *The Collected Essays of Ralph Ellison*. New York: Modern Library, 2003,

Ferrell, Robert H. *The Eisenhower Diaries*. New York: Norton, 1981.

Graham, Billy. *Just As I Am: The Autobiography of Billy Graham*. New York: Harper SanFransico/Zondervan, 1997.

Hagerty, James. "Dewey Far in Lead; A Tie in the Senate Strong Possibility." *The New York Times*, July 5, 1948.

Halberstam, David. *The Fifties*. New York: The Random House Publishing Group, 1993.

Hamby, Alonzo L. *Man of the People: A Life of Harry S Truman*. New York: Oxford University Press, 1995.

Hamilton, Charles V. *Adam Clayton Powell, Jr: The Political Biography of an American Dilemma*. New York: Atheneum MacMillan Publishing, 1991.

Hegel, George. *Hegel: The Essential Writings*. New York: Harper Perennial, 1977.

Hughes, Emmet John. *Ordeal of Power*. New York: MacMillan, 1975.

Jacobs, Travis Beal. *Eisenhower at Columbia.* New Brunswick, NJ: Transaction Publishers, 2001.

Johnson, David E. *Douglas Southall Freeman.* Gretna: Pelican Publishing Company, 2002.

King, M. L. *A Testament of Hope: The Essential Writings and Speeches of Martin Luther King Jr.* New York: Harper SanFransico, 1986.

------. *Why We Can't Wait.* New York: Mentor Book, 1964.

Larson, Arthur. *Eisenhower: The President Nobody Knew.* New York: Charles Scribner's Sons, 1968.

Lee, Ulysses. *The Employment of Negro Troops: Special Studies: United States Army in World War II.* 1966.

Leuchtenburg, William E. *In the Shadow of FDR: From Harry Truman to Bill Clinton.* Ithaca, NY: Cornell University Press, 1993.

Manchester, William. *American Caesar: Douglas MacArthur 1880–1964.* New York: Little, Brown and Company, 1978.

------. *The Glory and the Dream: A Narrative of America 1932–1972.* New York: Bantam Books, 1990.

Martin, John Bartlow. *Adlai Stevenson and the World: The Life of Adlai E. Stevenson.* Garden City, New York: Doubleday, 1977.

------. *Adlai Stevenson of Illinois: A Life of Adlai E. Stevenson.* New York: Anchor Books, 1976.

Meyers, Jeffrey. *Robert Frost: A Biography.* New York: Houghton Mifflin, 1996.

Morgan, Kay Summersby. *Past Forgetting: My Love Affair with Dwight D. Eisenhower.* New York: Golden Apple Publishers, 1976.

Morgan, Ted. *FDR: A Biography.* New York: Simon and Schuster, 1985.

Morris, Edmund. *Theodore Rex.* New York: Random House, 2001.

Myrdal, Gunnar. *An American Dilemma: The Negro Problem and Modern Democracy.* New Brunswick, NJ: Transaction Publishers, 1996.

Neal, Steve. *Harry and Ike: The Partnership that Remade the Postwar World.* New York: Simon and Schuster, 2001.

The New York Times, September 13, 1952.

The New York Times, September 28, 1962.

Oates, Stephen. *Let the Trumpet Sound: A Life of Martin Luther King, Jr.* New York: HarperPerennial, 1982.

Owen, David. *The Making of the Masters: Clifford Roberts, Augusta National, and Golf's Most Prestigious Tournament.* New York: Simon and Schuster, 1999.

Parmet, Herbert S. *Eisenhower and the American Crusades.* New Brunswick, NJ: Transaction Publishers, 1999.

Patterson, James T. *Mr. Republican: A Biography of Robert A. Taft.* Boston: Houghton Mifflin Company, 1972.

Perlstein, Rick. *Before the Storm: Barry Goldwater and the Unmaking of the American Consensus.* New York: Hill and Wang, 2001.

Perret, Geoffrey. *Eisenhower.* New York: Random House, 1999.

Persico, Joseph E. *Edward R. Murrow: An American Original.* New York: Dell Publishing, 1988.

Rampersad, Arnold. *Jackie Robinson: A Biography.* New York: Ballantine Books, 1997.

Reagan, Ronald. *Speaking My Mind: Selected Speeches.* New York: Simon and Schuster, 1989.

Reed, Roy. *Faubus: The Life and Times of an American Prodigal.* Fayetteville: The University of Arkansas Press, 1997.

Robertson, David. *Sly and Able: A Political Biography of James F. Byrnes.* New York. W.W. Norton and Company, 1997.

Robinson, Jackie. *I Never Had It Made: An Autobiography.* New York: Harper Perennial, 2003.

Ross, Irwin. *The Loneliest Campaign: The Truman Victory of 1948.* New York: The New American Library, 1968.

Scranton, William. Interview with Author. November 4, 2005.

Shakespeare, William. *The Complete Works.* New York: Gramercy, 1990.

Siciliano, Rocco. *Walking on Sand: The Story of an Immigrant Son and the Forgotten Art of Public Service.* Salt Lake City: The University of Utah Press, 2004.

Slater, Ellis D. *The Ike I Knew.* Ellis D. Slater Trust (self-published), 1980.

Smith, Graham. *When Jim Crow Met John Bull: Black American Soldiers in World War II Britain.* New York: St. Martin's Press, 1987.

Smith, Richard Norton. *The Harvard Century: The Making of a University to a Nation.* Cambridge: Harvard University Press, 1986.

Smith, Richard Norton. *Thomas E. Dewey and His Times.* New York: Simon and Schuster, Inc., 1982.

Sulzberger, C. L. *A Long Row of Candles: Memoirs and Diaries 1934–1954.* Toronto: The MacMillan Company, 1969.

Time, October 30, 1944.

Time, October 12, 1962.

Van Natta, Don. *First Off the Tee: Presidential Hackers, Duffers, and Cheaters From Taft to Bush.* New York: Public Affairs, 2003.

Vidal, Gore. *United States: Essays 1952–1992.* New York: Broadway Books, 1993.

Voltaire. *The Portable Voltaire.* New York: Penguin, 1977.

Walsh, Kenneth T. *Air Force One: A History of the Presidents and Their Planes.* New York: Hyperion, 2003.

Walsh, Kenneth T. *From Mount Vernon to Crawford: A History of the Presidents and Their Retreats.* New York: Hyperion, 2005.

Walsh, Lawrence. Interview with Author. December 2, 2005.

Warren, Earl. *Memoirs of Chief Justice Earl Warren.* New York: Madison Books, 1977.

The Washington Post, August 7, 1953.

Weigley, Russell F. *Eisenhower's Lieutenants: The Campaigns of France and Germany, 1944–1945.* Bloomington: Indiana University Press, 1981.

White, Theodore H. *In Search of History: A Personal Adventure.* New York: Warner Books, 1978.

Williams, Juan. *Eyes on the Prize: American Civil Rights Years 1954–1965.* New York: Penguin Books, 1987.

------. *Thurgood Marshall: American Revolutionary.* New York: Three Rivers Press, 1998.

Woodward, C. Vann. *The Strange Career of Jim Crow.* Oxford: Oxford University Press, 2002.

Young, Andrew. *An Easy Burden: The Civil Rights Movement and the Transformation of America.* New York: Harper Collins, 1996.

NOTES

PROLOGUE
1. Bates, *Shadow of Little Rock*, 2.
2. Beals, *Warriors Don't Cry*, 41.
3. Ibid., 46.
4. Ibid., 49.
5. Bates, *Shadow of Little Rock*, 65–66.
6. Beals, *Warriors Don't Cry*, 49.
7. Halberstam, *Fifties*, 672.
8. Reed, *Faubus*, 208.
9. Oates, *Let the Trumpet Sound*, 125.
10. Cray, *Chief Justice*, 340.
11. Warren, *Memoirs of Chief Justice Earl Warren*, 298.
12. Cray, *Chief Justice*, 337.
13. Branch, *Parting the Waters*, 222.

CHAPTER ONE: THE IRON HEWER
1. Bradley, *A General's Life*, 373.
2. Ambrose, *Supreme Commander*, 320.
3. Air Marshall Robb, Pre-Presidential Papers, Dwight D. Eisenhower Library (Dwight D. Eisenhower Library hereafter cited as DDE).
4. Sergeant McKeough, Interview, August 23, 1942, Harry Butcher Papers.
5. Bradley, *A General's Life*, 373.
6. Dwight D. Eisenhower, *At Ease*, 52.
7. Ambrose, *Eisenhower*, 187.
8. *Time Magazine*, "Dwight Eisenhower: Person of the Year," Editorial, January 1, 1945.
9. Ann Whitman, Oral History, DDE.
10. Ambrose, *Eisenhower*, 51.
11. Sergeant McKeough, Interview, August 23, 1942, Harry Butcher Papers.
12. Sue Sarafian, Oral History, DDE.
13. Hughes, *Ordeal of Power*, 19.
14. Morgan, *Past Forgetting*, 20–21.
15. John S. D. Eisenhower, *Strictly Personal*, 72.
16. Harry Butcher Diary, Nov. 9, 1942, DDE.
17. Ibid.
18. Brinkley and Drez, *Voices of Valor*, 11.
19. Perret, *Eisenhower*, 282.

20. Harry Butcher Diary, Nov. 9, 1942, DDE.
21. D'Este, *Eisenhower: A Soldier's Life*, 527.
22. Winston Churchill, Speech to Parliament, June 6, 1944, DDE.
23. David Eisenhower, *Eisenhower at War*, 555.
24. Ibid., 557.
25. Ambrose, *Eisenhower*, 357.
26. John S. D. Eisenhower, *Bitter Woods*, 215.
27. Perret, *Eisenhower*, 327.
28. Dwight D. Eisenhower, *Crusade in Europe*, 350.
29. Ibid.

CHAPTER TWO: THE DILEMMA

1. Rampersad, *Jackie Robinson*, 93.
2. Oates, *Let the Trumpet Sound*, 17.
3. Woodward, *Strange Career of Jim Crow*, 17.
4. Black, *Franklin Delano Roosevelt*, 421.
5. Ibid., 584.
6. Morgan, *FDR*, 595.
7. Burns, *Roosevelt 1940–45*, 239.
8. Cray, *Chief Justice*, 118.
9. Dwight D. Eisenhower, *At Ease*, 38.
10. Dwight D. Eisenhower to Lucy Eldredge, January 17, 1946, DDE.
11. Morris, *Theodore Rex*, 455.
12. Davis, *Soldier of Democracy*, 142–143.
13. Fred Morrow, Oral History, DDE.
14. Dwight D. Eisenhower, *At Ease*, 112.
15. Manchester, *American Caesar*, 3.
16. Douglas A. MacArthur to Dwight D. Eisenhower, November 4, 1931, DDE.
17. Dwight D. Eisenhower, Diary, December 27, 1935.
18. Dwight D. Eisenhower to George C. Marshall, March 25, 1942, National Archives.
19. Harry Butcher Diary, July 14, 1942, DDE.
20. Harry Butcher Diary, August 15, 1942, DDE.
21. Dwight D. Eisenhower to Raymond Daniel, August 17, 1942, DDE.
22. Dwight D. Eisenhower to Brendan Bracken, August 18, 1942, DDE.
23. Persico, *Edward R. Murrow*, 199.
24. Harry Butcher Diary, August 15, 1942, DDE.
25. Winston Churchill, War Cabinet Meeting, October, 1942, National Archives of England, Wales, and the United Kingdom.
26. Graham Smith, *When Jim Crow Met John Bull*, 102.
27. Harry Butcher Diary, August 15, 1942, DDE.
28. Graham Smith, *When Jim Crow Met John Bull*, 26.
29. Ibid., 106.

30. Dwight D. Eisenhower, *Crusade in Europe*, 60.
31. Dwight D. Eisenhower to John Eisenhower, February 26, 1943, DDE.
32. Harry Butcher Diary, August 15, 1942, DDE.
33. Dwight D. Eisenhower, *Crusade in Europe*, 157.
34. Black, *Franklin Delano Roosevelt*, 917.
35. James Hagerty, Oral History, DDE.
36. Graham Smith, *When Jim Crow Met John Bull*, 1-4.
37. Ibid., 185–86.

CHAPTER THREE: THE REINFORCEMENTS
1. Graham Smith, *When Jim Crow Met John Bull*, 689.
2. Ibid., 690.
3. Ibid., 690.
4. Dwight D. Eisenhower, Eisenhower Directive, January 4, 1945, DDE.
5. Abdul-Jabbar and Walton, *Brothers in Arms*, 87.
6. Dwight D. Eisenhower to George C. Marshall, February 9, 1945, DDE.
7. Weigley, *Eisenhower's Lieutenants*, 527.
8. Dwight D. Eisenhower, *Crusade in Europe*, 366.
9. Dwight D. Eisenhower to George C. Marshall, February 9, 1945, DDE.
10. Graham Smith, *When Jim Crow Met John Bull*, 26.
11. Dwight D. Eisenhower, *Crusade in Europe*, 409.
12. Ibid.
13. Harry Butcher Diary, August 15, 1942, DDE.
14. Dwight D. Eisenhower, Guildhall Address, June 12, 1945, DDE.
15. Harry Butcher Diary, August 15, 1942, DDE.
16. Ibid.
17. David Eisenhower, *Eisenhower at War 1943–1945*, 822.
18. Claridge, *Norman Rockwell*, 407.

CHAPTER FOUR: THE AFTERMATH
1. Dwight D. Eisenhower, Speech to Congress, June 18, 1945, DDE.
2. Harry Truman, Letter to Bess Truman, June 19, 1945, Harry S Truman Library.
3. Neal, *Harry and Ike*, 92.
4. Harry Truman, K. Gibson Press Release, April 9, 1945, Harry S Truman Library.
5. Gillem Report, February 26, 1946, Harry S Truman Library.
6. Dwight D. Eisenhower, *At Ease*, 316.
7. Neal, *Harry and Ike*, 98.
8. Walter White, Letter to Dwight D. Eisenhower, March 28, 1946, DDE.
9. Philleo Nash to David K. Niles, July 26, 1946, Harry S Truman Library.
10. Donovan, *Conflict and Crisis*, 148.
11. Neal, *Harry and Ike*, 92.
12. Harry Truman, Press Conference, Nov. 6, 1947, Harry S Truman Library.

13. Myrdal, *An American Dilemma*, 1xxxiii.
14. Ellison, *Collected Essays of Ralph Ellison*.
15. Neal, *Harry and Ike*, 101.
16. Dwight D. Eisenhower, Testimony to Congress, April 2, 1948, DDE.
17. Hubert Humphrey, Letter to James Forrestal, April 26, 1948, Harry S Truman Library.
18. Harry Truman, Executive Order, July 26, 1948, Harry S Truman Library.
19. Eisenhower, Letter to *Manchester Union-Leader*, January 22, 1948, DDE.
20. Abels, *Out of the Jaws of Victory*, 77.
21. Neal, *Harry and Ike*, 127.
22. Donovan, *Conflict and Crisis*, 129.
23. Johnson, *Douglas Southall Freeman*, 291.
24. Neal, *Harry and Ike*, 71.
25. Hagerty, "Dewey Far in Lead," *New York Times*, July 5, 1948.
26. Dwight D. Eisenhower, Press Release, July 5, 1948, DDE.
27. Ambrose, *Eisenhower*, 481.
28. Sulzberger, *Long Row of Candles*, 649.
29. Rampersad, *Jackie Robinson*, 126.
30. Duram, *Moderate Among Extremists*, 42.

CHAPTER FIVE: THE CANDIDATE

1. Edwards, *Conservative Revolution*, 37.
2. Richard Norton Smith, *Thomas E. Dewey and His Times*, 543.
3. Dwight D. Eisenhower, Diary, July 7, 1949.
4. Owen, *Making of Masters*, 165.
5. Jacqueline Cochran, Oral History, DDE.
6. Dwight D. Eisenhower, Letter to Herbert Brownell, March 18, 1952, DDE.
7. Brownell, *Advising Ike*, 94–101.
8. Sulzberger, *Long Row of Candles*, 649.
9. Ibid., 616.
10. Brownell, *Advising Ike*, 103.
11. Neal, *Harry and Ike*, 240.
12. White, *In Search of History*, 352.
13. Williams, *Thurgood Marshall*, 180.
14. Ibid., 183.
15. Ibid., 183.
16. Ibid., 183.
17. Ibid., 184.
18. Ibid., 185.
19. Donovan, *Confidential Secretary*, 7.
20. Ibid.
21. Graham, *Just As I Am*, 191.
22. Ibid., 191–92.
23. Patterson, *Mr. Republican*, 437.

24. Parmet, *Eisenhower and the American Crusades*, 96.
25. Cray, *Chief Justice*, 246.
26. Martin, *Adlai Stevenson of Illinois*, 611.
27. NAACP Meeting Minutes, August 7, 1952, DDE.
28. NAACP Meeting Minutes, August 26, 1952, DDE.
29. Hughes, *Ordeal of Power*, 25.
30. Robertson, *Sly and Able*, 504.
31. Donovan, *Confidential Secretary*, 13.
32. Robertson, *Sly and Able*, 512.
33. Martin, *Adlai Stevenson of Illinois*, 657.
34. Dwight D. Eisenhower, Speech in Harlem, October 25, 1952, DDE.
35. Neal, *Harry and Ike*, 275–76.
36. Martin, *Adlai Stevenson of Illinois*, 676.
37. *The Washington Post*, August 7, 1953.
38. Hughes, *Ordeal of Power*, 22.
39. Fred Morrow, Oral History, DDE.
40. Ibid.
41. Ibid.
42. Ibid.
43. Cray, *Chief Justice*, 247.
44. Dwight D. Eisenhower, Speech in Little Rock, September 3, 1952, DDE.

CHAPTER SIX: THE PRESIDENT
1. Ibid.
2. Robertson, *Sly and Able*, 516.
3. Williams, *Thurgood Marshall*, 216.
4. Eisenhower, Cabinet Meeting Minutes, January 12, 1953. DDE.
5. Dwight D. Eisenhower, *At Ease*, 200.
6. Larson, *Eisenhower*, 5.
7. Stephen Benedict, Oral History, DDE.
8. Dwight D. Eisenhower, Speech, April 16, 1953, DDE.
9. Clements, *Woodrow Wilson*, 100.
10. James Hagerty, Oral History, DDE.
11. Dwight D. Eisenhower, *Mandate for Change*, 234.
12. Dwight D. Eisenhower, Speech to Congress, February 2, 1953, DDE.
13. Dwight D. Eisenhower, Press Conference, March 19, 1953, DDE.
14. James Hagerty Diary, July 17, 1954, DDE.
15. Dwight D. Eisenhower, Memo to Secretary Wilson, March 25, 1953, DDE.
16. Dwight D. Eisenhower, Speech to United Negro College Fund Campaign, May 19, 1953, DDE.
17. Hamilton, *Adam Clayton Powell, Jr.*, 201–02.
18. Max Rabb, Oral History, DDE.
19. Ibid.
20. Ibid.

21. Ibid.
22. Ibid.
23. Brownell, *Advising Ike*, 190.
24. Stephen Benedict, Oral History, DDE.
25. Dwight D. Eisenhower, Diary, August 19, 1953.
26. Gov. Allen Shivers, Letter to President Eisenhower, July 16, 1953, DDE.
27. Dwight D. Eisenhower, Diary, July 24, 1953.
28. Dwight D. Eisenhower, Letter to Richard Nixon, August 15, 1953, DDE.
29. Dwight D. Eisenhower, Radio Address, August 6, 1953, DDE.
30. *The Washington Post*, Editorial, August 7, 1953.
31. Dwight D. Eisenhower, Letter to Jim Byrnes, August 14, 1953, DDE.
32. Jim Byrnes, Letter to President Eisenhower, August 27, 1953, DDE.
33. Dwight D. Eisenhower, Telephone conversation with Jim Brynes, September 3, 1953, DDE.
34. Cray, *Chief Justice*, 252.
35. Dwight D. Eisenhower, Speech to B'nai B'rith, November 23, 1953, DDE.
36. Rampersad, *Jackie Robinson*, 261.
37. Dwight D. Eisenhower, Speech to the UN, December 8, 1953, DDE.

CHAPTER SEVEN: THE RULING

1. Larson, *Eisenhower*, 20.
2. Brownell, *Advising Ike*, 256.
3. Ibid.
4. Williams, *Thurgood Marshall*, 224.
5. Brownell, *Advising Ike*, 194.
6. Ibid.
7. Ibid.
8. Dwight D. Eisenhower, Letter to Jim Byrnes, December 1, 1953, DDE.
9. Herbert Brownell, Telephone conversation with President Eisenhower, December 2, 1953, DDE.
10. Robertson, *Sly and Able*, 519.
11. Williams, *Thurgood Marshall*, 224.
12. Van Natta, *First Off the Tee*, 58.
13. Hughes, *Ordeal of Power*, 116.
14. Warren, *Memoirs of Chief Justice Earl Warren*, 291.
15. Ann Whitman, Oral History, DDE.
16. Robert Kennon, Letter to President Eisenhower, November 20, 1953, DDE.
17. James Hagerty Diary, January 24, 1954, DDE.
18. Williams, *Thurgood Marshall*, 227.
19. Robertson, *Sly and Able*, 520.
20. Stephen Benedict, Oral History, DDE.
21. Herbert Brownell, Oral History, DDE.
22. Ibid.
23. Ibid.

24. Dwight D. Eisenhower, Press Conference, May 19, 1954, DDE.
25. Gallup Poll #531, May 21–26, 1954.
26. Williams, *Thurgood Marshall*, 230.
27. Larson, *Eisenhower*, 21.
28. Hamilton, *Adam Clayton Powell, Jr.*, 206.
29. Max Rabb, Memo to Ann Whitman, November 2, 1953, DDE.
30. Stanley High, Letter to Max Rabb, July 16, 1954, DDE.
31. Ann Whitman, Memo to Max Rabb, July 24, 1954, DDE.
32. Dwight D. Eisenhower, Press Conference, July 7, 1954, DDE.
33. Cray, *Chief Justice*, 292.
34. Dwight D. Eisenhower, Letter to Swede Hazlett, October 23, 1954, DDE.

CHAPTER EIGHT: THE RUMBLING

1. Brownell Papers, DDE.
2. Dwight D. Eisenhower, Press Conference, November 23, 1954, DDE.
3. Williams, *Thurgood Marshall*, 233.
4. Cray, *Chief Justice*, 294.
5. Ibid.
6. Herbert Brownell, Oral History, DDE.
7. Williams, *Eyes on the Prize*, 44.
8. Ibid., 51.
9. Mamie Bradley, Letter to President Eisenhower, September 2, 1955, DDE.
10. William Barba, Letter to *The Chicago Defender*, September 2, 1955, DDE.
11. J. Edgar Hoover, Memo to Dillon Anderson, September 6, 1955, DDE.
12. J. Edgar Hoover, Memo to Dillon Anderson, September 13, 1955, DDE.
13. Max Rabb, Memo to Howard Pyle, October 23, 1956, DDE.
14. Dwight D. Eisenhower, Letter to Lyndon Johnson, September 23, 1955, DDE.
15. Gallup Poll, September 23, 1955.
16. Max Rabb, Memo to Howard Pyle, August 8, 1955, DDE.
17. Dwight D. Eisenhower, Press Conference, February 8, 1956, DDE.
18. Dwight D. Eisenhower, Cabinet Meeting, March 9, 1956, DDE.
19. Dwight D. Eisenhower, Cabinet Meeting, March 23, 1956, DDE.
20. Dwight D. Eisenhower, Press Conference, March 21, 1956, DDE.
21. Dwight D. Eisenhower, Legislative Leaders Mtg., January 10, 1956, DDE.
22. Brownell, *Advising Ike*, 199.
23. Dwight D. Eisenhower, Press Conference, March 14, 1956, DDE.
24. Dwight D. Eisenhower, Press Conference, March 21, 1956, DDE.
25. Ambrose, *Eisenhower*, 307.
26. Dwight D. Eisenhower, Cabinet Meeting, March 9, 1956, DDE.
27. Dwight D. Eisenhower, Legislative Leaders Mtg., April 17, 1956, DDE.
28. Branch, *Parting the Waters*, 192.
29. Dwight D. Eisenhower, Letter to Billy Graham, March 22, 1956.
30. Martin, *Adlai Stevenson and the World*, 302.

31. Dwight D. Eisenhower, Telephone conversation with William Rogers, August 13, 1956, DDE.
32. Dwight D. Eisenhower, Telephone conversation with Herbert Brownell, August 14, 1956, DDE.
33. Ann Whitman Diary, August 14, 1956, DDE.
34. Ibid.
35. Hughes, *Ordeal of Power*, 176.
36. Bernard Shanley, Notes of Eisenhower meeting with Adam Clayton Powell, October 11, 1956, DDE.
37. Adam Clayton Powell, Statement, October 23, 1956, DDE.
38. Hughes, *Ordeal of Power*, 176.
39. Dwight D. Eisenhower, Press Conference, September 11, 1956, DDE.
40. Brownell, *Advising Ike*, 205.

CHAPTER NINE: THE INSURRECTION

1. Branch, *Parting the Waters*, 203.
2. Vidal, *United States*, 797.
3. Dwight D. Eisenhower, Press Conference, February 6, 1957, DDE.
4. Ann Whitman Diary, January 3, 1957, DDE.
5. Martin Luther King, Jr., Telegram to President Eisenhower, February 14, 1957, DDE.
6. Branch, *Parting the Waters*, 213.
7. Dwight D. Eisenhower, Legislative Leaders Meeting, July 30, 1957, DDE.
8. Dallek, *An Unfinished Life*, 216.
9. Branch, *Parting the Waters*, 217.
10. Ibid., 219.
11. Caro, *Master of the Senate*, 711.
12. Ibid, 713.
13. Ibid, 717.
14. Dwight D. Eisenhower, Press Conference, July 3, 1957, DDE.
15. Dwight D. Eisenhower, Letter to Swede Hazlett, July 22, 1957, DDE.
16. Dwight D. Eisenhower, Press Conference, July 17, 1957, DDE.
17. Dwight D. Eisenhower, Letter to Jim Byrnes, July 23, 1957, DDE.
18. Dwight D. Eisenhower, Press Conference, July 17, 1953, DDE.
19. Dallek, *An Unfinished Life*, 217.
20. Dwight D. Eisenhower, Cabinet Meeting, August 2, 1957, DDE.
21. Reed, *Faubus*, 197.
22. Williams, *Eyes on the Prize*, 97.
23. Reed, *Faubus*, 198.
24. Williams, *Eyes on the Prize*, 97.
25. Ibid., 100.
26. Ibid., 99.
27. Reed, *Faubus*, 209.
28. Williams, *Eyes on the Prize*, 101.

29. Dwight D. Eisenhower, Speech, September 4, 1957, DDE.
30. Dwight D. Eisenhower, Telegram to Gov. Faubus, September 5, 1957, DDE.
31. Eisenhower, *Waging Peace*, 164.
32. Ibid., 165.

CHAPTER TEN: THE RECKONING

1. Adams, *Firsthand Report*, 341–42.
2. Ibid., 343.
3. Ibid., 343.
4. Ibid., 344.
5. Ibid., 344.
6. Dwight D. Eisenhower, Telephone conversation with Herbert Brownell, September 11, 1957, DDE.
7. Ibid.
8. Eisenhower, *Waging Peace*, 166.
9. Adams, *Firsthand Report*, 345.
10. Ibid., 345–46.
11. Dwight D. Eisenhower, Diary, October 8, 1957.
12. Ibid.
13. Ibid.
14. Ibid.
15. Ibid.
16. Baker, *Brooks Hays*, 165–66.
17. Dwight D. Eisenhower, Press Release, September 14, 1957, DDE.
18. Governor Faubus, Press Release, September 14, 1957, DDE.
19. Dwight D. Eisenhower, Press Release, September 14, 1957, DDE.
20. Governor Faubus, Press Release, September 14, 1957, DDE.
21. Dwight D. Eisenhower, Press Release, September 14, 1957, DDE.
22. Governor Faubus, Press Release, September 14, 1957, DDE.
23. Ann Whitman Diary, September 14, 1957, DDE.
24. Eisenhower, *Waging Peace*, 167.
25. Brownell, *Advising Ike*, 210.
26. Goodpaster, Memo to Dwight D. Eisenhower, September 19, 1957, DDE.
27. Reed, *Faubus*, 222.
28. Dwight D. Eisenhower, *Waging Peace*, 167–68.
29. Dwight D. Eisenhower, Telephone conversation with Herbert Brownell, September 20, 1957, DDE.
30. Slater, *The Ike I Knew*, 160–62.
31. Williams, *Eyes on the Prize*, 105.
32. Reed, *Faubus*, 227.
33. Williams, *Eyes on the Prize*, 105.
34. Beals, *Warriors Don't Cry*, 110.
35. Bates, *Long Shadow of Little Rock*, 93.
36. Dwight D. Eisenhower, *Waging Peace*, 168.

37. Dwight D. Eisenhower, Speech, September 23, 1957, DDE.

38. Ambrose, *Eisenhower*, 418.

39. Williams, *Eyes on the Prize*, 106.

40. Dwight D. Eisenhower, Proclamation, September 23, 1957, DDE.

41. Woodrow Mann, Telegram to President Eisenhower, September 23, 1957, DDE.

42. Manchester, *The Glory and the Dream*, 805.

43. Ibid.

44. Dwight D. Eisenhower, Telephone conversation with Herbert Brownell, September 24, 1957, DDE.

45. Dwight D. Eisenhower, Letter to General Al Gruenther, September 24, 1957, DDE.

46. Dwight D. Eisenhower, Telephone conversation with Herbert Brownell, September 24, 1957, DDE.

47. Woodrow Mann, Telegram to Dwight D. Eisenhower, September 24, 1957, DDE.

48. Larson, *Eisenhower*, 146.

49. Dwight D. Eisenhower, Speech Notes, September 24, 1957, DDE.

50. John Foster Dulles, Telephone conversation with Dwight D. Eisenhower, September 24, 1957, DDE.

51. Dwight D. Eisenhower, Speech, September 24, 1957, DDE.

52. Williams, *Eyes on the Prize*, 110.

53. Beals, *Warriors Don't Cry*, 135.

54. Reed, *Faubus*, 230.

55. John L. Steele, Memo, September 25, 1957, DDE.

56. Louis Armstrong, Telegram to Dwight D. Eisenhower, September 24, 1957, DDE.

57. James Roosevelt, Telegram to Dwight D. Eisenhower, September 27, 1957, DDE.

58. Monty Moncrief, Telegram to Dwight D. Eisenhower, September 25, 1957, DDE.

59. Harry Ashmore, Telegram to Dwight D. Eisenhower, September 24, 1957, DDE.

60. Senator John Sparkman, Telegram to Dwight D. Eisenhower, September 30, 1957, DDE.

61. Dwight D. Eisenhower, Letter to Richard Russell, September 27, 1957, DDE.

62. Eisenhower, *Mrs. Ike*, 296.

63. Lyndon Johnson Letter to Bob Nobles, October 3, 1957, Lyndon B. Johnson Library.

64. Lyndon Johnson, Letter to Dean Acheson, October 7, 1957, Lyndon B. Johnson Library.

65. Bryant, *Bystander*, 83.

66. Dwight D. Eisenhower, Press Release, October 1, 1957, DDE.

67. Dwight D Eisenhower, Letter to Richard Nixon, October 2, 1957, DDE.
68. Young, *An Easy Burden*, 96.
69. Branch, *Parting the Waters*, 228.

CHAPTER ELEVEN: THE FALLOUT

1. Larson, *Eisenhower*, 124–28.
2. Cliff Roberts, Oral History, DDE.
3. Jim Wright, Letter to Dwight D. Eisenhower, October 14, 1957, DDE.
4. Dwight D. Eisenhower, Letter to Jim Wright, October 14, 1957, DDE.
5. Dwight D. Eisenhower, Letter to Jim Wright, November 18, 1957, DDE.
6. Larson, *Eisenhower*, 31.
7. Ambrose, *Eisenhower*, 436.
8. Gerald Ford, Letter to Dwight Eisenhower, November 4, 1957, DDE.
9. Max Rabb, Memo to Chief of Staff Adams, November 12, 1957, DDE.
10. Martin, *Adlai Stevenson and the World*, 418.
11. Siciliano, *Walking on Sand*, 157.
12. Ibid., 162.
13. Ibid., 164.
14. Oates, *Let the Trumpet Sound*, 134.
15. Branch, *Parting the Waters*, 236.
16. King, *Why We Can't Wait*, 143.
17. Fred Morrow, Oral History, DDE.
18. Hamby, *Man of the People*, 631.
19. Dwight D. Eisenhower, Press Conference, March 16, 1960, DDE.
20. Hamby, *Man of the People*, 624.
21. Rampersad, *Jackie Robinson*, 342.
22. Ibid., 345.
23. Robinson, *I Never Had It Made*, 137.
24. Rampersad, *Jackie Robinson*, 351.
25. Lawrence Walsh, Draft Statement, October 31, 1957.
26. Lawrence Walsh, Interview with author, December 2, 2005.
27. Branch, *Parting the Waters*, 361.
28. Ibid., 362.
29. Ibid., 370.
30. Gallup Poll #614, May 29–June 3, 1959.
31. Slater, *The Ike I Knew*, 230.
32. Dwight D. Eisenhower, Meeting Notes, December 28, 1960, DDE.
33. Fred Morrow, Oral History, DDE.

CHAPTER TWELVE: THE ENDING

1. Kenneth Walsh, *From Mount Vernon to Crawford*, 128.
2. Branch, *Parting the Waters*, 657.
3. *The New York Times*, September 28, 1962.
4. Branch, *Parting the Waters*, 659.

5. *Time* Magazine, October 12, 1962.
6. King, *A Testament of Hope*, 292.
7. Dwight D. Eisenhower, Letter to Everett Dirksen, June 14, 1963, DDE.
8. Dwight D. Eisenhower, Oral History, November 8, 1966, DDE.
9. John Fitzgerald Kennedy, Letter to Dwight D. Eisenhower, June 10, 1963, DDE.
10. Dwight D. Eisenhower, Letter to President Kennedy, June 14, 1963, DDE.
11. Dwight D. Eisenhower, Letter to Everett Dirksen, June 14, 1963, DDE.
12. Branch, *Parting the Waters*, 885–86.
13. Dwight D. Eisenhower, Letter to Eugene Blake, October 9, 1963, DDE.
14. Larson, *Eisenhower*, 6.
15. Scranton, Interview with author, November 4, 2005.
16. Dwight D. Eisenhower, Letter to Hubert Humphrey, August 7, 1964, DDE.
17. Perlstein, *Before the Storm*, 442.
18. Reagan, *Speaking My Mind*, 24.
19. Fred Morrow, Oral History, DDE.
20. Eisenhower, Letter to Sam Vaughan, April 20, 1965, DDE.
21. Dwight D. Eisenhower, *Waging Peace*, 150.
22. Herbert Brownell, Letter to Dwight D. Eisenhower, March 4, 1964, DDE.
23. Ambrose, *Eisenhower*, 190.
24. Warren, *Memoirs of Chief Justice Earl Warren*, 5.
25. Dwight D. Eisenhower, Letter to Hubert Humphrey, March 28, 1968, DDE.
26. Dwight D. Eisenhower, *Mandate for Change*, 236.
27. Beschloss, *Eisenhower: A Centennial Life*, 208.
28. Ibid., 210.

INDEX